TRIBAL ADMINISTRATION
HANDBOOK

Makwa Enewed is an imprint of the American Indian Studies Series, at Michigan State University Press.

Gordon Henry, *Series Editor*

Makwa Enewed stands dedicated to books that encompass the varied views and perspectives of people working in American Indian communities. In that light, books published under the Makwa Enewed imprint rely less on formal academic critique, argument, methodology, and research conventions and more on experientially grounded views and perspectives on issues, activities, and developments in Indian Country.

While work published in Makwa Enewed may resound with certain personal, speculative, conversational, political, and/or social concerns of individuals and groups of individual American Indian people, in a larger sense such concerns and their delivery reflect the import, strength, uniqueness, and potential viability of the imprint.

The imprint will gather its strength from the voices of tribal leaders, community activists, and socially engaged Native people. Thus, each publication under the Makwa Enewed imprint will call forth from tribally based people and places, reminding readers of the varied beliefs and pressing interests of American Indian tribal people and communities.

TRIBAL ADMINISTRATION HANDBOOK

A Guide for Native Nations in the United States

Edited by Rebecca M. Webster and Joseph Bauerkemper

MAKWA ENEWED | EAST LANSING, MICHIGAN

⊗ The paper used in this publication meets the minimum
requirements of ANSI/NISO Z39.48-1992 (R 1997) (Permanence of
Paper).

makwa
enewed

Makwa Enewed
Michigan State University Press
East Lansing, Michigan 48823-5245

Library of Congress Cataloging-in-Publication Data
Names: Webster, Rebecca M., editor. | Bauerkemper, Joseph, editor.
Title: Tribal administration handbook : a guide for Native nations
in the United States / edited by Rebecca M. Webster and Joseph
Bauerkemper.
Description: East Lansing, Michigan : Makwa Enewed, [2022] |
Includes bibliographical references and index.
Identifiers: LCCN 2021062379 | ISBN 9781938065149 (paperback)
| ISBN 9781938065156 (PDF) | ISBN 9781938065163 (ePub) | ISBN
9781938065170 (Kindle)
Subjects: LCSH: Tribal government—United States—Handbooks,
manuals, etc. | Indians of North America—Politics and
government—Handbooks, manuals, etc. | LCGFT: Handbooks and
manuals.
Classification: LCC E98.T77 T748 2022 | DDC 323.1197—dc23/
eng/20220124
LC record available at https://lccn.loc.gov/2021062379

Cover design by
Cover art is *Celestial Growth* by Jessica Powless.

Visit Michigan State University Press at www.msupress.org

Contents

Acknowledgments

SINCE ITS INCEPTION, THIS HANDBOOK HAS BEEN A COLLABORATIVE AND community effort. We owe many debts of gratitude to so many who made it possible.

The Department of American Indian Studies and the Tribal Sovereignty Institute at the University of Minnesota Duluth serve as our shared professional and intellectual home, and we thank our colleagues Jill Doerfler, Linda Grover, Tadd Johnson, Wendy Todd, Carter Meland, Doug Thompson, Tami Lawlor, and Holly Rosendahl.

This project would not have been possible without the extensive support of the Bush Foundation and Eileen Briggs. The vague idea of a tribal administration handbook gained its initial traction toward reality during a meeting sponsored by the Bush Foundation and attended by Laural Ballew, Jill Doerfler, Wayne Ducheneaux, Amy Gould, Wendy Helgemo, Tadd Johnson, Miriam Jorgensen, Joseph Kalt, Ian Record, Joan Timeche, and Eric Trevan.

As the project gathered steam, it was guided in key moments by an advisory group consisting of Laural Ballew, Wayne Ducheneaux, Amy Gould, Annamarie Hill, Tadd Johnson, Lorna LaGue, Paul Ninham, and Joan Timeche.

We are also, of course, deeply grateful to all of the handbook's chapter authors whose generosity of knowledge and hard work make this project what it is. And many thanks to Michigan State University Press, especially Catherine Cocks and Julie Loehr, for providing the handbook a home and agreeing to make it freely available to Native nations.

Introduction

THIS HANDBOOK ARISES OUT OF AN ONGOING COLLABORATION INVOLVING scholars and practitioners from tribal nations, universities, tribal colleges, and nonprofit organizations who are working together to develop practical and teaching resources in the field of tribal administration and governance. With 574 federally recognized tribes in the United States, we understand that each tribe has unique social, political, and cultural histories. Despite such differences, there are many shared commonalities and there is much to learn from one other.

The concept, structure, content, and editorial approach for this handbook emerged through extensive tribal consultation, a thorough review of existing literature, and a survey of over one hundred scholars and practitioners in the field. The handbook aspires to simultaneously meet the needs of multiple audiences: undergraduate and graduate students pursuing training and degrees in tribal administration; professional practitioners and elected officials engaging in the work of tribal administration and governance; practitioners working in governments and institutions that interface with tribes; scholarly researchers and teachers, whether focused specifically on tribal contexts or more broadly in public administration; and tribal community members seeking to enhance their capacity and impact as engaged citizens.

OBJECTIVES

- This book is designed as a readable, accessible volume focused on key areas of tribal administration and governance.
- Each chapter is grounded in specific tribal contexts, respecting intellectual authority and emphasizing tribal knowledge.
- Each chapter links its specificity to broadly resonant concepts and patterns in tribal administration.
- Each chapter accounts for impacts of tribal decision-making on elders, women, children, veterans, and other specific populations as may be relevant to each topic.
- Each chapter emphasizes best practices, provides a quick-reference executive summary, and includes practitioner notes to aid application.

CHAPTER FORMAT AND PROTOCOL

Each chapter begins with a brief summary of the topic at hand and a bulleted list presenting research-based best practices. Chapters then pursue illuminating case studies and analyses of key problems, opportunities, strategies, concepts, and skills relevant to the topic at hand. Each chapter concludes with a section titled "Practitioner Perspective" generated by a practitioner in the field, along with references to additional resources. To ensure the influential presence of relevant practitioner perspectives, each chapter author has partnered with a tribal administration professional to develop the chapter and create the "Practitioner Perspective" section. In several cases, chapter authors are themselves tribal administrators.

DEVELOPMENT CONTEXTS AND CONTENT

During 2018 the Bush Foundation awarded a planning grant to the Department of American Indian Studies (AIS) at the University of Minnesota Duluth (UMD). This funding supported research and relationship-building with other institutions, organizations, and tribal nations in order to assess the need for, and existing availability of, curricular and directly applicable resources for tribal administration and governance. UMD AIS faculty created and deployed a survey—based itself on tribal consultation—to determine which areas of tribal administration and governance were most important to practitioners, leaders, and scholars. UMD AIS faculty also completed a thorough review of existing literature in the field, revealing areas that are particularly understudied. The table and graph below feature core findings of the literature review and survey.

AIS at UMD hosted a planning meeting with participants from several tribal nations, The Evergreen State College, George Washington University, University of Arizona, Washington University (St. Louis), the Harvard Project on American Indian Economic Development, National Congress of American Indians, Native Governance Center, and the Native Nations Institute. The handbook project arose as an outcome initiative of this planning meeting, and a provisional advisory group emerged to steer its development. The Bush Foundation awarded a subsequent grant allowing for the project's editors, chapter contributors, and advisory group to collaboratively develop the handbook and to make it freely available to tribal practitioners. This process included a spring 2020 symposium during which contributors presented their drafts and received feedback from one another and from the advisory group.

Considered in relation to one another, the literature review and survey allowed for the identification of key topics in tribal administration and gaps in available research, reference, and practical materials addressing those topics. The survey also generated insight regarding specific subtopics perceived as particularly important, and detailed graphs of this data can be made available upon request. The literature review and survey responses were combined with further direct input from tribal practitioners and leaders, as well as curricular considerations from programs associated with tribal colleges and public universities. This constellation of influences led to the table of contents that comprises this handbook. Moreover, these same factors shaped the perspectives, structure, and formatting of the chapters.

While this handbook presents a coherent and unified constellation of voices illuminating a shared terrain of practical Indigenous governance, and while chapters complement one another, each chapter ultimately stands alone to serve students, practitioners, scholars, community members, and other readers with specific needs and interests.

The collection is organized into three broad clusters. The first illuminates "Tribal Management." Reflecting on historical knowledge and traditional ways

Key Tribal Administration Topics Categorized by Level of Existing Coverage

SUFFICIENTLY STUDIED	UNDERSTUDIED	NOT STUDIED
• Economic & energy development	• Tribal laws	• Project management
• Sovereignty & federal Indian law	• Cultural match between government & traditions	• Operations management
• Natural resources		• Finance & budgeting
• Leadership & ethics	• Human resources	
• Human services	• Strategic management	
• Community wellness		

of governing, chapters in this section consider how to engage in best collective decision-making practices, how to plan for the future, and how to handle our employee base with care and compassion. The handbook opens with a chapter on citizen engagement from Toni M. House, a faculty member in the Department of Human Services Leadership at the University of Wisconsin Oshkosh who also has vast experience as a staffer with the Oneida Nation, and Jo Anne House, the Oneida Nation's chief counsel and parliamentarian. Lois Stevens, a faculty member in First Nations Studies and the First Nations Education Doctoral Program at the University of Wisconsin-Green Bay, and Brandon Yellowbird-Stevens, vice-chairman of the Oneida Nation of Wisconsin, provide a chapter on tribal structures, operations, and decision-making. This is followed by a chapter from Kris Peters, chairman of the Squaxin Island Tribe, and Amy Gould, a faculty member at Evergreen State College, exploring and explaining the authorizing environment at the root of tribal administration. Laural Ses yehomia Ballew, a Swinomish scholar currently serving Western Washington University as the first executive director of American Indian/Alaska Native and First Nation Relations, offers a vital consideration of Indigenous leadership and ethics. This first cluster of chapters concludes with a trio of contributions addressing strategic, project, and human resources management. Rebecca M. Webster, a faculty member in the Department of American Indian Studies at the University of Minnesota Duluth and elected member of the Oneida Land Commission, and Julie Clark, organizational development specialist with the Oneida Casino, offer a chapter on culturally appropriate strategic planning. Joseph Bauerkemper, a faculty member in the Department of American Indian Studies at the University of Minnesota Duluth, and Jason Hollinday, planning director for the Fond du Lac Band of Lake Superior Chippewa, present a chapter on project management. The chapter on human resources comes from Rebecca

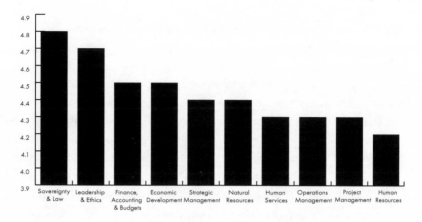

Figure 1. Top Ten Tribal Administration Topics Rated by Perceived Importance

M. Webster; Paul Ninham, former tribal councilman for the Oneida Nation; and Michael J. Poitra, a faculty member in the Ogimaawiwin Leadership and Business Management Program at the Turtle Mountain Community College.

The handbook's second cluster of chapters addresses "Funding and Delivering Core Services." Positing economic development as a primary enabling underpinning of government programs and services, chapters in this section consider how to allocate limited resources in ways that best meet the physical and spiritual needs of Indigenous peoples and lands. The first pair of chapters, one on tribal finance and the other on economic development, are from Eric S. Trevan, a faculty member at California State University San Marcos, and Jon Panamaroff, chief executive officer of Command Holdings, an economic development arm of the Mashantucket Pequot Tribal Nation. Katie Johnston-Goodstar, a faculty member and director of Undergraduate Studies in the School of Social Work at the University of Minnesota; Donald Eubanks, a faculty member and field director for the social work program at Metropolitan State University and former commissioner of Health and Human Services for the Mille Lacs Band of Ojibwe; and Cary B. Waubanascum, a doctoral student in the School of Social Work at the University of Minnesota offer a chapter on human services. The chapter on community wellness is from Linda Bane Frizzell, faculty member in the University of Minnesota School of Public Health, and Candice Skenandore, self-governance coordinator for the Oneida Nation. The section concludes with a chapter on natural resources from Kekek Jason Stark, a faculty member in the Alexander Blewitt III School of Law at the University of Montana.

The handbook's third and final cluster of chapters contemplates "Sovereign Tribes Engaging Settler Governments." Emphasizing intergovernmental diplomacy contextualized by ongoing colonization, chapters in this section consider how tribal nations navigate complex layered jurisdictions, federal lawmaking processes, and mutually beneficial agreements with settler governments. Krystal L. John, an attorney with the Oneida Law Office, provides a foundational chapter on jurisdiction and law. This is followed by a chapter on federal legislative policy by Kirsten Matoy Carlson, a faculty member in law and political science at Wayne State University; Wendy Helgemo, senior legislative attorney at Big Fire Law & Policy; Tadd M. Johnson, senior director of American Indian Tribal Nations Relations for the University of Minnesota; and Laura Paynter, a recent graduate of the University of Minnesota's Humphrey School of Public Affairs. Lawrence S. Roberts, faculty member and executive director of the Indian Gaming and Tribal Self-Governance Programs at Arizona State University, chief of staff for Secretary of the Interior Deb Haaland, and former principal deputy assistant secretary of Indian Affairs, provides a chapter on the federal budget process. Nicholas C. Zaferatos, a faculty member in urban planning at Western Washington University's Huxley College of the Environment, presents a chapter on intergovernmental agreements. Finally, a chapter on tribal influence in federal and state politics comes from Michael D. O. Rusco, faculty member in the Southern University Law Center; Kirsten Matoy Carlson; and Patrice Kunesh, the founder and director of Peȟíŋ Haha Consulting and the major gifts officer at the Native American Rights Fund.

Responding directly to the needs and ambitions articulated by tribal administrators and leaders, these chapters seek to serve practitioners, students, researchers, and community members alike. This humble collection of remarkable voices initiates a conversation about tribal administration that we all hope will continue to grow in service to Native nations.

PART 1

Tribal Management

PRIOR TO EUROPEAN CONTACT, COMMUNITY MEMBERS HAD DIFFERENT ROLES and responsibilities from hunting to storytelling, and from negotiating agreements to caring for children. Today, within our modern tribal governments, community members still have various roles and responsibilities; it just looks quite a bit different. Reflecting on our historical knowledge and our traditional ways of governing, we can learn how to bring those practices into contemporary governance. These lessons can help us determine how to engage in the best collective decision-making practices, how to plan for the future, and how to handle our employee base with care and compassion.

From Citizen Engagement to Haudenosaunee Governance

Bringing an Ancient Participatory Governing System Forward

Toni M. House and Jo Anne House

THIS CHAPTER WILL INTRODUCE, ILLUSTRATE, AND DISCUSS A SIMPLIFIED version of the Haudenosaunee Kayanlásla?kowa (Great Law of Peace) with the intention to encourage readers to explore these ancient participatory governing principles still practiced today, reflect upon, then promote how these principles can be applied within the self, clan, community, and nation. The governing principles are ka?nikuhli·yó, kanolukhwátsla, and ka?satstʌ́sla? (peace of mind, love, and power), which support a structure to organize clan systems and nations through diverse responsibilities/functions, processes, and community participation. These interdependent principles promote a balanced system respecting all people from ancestors, to those yet to be born, to those of us in between from the youngest to the oldest; diverse characteristics of leadership; and community participatory decision-making with the intent of creating a governing process unifying nations to create Skanúhsat (one house).

BEST PRACTICES

- Utilizing self-reflection to foster self-awareness promoting a peaceful mind
- Maintaining awareness of the power in having a peaceful mind and peaceful actions toward self and others

- Recognizing clans systems as our "family," which create identity and belonging
- Recognition of the necessity of complementary functions within systems/processes
- Recognizing the clan system as an organizational decision-making process
- Recognition of the necessity of diverse leadership styles
- Reestablishing the importance of inviting all, from the youngest to the oldest, to community meetings as one of our strongest educational practices
- Sharing of Indigenous foods to promote a good mind at community gatherings

BACKGROUND

There is an ancient story referred to as Kayanlásla?kowa, also known in English as the Great Law of Peace, that has its origins among the Haudenosaunee (They Make a House). This story tells how the Peacemaker journeyed throughout the Kanyʌ?keha·ká·, Onʌyote?a·ká·, Onuta?keha·ká·, Khayuka?a·ká·, and Tsi?twana?a·ká·territories, to bring the message of peace.[1] The Five Nations accepted the principles of ka?nikuhli·yó, kanolukhwátsla, and ka?satstásla? (peace of mind, love, and power) and unified to become Skanúhsat (one house). These interdependent principles promote a balanced system respecting all people, from ancestors to those yet to be born, to those of us in between from the youngest to the oldest; diverse characteristics of leadership; and community participatory decision-making with the intent of creating a governing process unifying nations to create Skanúhsat (one house).

It takes many days to recite this story. There are many protocols to be observed. Due to the impacts of colonization and oppression, many of the Haudenosaunee no longer speak our languages. This has required the Kayanlásla?kowa to be told in the Haudenosaunee language of the speaker and often interpreted into English.

For the purposes of this chapter, I will provide a simplified summary of the Kayanlásla?kowa. While there are a number of written versions of the Kayanlásla?kowa, I did not provide any citations to any of them to keep with the concept of oral culture where it is the teller's perspective of what was passed to them. I have heard the Kayanlásla?kowa recited multiple times and have had many discussions with various clan mothers, chiefs, faithkeepers, and various people throughout Haudenosaunee communities in order to learn and understand this story. Every time I hear this story, I am amazed by how much more I have to learn.

The multiple variations of the story make sense when one considers various speakers' perspectives, environment, era in time, upbringing, and their developmental stage at the time of the telling. Furthermore, it changes by translation, interpretation, and magnitude of understanding when the story is told in the Haudenosaunee languages. Many people resist the concept that one needs to understand the Haudenosaunee language in order to fully embrace the story. On the other hand, those who understand the implications of how language holds many cultural nuances will understand how this may be true.

INTRODUCTION OF THE KAYANLÁSLA?KOWA

The story of how the Haudenosaunee Confederacy formed begins by describing the context of the violent times just prior to the birth of the Peacemaker. The Peacemaker's given name is not utilized casually as there are specified times to use it. He was assigned the task of bringing the good message of peace to the people. The story goes into great detail regarding the Peacemaker's mother and grandmother, their journey to seek refuge from the warfare, to bring him into the world, and the unique upbringing provided by his matrilineal line. This upbringing was essential in order to fulfill the task of bringing peace through respect for all people.

The story then shifts to describing the preparations the Peacemaker makes in order to begin his journey. He introduces three principles of peace as he journeys through the territories. These principles change according to time and the teller. English interpretations commonly used are peace of mind, peace, power, righteousness, love, compassion, and good message. The two most consistent principles are peace of mind and power. The Peacemaker names a head clan mother and ten chiefs to help take the message out to the nations. They are faced with many challenges.

The last part of the story includes the Peacemaker, the head clan mother,

Tsikúhsase,[2] chiefs, and the Five Nations identifying and giving official title to all of the forty-nine clan mothers and fifty chiefs. He also provides detailed roles, responsibilities/functions, and processes to facilitate peaceful governance within their clans and nations, with governing protocols promoting participatory decision-making, fostering balance.

Respect for All People

The beginning of the story begins with conflict, which presents itself as war. The mother and daughter seek refuge in isolation for safety. During this time the daughter conceives a child, causing conflict between the mother and daughter. The grandmother attempts to vanquish the baby three times, to no avail. Shortly after, she receives a dream telling her how the baby came to be, what his purpose is, how to care for him, and to make right with her daughter. They are instructed to take him back to their village to begin sharing the message he is bringing.

Some primary themes become evident. The story begins illustrating the consequences of avoiding conflict between individuals, and within relationships, community, and nations. The birth of the child illustrates the powerful role of the intergenerational responsibility of women providing the nurturance of children from conception to young adulthood. Furthermore, the dream reinforces the importance of trusting dreamtime.

Diverse Characteristics of Leadership

The Peacemaker's journey begins by approaching various individuals, beginning with the KanyʌʔÊkeha·ká·/Mohawk. The Peacemaker makes it explicitly clear he is looking for notorious people, the worst, in order to change their minds and to assist with taking his message out to the nations. He takes great precaution, yet he risks enough to show compassion and courage, to listen, and to share his message with these individuals. His path includes multiple challenging events testing his perseverance and strength.

Throughout this beginning journey, the Peacemaker models powerful leadership characteristics. For instance, the Peacemaker is nonjudgmental, a good listener, and courageous in taking risks for the greater good. More importantly, he models respect for all through his leadership. He acquires a team of ten chiefs and Tsikúhsase to assist him in taking his message of peace out to the various nations he encounters.

The Peacemaker also renames each of these individuals with titles symbolizing their responsibilities. The titles of each of these clan mothers and chiefs give great meaning to the diverse leadership qualities critical for promoting and implementing peace as a governing practice. This appears to foster balance rather than hierarchy.

COMMUNITY DECISION-MAKING FOSTERING BALANCE

In the final section, respect for all is denoted in the decision-making processes necessary to work together. Processes were taught in order to govern themselves as individuals, clans, nations, and most importantly, One House. A critical inclusion is the process of how the people get their issues to council. The people of the clan must know their clan mother and chief. Issues are taken to the chief, then to the clan mother. It is the responsibility of the chief to know and understand the issues within his clan, provide counsel, and represent their voices in council both at the nation level and the Five Nation level at what is known as Grand Council. Through the nation and Grand Council, matters are addressed in a participatory manner.

CIRCLE WAMPUM

Some say the Circle Wampum is as old as the Kayanlásla?kowa. The circle denotes equality in that all chiefs have an equal voice in council. It is an illustration of how the Five Nations are to sit together in council. Each of the strings represent a chief, and they are grouped by nation. Some say the longest string represents the people, while others believe it represents one of the Chiefs Tehototálho or Honawiyétu. The edge of the circle has two interlocking strings representing when the Peacemaker directed the chiefs to interlock their arms, utilizing governing and spirituality to hold the Great White Pine up. The Peacemaker warned them to never let it fall so as to protect the people, the ways, and prevent calamity from falling upon the confederacy.

DECISION-MAKING FUNCTIONS

Seating and function are assigned by nation when all five nations come together and by clan for individual nation councils. Only the Grand Council, as shown in figure 1, and the individual Oneida Nation Council, shown in figure 2, will be explained and illustrated. Both councils sit in three parties with similar responsibilities during both types of councils.

In the Grand Council in figure 2, the Older Brothers, the Younger Brothers, and the Fire Keepers are the grouped titles. The Fire Keepers/Onuta?kehákʌ́/ Onondaga will open council and provide the agenda. The Older Brothers are the first to consider and give opinion on any matter brought to council. The Kanyʌ?keha·ká·/Mohawk make their considerations and pass to the Tsi?twana- ?a·ká·/Seneca for consideration. Once the Tsi?twana?a·ká· are done, they report to the Kanyʌ?keha·ká· to send the matter across the fire to the Younger Brothers to consider. The Onʌyote?a·ká·/Oneida make their considerations pass to the Khayuka?a·ká·/Cayuga for consideration. Once the Khayuka?a·ká· are completed they report out to the Onʌyote?a·ká· and the Onʌyote?a·ká· send the matter and decision back across the fire to the Older Brothers. The Kanyʌ?keha·ká· then send the matter back over to the Fire Keepers to strengthen/ratify the matter. An issue can cycle in this manner three times for agreement before being dropped. Finally, the Fire Keepers will close the council.

In the Onʌyote?a·ká·/Oneida Council it is the turtle, bear, and wolf clans that act in place of nation responsibilities. The wolves have the same function as the Fire Keepers. The turtle clan has responsibilities like the Older Brothers. The bear clan has the same function as the Younger Brothers.

Most significant, at both councils it is proper protocol for every speaker to begin by summarizing their understanding of what they heard before making recommendations or reporting out. This is to assure your group has heard, understands, and addresses the issue. This example highlights the importance of creating an environment promoting belonging and respect.

KAYANLÁSLA?KOWA PARADIGM

The protocol of summarizing what you have heard before making your point, and many others not mentioned here, prioritize an environment that many

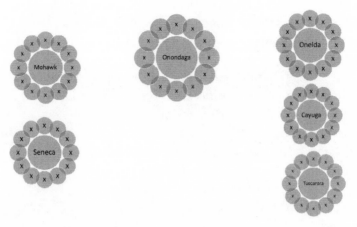

Figure 1. Haudenosaunee Grand Council Seating Arrangement

SOURCE: CREATED BY REBECCA M. WEBSTER

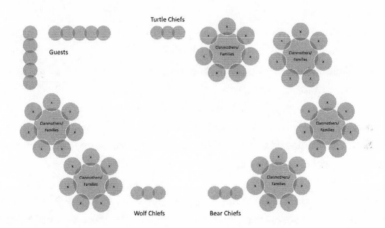

Figure 2. Oneida Nation Council Seating Arrangement

SOURCE: CREATED BY REBECCA M. WEBSTER

colonized Indigenous people have not experienced today or have forgotten. Learning the Kayanlásla?kowa can be a difficult task because of how different our minds have become through colonization. Below are some assumptions one may need to consider in order to open our minds to the different cultural paradigms and lessons embedded in the Kayanlásla?kowa.

- A practice of giving a recap of what people have said before responding is proper in this culture; the Haudenosaunee languages all reflect this.
- One mind is not thinking all the same, but recognizing how bringing diverse perspectives together increases the potential of bringing a group to one mind.
- Having one body, one head, and one life recognizes the importance of different responsibilities/functions within the whole.
- It was intended that acceptance and practice of this way of life determines membership, not blood quantum.
- Each of the clans and nations has different responsibilities in council.
- A clan is a much larger family than the common nuclear family.
- The clan system remains the foundation for organization throughout individual nations, as well as across the whole confederacy.
- No matter which of the nations one visits, there is always a clan/family to sit with.
- Working in a clan system is organizational, not nepotism.
- Each clan provides a clan mother and chief as individual council for all clan members and a voice in participatory governance at the nation and Grand Council levels.
- Clan mothers and chiefs have lifetime appointments and meet in council still today, even though ira governments are in operation.
- The Kayanlásla?kowa has an adoption process for whole nations and individuals based upon the acceptance of the law, hence the Tuscarora and individuals.
- The Kayanlásla?kowa has many language differences with both literal translations and interpretations, which cause great variability.

MODERN TRIBAL GOVERNANCE IN RELATION TO THE GREAT LAW

In order to understand the state of modern governance of the Oneida people in Wisconsin, one of the three Oneida communities today, a brief explanation of their history of Oneida governance is in order. After European contact, the entire Haudenosaunee confederacy suffered great losses at the hands of French, British, and American military campaigns.[3] The worst of these military confrontations was the Revolutionary War, leaving Haudenosaunee crops, orchards, and homes destroyed, and the nations scattered and factionalized. During this time, the State of New York also entered into a number of illegal treaties, dispossessing the Haudenosaunee of almost all of their land. Many Haudenosaunee people had no choice but to relocate within the new countries of the colonizers, the United States and Canada. A few groups of Oneida people moved to what would later become the State of Wisconsin in the early 1820s. Although challenged at every turn, the Oneida people persevered and continued to rebuild as a nation.

While the traditional systems of governance were still in place in their new home, some people began to introduce new ways of making decisions.[4] This caused tensions among the community. Exacerbating those tensions was the General Allotment Act of 1887.[5] This act broke up Oneida landholdings and gave title to individual tribal members. The act also was designed to undermine the powerful role of Haudenosaunee women as key decision-makers within their families, clans, and nations. After a period of time, this land became taxable, and could be mortgaged and sold. Within one generation, the Oneida people lost title to over 90 percent of the Oneida land on the reservation, often through illegitimate means.

Preexisting tensions became even more intense leading up to the passage of the Indian Reorganization Act (ira) in 1934.[6] The ira asked tribes to reorganize their governments in order to be eligible for certain federal programs, including reacquisition of land lost through allotment. When it came time to vote on acceptance of the ira, the Oneida people who followed their traditional form of government did not support it and refused to participate in the vote. Of those Oneida people who did vote, the majority voted to accept the ira. This federal voting and reorganization process further factionalized the Oneida people by overlooking the voices of those following their existing form of traditional government. This process acknowledged and empowered voters who did not follow the traditional form of government. The result was a new constitution almost identical to other tribal constitutions newly adopted under the ira. As a general rule, these "boilerplate" constitutions failed to reflect traditional governing principles or the unique cultural identity of the tribes except for the participatory part of governance.

MODERN GOVERNANCE PARTICIPATORY
DECISION-MAKING EXAMPLE

Oneida's General Tribal Council (gtc) has a long history of making decisions concerning the reacquisition of land on the Oneida Reservation, starting with the adoption of the constitution in 1934. Then in 1987, the gtc decided to dedicate $.30 from every carton of cigarettes to land acquisition.[7] A few months later, the gtc wanted to stabilize the land acquisition fund, so they adopted a new resolution to dedicate $500,000 per year to land acquisition plus 20 percent of all net profits in excess of the annual budget.[8]

As the years went on, and Oneida's overall budget increased, GTC passed a number of resolutions dedicating progressively more money for land acquisition. The most recent budgets included tens of millions of dollars toward land acquisition. The body currently responsible for deciding what land to purchase and at what price is the Oneida Land Commission. Tribal members elect individuals to serve on the Land Commission. The Land Commission delivers reports twice a year to GTC on acquisitions, and more frequently when the Land Commission acquires controversial properties.

Decision-Making in Oneida

Under Oneida's boilerplate constitution, there is a single governing body consisting of all the tribal members aged twenty-one and older.[9] This body is called the gtc. This body elects individuals to serve on the Business Committee (bc) to carry out tribal business when the gtc is not in session. In order for the gtc to conduct business, they need seventy-five people to constitute a quorum.

Due to difficulties in securing and maintaining a quorum, the gtc passed a policy in 2007 to pay tribal members $100 to attend gtc meetings.[10] Since 2007, meetings generally have between fifteen hundred and two thousand people in attendance. GTC makes decisions on the annual tribal budget, reports from areas within the tribal government, and special topics that arise through a petition process.

This action increased participation based upon a stipend for every member that attends the GTC. Now we have participation with many people who do not understand the functions, processes, and protocols of our GTC, the United States,

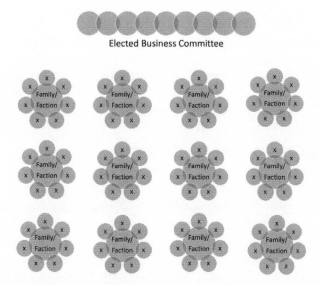

Figure 3. Oneida General Tribal Council Seating Arrangement
SOURCE: CREATED BY REBECCA M. WEBSTER.

and our ancient governing systems. This dynamic highlights the importance of reinstilling educational methods to teach governance from the youngest to the oldest once again. Without understanding governance, by default, people will gather at the meetings according to family or other groups where they have a sense of belonging, as shown in figure 3. People support elected officials who they feel represent their group.

This natural group behavior may relate back to why the Peacemaker supported the clan systems because it appears to be human nature to group this way. Ironically, when the Peacemaker brought this message and titled our nine clan mothers and chiefs, we had lost our clan system through warfare back then too. Researching this group dynamic further within our nation meetings today may indicate other innate qualities of participatory governance.

POTENTIAL APPLICATION FOR THIS DECISION-MAKING PROCESS

Innate qualities of participatory governance also link to the importance of sustenance as a critical responsibility woven into the Kayanlásla?kowa. This has origins back to when the Peacemaker identified a group of the first ten chiefs to help introduce Kayanláslaʔkowa across the nations. The first three Oneida chiefs named were all guarding the corn. The first was Hoʔtatshehteʔ, meaning Quiver Bearer was assigned the responsibility to sustain/support them. The second, Kanuhkweʔyo·tú·, Standing Ears of Corn, was assigned the responsibility to sustain all of life. The third, Teyohakwʌ·tí·, Through the Opening, was assigned the responsibility to carry traditions into the future. None of the other Five Nations chiefs' titles are related to the subject of corn.

Sustenance is a critical piece of the Kayanláslaʔkowa. This is further supported when the Peacemaker sent the first ten chiefs out to help spread the message. He made it clear when they shared the message that there would be a feast prepared for the whole community, from the youngest to the oldest. So how does this governing process apply to how Haudenosaunee organizes to grow corn today?[11] At the time of this writing, we are approaching the harvest of our corn this season in the midst of a worldwide pandemic. We have had to rethink our structure, responsibilities/functions, and processes as individuals, families, organizations, and nations. Many of our nations have suffered in multiple ways. Does the matter of growing corn belong at all levels of governance—the individual, clan, nation, and Grand Council? Is this not a national matter?

As corn growers, many of us are new to growing, protecting, and preparing our corn as well as other Indigenous foods. Through this endeavor, we have had many lessons. We are coming to understand that we have to make mistakes to learn. Most important, we have to have kaʔnikuhli·yó, kanolukhwátsla, and kaʔsatstásla? (peace of mind, love, and power) to grow and harvest, nurture, and prepare our foods together. This process requires a respectful participatory decision-making process in order to be able to work together to feed our nations.

Growing our corn helps to understand our cycle of creation and ceremonies. This has provided an experience of addressing our disconnection to creation by reconnecting through growing our foods and making relationships with all of creation. We are fortunate today our ways are still lying here for us to stand them up.

There is no doubt in my mind that utilizing the Kayanláslaʔkowa decision-making process could be very instrumental in helping various groups to grow corn for our nations once again in order to promote participation of the community while also teaching and practicing an ancient governing system promoting peace.

Conclusion

In my view there needs to be foundational work in the area of teaching governance. This can be done by utilizing the Kayanláslaʔkowa to assist in educating, practicing, and applying this way to community initiatives. It would support practice in governance from the youngest to the oldest. With an increase in people identifying with their clan, opportunities emerge to organize and function according to clan systems. In turn, we will be promoting a sense of belonging and cultural identity by understanding how clanship relates directly to participatory governance. This way honors the gifts of all. Why not start utilizing this way and open up to our foods helping us to remember our ways? They are both ancient, intergenerational, and interdependent.

A final note: A man who has taught many people about our ancient governing system and ways expressed how in his upbringing, he often heard other speakers state it is important to always share how you came to an understanding, because somewhere among us someone is sitting there listening and they are taking it all in. A strong reminder that we have a responsibility to the faces still coming from the ground to bring what is here, today, forward.

Practitioner Perspective

As we wander away from our truth, our history, and our culture, we become more dysfunctional.[12] Our community was built on networks and communication. The Great Law is the embodiment of that system. We moved from small communities based on discussion and awareness of the needs of the family and community group, to aggregates of communities meeting and talking, understanding each other, and being aware of the needs of the whole, to aggregates of all the Native nations. This took time, it took understanding, it took patience. When we move away from these things, we become less aware of the needs of the community, the family, the group, and we end up not meeting any needs of ourselves or others.

NOTES

1. Literal translations and English names for the Five Nations consecutively: Flint People/ Mohawk, Standing Stone People/Oneida, Hill People/Onondaga, People of the Swamp/ Cayuga, and Mountain People/Seneca.
2. Literal translation: New Face.
3. Jack Campisi and Laurence M. Hauptman, eds., *The Oneida Indian Experience: Two Perspectives* (Syracuse, NY: Syracuse University Press, 1988).
4. Campisi and Hauptman, *The Oneida Indian Experience*.
5. Laurence M. Hauptman and L. Gordon McLester, eds. *The Oneida Indians in the Age of Allotment, 1860–1920*, vol. 253 (Norman: University of Oklahoma Press, 2006).
6. Locklear, Arlinda. "The Allotment of the Oneida Reservation and Its Legal Ramifications." In Campisi and Hauptman, *The Oneida Indian Experience*, 83–93.
7. Oneida General Tribal Council Resolution 1-06-87-A.
8. Oneida General Tribal Council Resolution 10-29-87-A. See https://oneida-nsn.gov/ wp-content/uploads/2016/03/10-29-87-A-GTC-FY-88-Budget-for-Land-Acquisition-Expenditures.pdf.
9. In 2015, Oneida tribal members amended the constitution to lower the voting age to eighteen.
10. General Tribal Council Meeting Stipend Payment Policy, BC-12-07-07-A. See https:// oneida-nsn.gov/wp-content/uploads/2020/10/Chapter-111-General-Tribal-Council-Meeting-Stipend-Payment-Policy-BC-09-23-20-B.pdf.
11. This whole chapter was inspired by the frustration experienced through unaddressed conflict in a corn-growing cooperative. The group avoided passive conflict, which over time was destructive to the whole group, thus impacting the corn harvest and the community. In order to work through my anger, frustration, and pain, I looked for a solution to propose. I thought: we are growing our ancestral corn; should we not be able to govern ourselves with the processes that were given to us from the Peacemaker, also passed to us through our ancestors? This story helped me to heal and see a governing process that could be utilized in our corn co-op. And although ancient, this is applicable because it is principle-centered.
12. Jo Anne House, Oneida chief counsel and parliamentarian at GTC meetings.

GLOSSARY

Clan systems. Categorization of families of turtle, wolf, and bear clans.
Haudenosaunee. They Make a House. Refers to the Five Nations of Mohawk, Oneida, Onondaga, Cayuga, and Seneca. (Later the Tuscarora would join.)

Honawiyétu. He Disappeared.

Ho?tatshehte?. Quiver Bearer.

Ka?nikuhli·yó. Peace of mind.

Kanolukhwátsla. Love.

Kantsyokwanhasta?. People–the group–the thing that binds us together.

Kanuhkwe?yo·tú·. Standing Ears of Corn.

Kanyʌ?keha·ká·. People of the Flint/Mohawk.

Ka?satstásla?. Power.

Kayanlásla?kowa. Great Law of Peace.

Khayuka?a·ká·. People of the Swamp/Cayuga.

Oneida General Tribal Council (GTC). Indian Reorganization governing council for Oneida.

Onuta?keha·ká·. Hill People/Onondaga.

Onʌyote?a·ká·. Standing Stone People/Oneida.

Peacemaker. Because we only use his name at certain times, this is the replacement name for him in English.

Skanúhsat. One house.

Tehototálho. Entangled One.

Teyohakwʌ·tí·. Through the Opening.

Tsikúhsase. New Face.

Tsi?twana?a·ká·. Mountain People/Seneca.

Operations Management Roles and Responsibilities

Providing a Space for Haudenosaunee Decision-Making

Lois Stevens and Brandon Yellowbird-Stevens

THE HAUDENOSAUNEE ARE OFTEN CREDITED WITH BEING THE INSPIRATION FOR the U.S. governmental structure when the Constitution was first penned. The Great Law of the Haudenosaunee had governed the people long before European contact, and while many factions of our initial colonizers sought to destroy our way of living and nearly succeeded, they understood that our structure was successful. The purpose of this chapter is to first discuss the Great Law and its importance to the Haudenosaunee people. Secondly, looking specifically at the Oneida Nation in Wisconsin this chapter briefly examines the tribe's government structure, focusing specifically on the psychological biases associated with the decision-making process of the General Tribal Council and how this has contributed to the weakening of Oneida's commitment to One Mind. Finally we will discuss how restructuring the process in a safe space can revitalize the principles of the Great Law and develop decisions that best serve the people.

BEST PRACTICES

- Incorporate Great Law principles for more efficient tribal operations.
- Address psychological biases in the tribal member decision-making process.

- Discontinue financial rewards for negative behaviors.
- Adopt ancestral knowledge systems to outline the roles and responsibilities of all tribal members.
- Provide a safe space for compassionate and effective community engagement.

INTRODUCTION

Operational management refers to practices that create the highest level of efficiency possible within an organization. The Oneida Nation is grounded on the values of "a good mind, a good heart, and a strong fire." These values were born out of the Haudenosaunee Great Law; however, the tribe operates under a governmental structure that is foreign to our ancestral knowledge system. I was once told that the more you try to define sovereignty, the more it is weakened. So I will not try to define this term, but merely express that sovereignty is enacted every time we make a decision. Tribal operations management refers to the policy and procedure aspect of sovereignty—that is, how a nation addresses and responds to the decisions of our people. Therefore, this chapter looks at the core of the Oneida Nation's decision-making process to address how the current government structure may be obstructing growth due to the lack of our Great Law roles and responsibilities in place.

THREE PRINCIPLES OF THE GREAT LAW

One of the oldest and most important stories told among the Haudenosaunee is the story of the Peacemaker and his powerful journey to unify the people during a time of great conflict. This story has been told to Haudenosaunee for generations, reminding us of our history, our responsibility, and the peace that once unified the original Five Nations of the Haudenosaunee. There are many variations of this long and complex story, as it was passed down through oral traditions. In addition to its complexity, there is no "official" written version of the Great Law to reference, and conveying its true beauty in limited words is difficult.[1] Nonetheless, this section will attempt to break down three guiding principles interpreted through the overall message of unity and to outline the roles and responsibilities that were assigned to the people. These three principles are often presented using different terminology, such as peace, power, equity, reason, health, good mind, righteousness, etc., so for the purpose of this chapter we will be using the terms Righteousness, Power, and Peace with Oneida translations: *Ka'nikuhli·yó*, *Katsatstʌ́hsla'*, and *Skano*.

Ka'nikuhli·yó—Righteousness

John Mohawk said righteousness refers to something akin to the shared ideology of the people using their purest and most unselfish minds.[2] Ka'nikuhli·yó translates to "the openness of the good spirit and mind" or "good mind" in Oneida. This principle tells us to put aside feelings of superiority, as we are all equal. This refers to relationships with all elements of the universe: human, animal, and nature. We are to exercise a reciprocal relationship so that all benefit.

Katsatstʌ́hsla'—Power

This principle refers to the power of those good minds to operate with reason and justice. We must use our minds to exercise a healthy path towards peace and to settle our differences without the use of force. Using five arrows to signify the power of unity, the Peacemaker referred to a single arrow being weak and easily broken, but when five arrows are tied together their collective strength cannot be broken (see figure 1).

Skano—Peace

While this principle may be self-explanatory, it refers to peace among the people and an agreement to end fighting, bloodshed, and warfare. True unity means laying down your weapons and making decisions that best serve the collective. However, peace does not only mean the absence of war or violence. Peace also refers to our own internal or spiritual peace: knowing ourselves and being able to peacefully engage in decision-making within the ideology of one mind.

These principles began the unification of the Five Nations of the

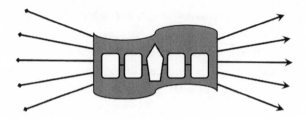

Figure 1. Strength in Unity based on community concepts. Five arrows are going behind the wampum belt, symbolizing the strength the Haudenosaunee Confederacy has by unifying together.

Haudenosaunee Confederacy, with Tuscarora joining later to form what is the Six Nations today. Another constant symbol is the circle, representing that these three principles do not stand alone but are tied together in a cyclical manner, continually complementing each other through the pursuit of one mind. (See figure 3 later in this chapter.)

ONEIDA NATION

Today, the Oneida Nation is the result of nearly two centuries of generational trauma founded on the displacement of traditional place and near abandonment of cultural self. Due to heavy Christian influence, the Oneida people were removed from their homelands in the state of New York to an area near what would become the city of Green Bay, Wisconsin. Christian influence meant this particular group of Oneidas abandoned much of their ceremonial and linguistic practices. This also meant the abandonment of Great Law ideology and adoption of hierarchical practices. Their situation was only aggravated by the Dawes Act of 1887, when allotments were created as a method to pulverize tribal land masses and led to the loss of 95 percent of Oneida land ownership.[3] And even more so with the Indian Reorganization Act of 1934, which stopped the allotment process but forced a mundane constitution, solidifying the loss of traditional Haudenosaunee governance.[4]

Today, the tribe is governed by the Oneida Constitution, which was first adopted in 1936, and states: "We, the people of the Oneida Nation, grateful to Almighty God for his fostering care, in order to reestablish our tribal organization, to conserve and develop our common resources and to promote the welfare of ourselves and our descendants, do hereby ordain and establish this Constitution."[5] The governing body of the Oneida Nation is referred to as the General Tribal Council (GTC) and is composed of all the qualified voters of the Oneida Nation, with all members eighteen years and older being considered qualified voters.[6] The Oneida Business Committee (OBC) is an elected body of officials that govern the nation when the GTC is not in session and is made up of nine individuals.

Within the government structure, there are three branches: executive, legislative, and judiciary. The executive branch consists of the supervisory authority of the OBC officers (chair, vice-chair, treasurer, and secretary). A subcommittee made of the five OBC at-large members is the Legislative Operating Committee (LOC), which represents the legislative body of the nation. The LOC was granted authority by the GTC through the Legislative Procedures Act with the purpose of drafting laws and policies and reviewing past and current laws.[7] Although new, having been adopted in 2013, the judiciary operates as an independent branch of the Oneida Nation government entrusted by the General Tribal Council as a neutral forum for the resolution of government and civil issues on the Oneida Nation reservation.[8] The Oneida Nation's current chart of organization honors the power of the people in the form of the General Tribal Council, yet lacks a proper separation of powers between executive and legislative. While the OBC members represent separate branches, neither can take independent action without the full OBC approval (see figure 2).[9]

According to the constitution, seventy-five qualified voters shall constitute a quorum at any meeting of the GTC. In 2008, the Oneida Nation adopted the "General Tribal Council Meeting and Stipend Payment Policy," which requires the tribe to pay each eligible GTC member a $100 stipend for their participation.[10] The original petition addressed the concern about low membership participation in meetings by offering compensation to members to cover costs associated with their attendance.[11] While this petition effectively addressed the need for higher participation rates by tribal members, it also created an environment of negativity within the community. Currently, GTC meetings operate in a forum setting, with several OBC members sitting on a stage, with microphones below giving the community opportunity for discussion. There is also an "overflow" room, where the rest of the OBC officials sit in front of the individuals who could

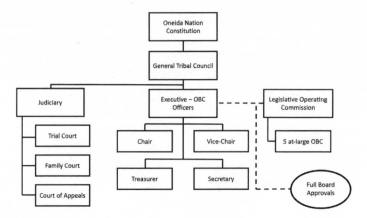

Figure 2. Oneida Nation Chart of Organization developed through consultation with Oneida Nation officials.

not fit in the large room. They watch the proceedings through live video feed, but it can often be hard to hear the full context of the proceedings in this room. These conditions are not ideal for thoughtful decision-making.

PSYCHOLOGY OF DECISION-MAKING

In *Basic Call to Consciousness,* John Mohawk acknowledged the creation of the Great Law as the evolutionary recognition that "vertical hierarchy creates conflict," and to combat that conflict, the Haudenosaunee dedicated themselves to a "complex organization of their society to function to prevent the rise internally of hierarchy."[12] While the Oneida Nation has given the power to the people, current governance has fostered the internal rise of hierarchy by perpetuating the negativity generated in the GTC meetings. The decision-making process associated with the GTC meetings has contributed to the rise of conflict among tribal members.

As individuals, we want to believe that we operate logically, yet our societal norms have much more influence on our decisions than we care to admit.[13] Decisions are often motivated by the group, not the individual. Each of us has our own social reference group—a group of friends, family members, even neighbors—who inadvertently pressure us into conforming to their attitudes and beliefs, therefore maintaining the balance of said group.[14] This social bias is readily on display at every GTC meeting held when our votes are influenced by our closest family members and friends. This happens because there is a vast amount of information for us to process in a short amount of time, so we actually fail to do so and cast a vote that makes us most comfortable. At this point, we are not operating logically but aligning ourselves with the norms of our closest reference group.

In addition, those of us who may acknowledge that this is an accurate description of our decision-making process at GTC meetings may still be making psychological arguments in our heads that serve our own ego. Cognitive dissonance is the unsettling feeling that the world does not fit because we are trying to reconcile two or more contradictory beliefs or values in our minds and this may result in painting a prettier picture of ourselves than is created by our actions.[15] For instance, as human beings we have a tendency to judge those who do not hold the same beliefs as ourselves. Therefore, when we witness others that are voting with their reference groups or verbally supporting other reference groups, we are quick to judge them for their fealty to that group and label them as the bad ones or the followers. We rationalize our decisions by defending the character of the elected officials or enrolled individuals within our reference groups. We are then judging others while letting ourselves off the hook because it is more consistent with our self-image. In an effort to reduce these contradictory beliefs we opt for a self-serving bias that holds ourselves in higher esteem than others.[16]

Even when we have all the information and we acknowledge dissonance, it may still not be enough to respond logically. Regardless of how much information we possess, we are still faced with the limited amount of time to process that information coupled with the limited choices given (yea, nay, or abstain); therefore information alone does not change our behavior on a rational level. Operant conditioning states that a favorable consequence from a past act imprints itself in our minds, while a punishment associated with that action stamps it out of our minds.[17] While this paper does not recommend punishment, it is merely pointing out that in our current governmental structure, tribal members are consistently rewarded financially for their participation in the GTC meetings, no matter how much, how little, or even how negative that participation is. Therefore those actions are imprinted in their minds. The good minds that are in attendance are poisoned by this negativity, leading to feelings of anger, resentment, and hopelessness.

This negativity is synonymous with the Oneida Nation's GTC meetings when a tribal member can ignite anger with a microphone in a room full of unrest, or with a simple social media post. While social media is a great communication tool, it can also create negativity when we have a platform at our fingertips. The creation of a Facebook group for Oneida Nation members has the potential to be an online space for members to discuss current tribal issues and help develop strategies for change; however, this particular group has fostered negative emotions amongst the community. Attacking members of the OBC, tribal employees, and other community members because of their beliefs, actions, or familial ties has been a consistent trend. Kristofferson et al. refer to the notion that once an individual has felt they have made a positive impression on a social media audience, they are less willing to engage again for the same cause. Meaning these quick online "actions" address our personal satisfaction, therefore disrupting actual offline participation.[18] So, then, not only does this create feelings of unrest in the community, it could also contribute to community inaction in relevant settings. There must be a safer process.

RESTRUCTURING THE GTC PROCESS

The GTC petition that called for the $100 had originally included an initial step towards bettering the GTC function: it requested the "establishment of an office of General Tribal Council to review/monitor all aspects of tribal operations." This office would consist of one individual to review issues requested by the GTC, taking assignments from the GTC and reporting information directly back to them.[19] The petition was headed in the right direction; there is a need for improvement in how the current GTC functions and there is a need for better processing of vast amounts of information entrusted to the GTC. The issues addressed in the original petition were valid; however, one major issue is that it wanted to put this power into the hands of one person rather than into the hands of the community. For the community to better process information, it would be more beneficial for this information to be disseminated into smaller groupings/agendas that can be reviewed, discussed, and monitored by tribal members.

Perhaps the adoption of our complex clan system into the gtc structure would address this current issue in Oneida governance. Within the Oneida

Nation clan system, each tribal member belongs to either the Turtle, Bear, or Wolf Clan, and each clan has roles and responsibilities they must fulfill within the nation as a whole. The role of the Wolf Clan is to be the Pathfinders and guide the people to live the way of life the Creator intended; the Bear Clan are the Keepers of Medicine, known as healers with the knowledge of medicinal plants; and the Turtle Clan are the Keepers of the Knowledge, who represent all of the environment and the cycles of the moon. Within a meeting setting, the clan system operates by breaking up responsibilities in a cyclical manner for each clan to develop a consensus. The responsibilities are as follows:

- The Wolf Clan receives the issues, sets an agenda, and then sends the agenda to the Turtle Clan.
- The Turtle Clan researches necessary topics and concerns according to the agenda and then sends the information to the Bear Clan.
- The Bear Clan reviews the information and makes recommendations that establish a dialogue between the Turtles and Bears.
- The two clans send a unified recommendation to the Wolf Clan, who then details additional concerns or ratifies the decision by establishing full consensus, and the circle is complete.[20]

The sole purpose of this system is to establish a decision-making process where all come to one mind and all are in agreement.[21]

SAFE SPACE FOR COMMUNITY ACTION

So then, we are faced with the true challenge in applying this ancestral knowledge system to our current government structure. Understanding how to bring our minds together as one is the first step; the next step is developing spaces where the community can make unbiased and thoughtful decisions. During times of uncertainty, recognizing our shared values and aligning our decision-making process creates a safe space for discussion. This section proposes the creation of a safe space for such dialogue. Cree philosopher Willie Ermine refers to this as an ethical space: a place between two worldviews that offers the potential for new models of research and knowledge production codeveloped through respect, yet guided by a community's past.[22] We have already acknowledged the Oneida Nation's place-based struggles that separated them from other Haudenosaunee nations; for this reason, adopting the Great Law into governance will not be an easy task. However, providing the Oneida community with a safe space (separate from the OBC and other governmental structures) to research issues concerning the tribe will help the people take that first step in returning to one mind by developing viable solutions not heavily influenced by their reference groups.

When tribal members are broken into their reference groups, they forget their place in the community as a whole. Bringing them together where they are giving and receiving support from other tribal members may rebuild that sense of community that was lost. But this space is much more than a shared concept; it can be a physical meeting place. The Indigenous Gathering Place Committee out of Canada brought this idea into fruition by creating an ethical space as a place where everyone can "explore ideas, aspirations, and thoughts, and reconnect with traditions, protocols, and practices to define a new future and preserve the unique perspectives, cultures, language and ways of knowing and doing."[23] Such places allow for a safe environment where people feel respected and valued through the expression of their shared place. Developing a sense of control over the whole process by exercising their voice in smaller settings within their outlined clan responsibilities allows their voice to be heard in a constructive manner.

The creation of an Oneida Nation Research Center would serve this need for a safe and ethical space by providing the community with a physical place to meet, explore ideas, research problems/solutions, and feel welcome regardless of reference groups or familial ties. This center would fit into the three principles of the Great Law and provide needed change for the gtc process in the following ways (see figure 3):

- Roles and responsibilities clearly laid out for each tribal member.
- Proper amount of time to research and analyze information.
- Freedom from tribal titles and social reference group labels.
- Creation of dialogue grounded on principles of one mind and fostered by the well-being of the nation.

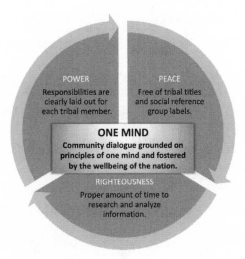

Figure 3. Practice of One Mind in a Safe Space

SOURCE: CREATED BY THE AUTHOR BASED ON COMMUNITY KNOWLEDGE.

Conclusion

According to the Haudenosaunee clan system, the people were entrusted long ago with research responsibilities to best serve the community as a whole. The creation of these safe spaces are essential for all Indigenous communities. This chapter goes further in suggesting that the creation of a physical place for the Oneida Nation would assist in adopting the principles of the Great Law by helping the community fulfill their clan responsibilities outside of the OBC and GTC influence. Moving forward, the Oneida community must think of the next seven generations and how we will leave this earth in a better state for their survival. The people have much work to do, however; if our history has taught us anything, it is that we are a resilient people. We will continue to use this resilience by revitalizing our true Haudenosaunee selves by first putting our minds together as one, then exercising our inherent role as researchers, and finally accepting our responsibility to make decisions that demonstrate Peace, Power, and Righteousness for our community.

PRACTITIONER PERSPECTIVE

In the current state of the GTC, it is paramount to provide a safe environment for every GTC member to participate in their government.[24] Transitioning to a traditional system may be uncomfortable and take time; however, we should consider the time it took for us to lose our knowledge of that system to begin with. Only when our own biases, on all levels, are set aside can a true One Mind be possible. One Mind decision-making creates an environment where all ideas are thoroughly vetted through a traditional process. While a similar process does exist now, one where each member has a chance to share their ideas, the current environment does not provide a setting conducive to openness while being void of negativity. Since the inception of the $100 GTC stipend in 2007, there has been a significant increase in attendance, but not an equally significant increase in valuable participation. In the years prior to 2007, there were eleven meetings per year with an average of 102 members in attendance. Post GTC stipend, the average attendance rate has easily surpassed one thousand members per meeting; however, the numbers of actual participants in the meetings are still drastically low. From 2013 to 2020, the Oneida Nation spent $10.2 million on GTC stipends alone. This practice needs to change. The goal should be to propose how ideas are first accepted, then nurtured with thoughtful consideration through our traditional way. This process of introducing a new, yet traditional structure would be best done in a slow manner and broken into many steps. With careful attention to detail, communication, and listening to the story of our history we will unwind generations of deliberate disconnection and return to our ways brought back to us by the Peacemaker.

NOTES

1. For the purpose of this chapter, the definition of official is "having the approval or authorization of an authority or public body." Lexico U.S. Dictionary, https://www.lexico.com/en/definition/official.

2. John Mohawk, *Basic Call to Consciousness*. ed. Akwesasne Notes (Summertown, TN: Book Pub. Co, 1991).

3. Laurence M. Hauptman and L. Gordon McLester, *The Oneida Indians in the Age of Allotment, 1860–1920* (Norman: University of Oklahoma Press, 2006).

4. Rebecca M. Webster, "This Land Can Sustain Us: Cooperative Land Use Planning on

the Oneida Reservation," *Planning Theory & Practice* 17, no. 1 (January 2, 2016): 9–34.

5. "Constitution and By-laws of the Oneida Nation," June 16, 2015, https://oneida-nsn. gov/wp-content/uploads/2018/05/2015-06-16-Tribal-Constitution.pdf.

6. Ibid.

7. Oneida Nation, "Legislative Procedures Act," n.d., https://oneida-nsn.gov/wp-content/uploads/2018/05/Chapter-109-Legislative-Procedures-Act-GTC-01-07-13-A. pdf.

8. Oneida Nation, "GTC Resolution # 03-19-17-A," n.d., https://oneida-nsn.gov/wp-content/uploads/2016/03/03-19-17-A-Designation-of-the-Oneida-Judiciary.pdf.

9. The chart is a general representation to illustrate lack of powers of separation; not all departments are listed.

10. "General Tribal Council Meeting and Stipend Payment Policy," February 13, 2013, https://oneida-nsn.gov/wp-content/uploads/2021/04/Chapter-111-General-Tribal-Council-Meeting-Stipend-Payment-Policy-BC-02-13-13-E-Updated-Footnote.pdf.

11. Oneida Nation, "Special General Tribal Council Meeting Notice," August 11, 2007.

12. Mohawk, *Basic Call to Consciousness*.

13. Susan M. Koger and Deborah Du Nann Winter, *The Psychology of Environmental Problems: Psychology for Sustainability*, 3rd ed. (New York: Psychology Press, 2010); Lois Lorraine Stevens, "Trusting the Culture in Our Food: Overcoming Barriers for Sustainable Indigenous Foodways" (master's thesis, University of Kansas, 2014), https://kuscholarworks.ku.edu/handle/1808/18096.

14. Ibid.

15. Frances Moore Lappé, *EcoMind: Changing the Way We Think, to Create the World We Want* (New York: Nation Books, 2013); Stevens, "Trusting the Culture in Our Food."

16. Koger and Winter, *The Psychology of Environmental Problems*; Stevens, "Trusting the Culture in Our Food."

17. Koger and Winter, *The Psychology of Environmental Problems*.

18. Anna Kende, Adrienn Ujhelyi, Adam Joinson, and Tobias Greitemeyer, "Putting the Social (Psychology) into Social Media," *European Journal of Social Psychology* 45, no. 3 (April 2015): 277–78; Kirk Kristofferson, Katherine White, and John Peloza, "The Nature of Slacktivism: How the Social Observability of an Initial Act of Token Support Affects Subsequent Prosocial Action," *Journal of Consumer Research* 40, no. 6 (April 2014): 1149–66.

19. Oneida Nation, "Special General Tribal Council Meeting Notice."

20. See link to further information and figures: Oneida Nation, "Clan System and Responsibilities," 2018, https://exploreoneida.com/culture-and-history/

clan-system-and-responsibilities/.

21. Bob Brown, "Clans of the Oneida People," ed. Tiffany Schultz, September 2013, https://oneida-nsn.gov/wp-content/uploads/2016/04/IROQUOIS-CLAN-SYSTEM-CLANS-OF-THE-ONEIDA-PEOPLE-9.13.pdf.

22. Willie Ermine, "The Ethical Space of Engagement," *Indigenous Law Journal* 6, no. 1 (2017): 11; Kelly Bannister, "From Ethical Codes to Ethics as Praxis: An Invitation," *Ethnobiology Letters* 9, no. 1 (July 11, 2018): 13–26.

23. Aaron Aubin Consulting Inc., "The Case for a Calgary Indigenous Gathering Place," n.d., https://www.sisn.ca/wp-content/uploads/2019/05/TheCaseforaCalgaryIGPPublic2017-2.pdf.

24. Brandon Yellowbird-Stevens, vice-chairman, Oneida Nation.

GLOSSARY

Cognitive dissonance. State of having inconsistent thoughts, beliefs, or attitudes, especially as relating to behavioral decisions and attitude change.

Displacement. The moving of a people from their ancestral or culturally connected place.

Ethical space. A place where traditional oral practices and Western written practices are paralleled, leveraging the strengths of the respective processes to co-create a safe place to design, develop, validate, and work together in harmony, bridging the gap between cultures and activating meaningful reconciliation.

General Tribal Council (GTC). The governing body of the Oneida Nation composed of all the qualified voters (all members 18 years and older) of the nation.

Legislative Operating Committee (LOC). The body granted authority by the GTC through the Legislative Procedures Act with the purpose of drafting laws and policies and reviewing past and current laws.

Oneida Business Committee (OBC). An elected body of officials that govern the nation when the GTC is not in session; it is made up of nine individuals.

One Mind. Haudenosaunee philosophy that the collective minds hold power; unity of the people.

Operant conditioning. A method of learning that employs rewards and punishments for behavior.

Social bias. Refers to being in favor of or against individuals or ideas based on their social identities/reference groups.

Social reference group. A standard by which we measure our behaviors and attitudes. Reference groups guide our behavior and attitudes and help us identify social norms.

Authorizing Environment

Making Decisions with People and Governments

Kris Peters and Amy Gould

WHAT ARE THE EXTENT AND LIMITATIONS OF YOUR AUTHORITY TO ACT? OUR authority to act comes from teachings, lifeways, traditions, and the mantle of responsibility for governing with our peoples. However, as tribal administrators swimming in multiple parallel government streams, we are simultaneously both constrained and reassured in our authority to act by our "operating environments": bureaucracies, tribal constitutions, laws, codes, and agreements. This chapter cannot get into the deep nuances of the operating environments established by each sovereign government. Instead, we will explore the meaning of our "authority to act" as tribal administrators from four leadership lenses: relationality, change, roles, and abilities.

BEST PRACTICES

- Situational awareness
- Ask the right questions, to the right people
- Know your role (not just your position)
- Know your ability: authority to say "no," but maybe not "yes"
- Humility: Who are you working for?

INTRODUCTION

Managing your authorizing environment is hard; sometimes it's hard to even nail down what the current authorizing environment is or is not. This said, "given the way authority constrains or supports certain behaviors, it must be said that authority structures have huge implications for what organizations do, how they do these things, when, where, and with whom."[1] This chapter addresses your authority to act within tribal governing processes (not just within the operating environment that is the day-to-day functions of administration, but within the authorizing environment that is rooted in the lived realities of leadership within tribal communities).

Our fundamental assumption is that many types of authority are needed for decision-making: formal authority and informal authority. Some days it may feel like any authority is difficult to attain; however, it is not usually located in only one position or person. This is because administrative actions usually have multiple decision-makers responding to different authorizers within a variety of contexts. Efforts to understand your authority to act should include personal leadership lenses to establish your specific appropriate authorizing environment based on the relational spheres of authority around you.

FIRST LEADERSHIP LENS: RELATIONALITY

Authority is based on who we are and where we are. For the purposes of this chapter, we define the authorizing environment in tribal administration as the personal, communal, and workplace shared understandings that allow all of us to invest in getting things done for our people. Synonyms for "authorizing" include: empower, license, bless, give the go-ahead, and say the word.[2] To this end, our environment to function within authority is place-based. Our authorizing environment shifts, ebbs, and flows based on where we are: in the administration building vs. in the youth center; in council chambers vs. out fishing; at the healing house on-rez vs. the county public-works department.

Leaders in any organization have limits on their authority. Mark Moore termed these limits the "authorizing environment" or "AE."[3] This refers to all the sources and strategies of authority with which the leader/administrator acts, both formal and informal, in order to create public value. An AE provides legitimacy and support to the decision-maker. Anyone expected to make decisions must have a clear comprehension of their authorizing environment.

Scenario

I worked for several years as a tribal administrator for my own tribe. I have wondered if it would have been easier to work for a different tribe or work for my own. As the boss, you are faced with difficult decisions from time to time. You may have a family member working for you; this is especially true for small tribes. What if that person is a difficult employee? What if the employee is part of a large, politically powerful family? If you choose to look the other way, you will lose the respect of your other employees and some of the community, and ultimately services could be negatively impacted. If you choose to reprimand and even terminate this employee, the political repercussions could be heavy. What if the employee who works for you is also one of the council members who you report to? These are real-life scenarios that are not uncommon in Indian Country. This is not something that you typically learn how to handle in a book, or in your graduate studies, or in any leadership seminar. As a young tribal administrator at my small tribe, I also learned quickly about some of the historical issues/rivalries between my family and some of the other families. There were some people who held a grudge against me or just did not like me because of my last name. And unfortunately they do not just come out and say it. They just give you the cold shoulder, or act passively resistant to what you are trying to do, and you have no idea what you did to make them upset. How do you handle that sort of thing?

The answer to all of this in the simplest terms is to be yourself; communicate, communicate, communicate; handle things in a consistent way; and be honest, respectful to others, hard-working, and compassionate towards the needs of others. Seems simple enough, right?

I think about my past ancestors, at times even more specifically of my late grandfather watching me. And I ask myself, "are the actions that I am taking or about to take or the words I am about to say going to make those ancestors, my grandfather, proud of the man I have become?" "Am I carrying on the legacy of these great people and are all the struggles they went through in vain?" I will also ask myself, "am I making my children proud?"

Best Practice: Situational Awareness

Working in a professional office, there are many rules, policies, ordinances, and standards that we must follow. Understanding budgets, logistics, leadership, how to run meetings, set agendas, get people in the right place, and do the work. These are operating environments that follow mostly set standards, written or unwritten. But, are there other factors that affect your daily decisions, direct you, guide you, determine course of action? Are these unique to your community? Would they fly in another community?

We argue that there are many personal or authorizing environments in the job of a tribal administrator within a tribal community that, if not taken into consideration, can make your job much more difficult. How does one make decisions with these authorizing environments in mind? Start by identifying two very obvious things. Who are you working for and who are you? What tribe is this? Is it a small or big tribe? Where is it located? What is important to the people of this tribe? What is their history and traditions? Who are the people and their families?

Know their connections with the local waterway and geography; know what is sacred to them (see figure 1). Understand their trials and tribulations with the local government, the state, and the federal government. These considerations will all play a role in what is important to the people of this community and in effect play a big role in how you run your government.

Next, openly identify to yourself who you are. If you are non-Indian, accept the fact that there will be an uphill battle in gaining the trust of some of the membership of this community, regardless of who you are. Accept this fact and move forward immediately. There are very good, deep-rooted reasons for this mistrust that are in no way personal to you. I know many non-Native allies who have put together long, distinguished careers in tribal government, and have gained great respect from the tribal community. Your job as a non-Native is to listen and learn from elders and cultural leaders, and to attend tribal events. Be respectful and open to tribal government norms and be prepared to put away non-tribal government norms. If you do not accept where you work and who you work for, then no amount of policies, leadership skills, or work ethic will protect you in the long run.

Try living and working with the "seven generations" mindset. Respect, honor, and carry on the ways of our ancestors; teach our youth and protect and ensure

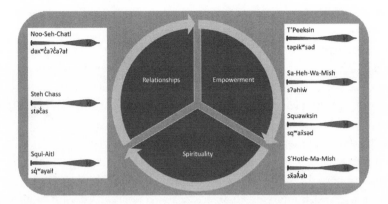

Figure 1. The seven names above each paddle represent the names of each band who made up the Squaxin Island Tribe. Each lived on separate inlets in the South Salish Sea (Puget Sound). Under each paddle is the name written in Lushootseed, our native language.

SOURCE: L. GRENINGER, K. PETERS, M. ZIMMERMAN, "TALKING CIRCLES AT THE SQUAXIN ISLAND TRIBE," MASTER OF PUBLIC AFFAIRS CAPSTONE, EVERGREEN STATE COLLEGE, 2016.

a healthy environment; maintain our culture for future generations (see figure 1). You have to maintain your integrity in everything and have respect for the people whom you work for.

SECOND LEADERSHIP LENS: CHANGE

This section offers ideas for perspectives you could adopt to hone the nuances of your spheres of authority. We believe the best practices outlined here will equip readers to identify their own effective approaches to addressing complex challenges in their authorizing environment at their tribe. However, our authorizing environments are not static or permanent. Authority can change with each decision, policy, budget, crisis, community event, or political shift/maneuver. This is because the foundation for the concept of any government is governing. Just having formal structures of government to establish our operating environment isn't enough. We also have to humbly and inquisitively be in tune with people doing the actual governing, formally and informally (see figure 2); this is the authorizing environment and it is a world of constant change.

Scenario

Change is constant in tribal administration. Navigating the political, historical, and familial landscape can be tricky for anyone, especially if you are new to the position. I reached out to former tribal administrators and administrators at other tribes. When you are talking to others, asking questions, and getting the layout of the land through their lens, it is important to remember that it is just that. Through their lens. Try to find their biases and angles.

A big piece of this is learning how to navigate multiple bosses who are elected officials. I reported directly to Tribal Council. There are seven members led by a chair and vice-chair. These seven positions do not require any professional experience or formal education. From year to year, election to election, you have to learn how to manage seven wide-ranging personalities with wide-ranging experiences. It is very important to know in writing where you get your direction from. At my tribe, no one council member had the authority to give me direction. It had to come from the group by consensus.

At my tribe there are five people who directly report to Council. The tribal administrator who oversees governmental operations, the CEO of Little Creek Casino Resort & Golf Club, the CEO of Island Enterprises (who oversees all other economic enterprises), the governmental affairs liaison to Council, and the director of the Legal Department. These five "heads of state," if you will, play a game of political jockeying, push and pull, and at times are at odds with one or several others. Try to identify what other power dynamics are there at your particular tribe that you should know about. This type of knowledge will grow your political savvy and help you stay afloat at least a little longer. It is important for someone who is trying to navigate the many authorizing environments of a tribe.

Best Practice: Ask the Right Questions, to the Right People

How do you know what questions to ask? Who do you ask? Navigating the political, historical, and familial landscape can be tricky for anyone, especially if you are new to the position. Reach out to former tribal administrators and administrators at other tribes. Ask where the landmines are. What works, what doesn't? What do you wish someone would have told you when you first started?

It is even more important to recognize your own biases. What are your implicit biases? It is okay to have preconceived notions about things. But do you have the emotional intelligence to recognize them, and to question yourself? Talk with those who have countering opinions and have healthy debate and do some research on both sides of an issue. Are you willing and capable of changing your mind? Admitting you were wrong? If you master the skill of listening, you will actually show that you value what people say. Others will think of you as a thoughtful listener. Being a good listener is a huge step in the right direction for finding the right answers in your job.

You will need to learn how to navigate multiple bosses who are elected officials. These elected positions do not require any professional experience or formal education. From year to year, election to election, you have to learn how to manage multiple wide-ranging personalities with wide-ranging experiences. There can be some valuable experience and knowledge to be gained from your elected officials. Building a relationship with each council member is important. Ask questions; learn what their strengths and backgrounds are. Some may be able to give you valuable community insight.

Does the tribe have other branches with CEOs? How do you interact with those CEOs/administrators? Do you communicate and meet regularly? Their relationship with Council and the community may be a little different than yours, but you can gain much insight from building a relationship with them. Sometimes you can learn what not to do from other CEOs/administrators.

Community engagement is an important step to finding the "truth" through constant change. Through both community forums and individual connections with community members, make sure you take the time to engage and take input. Show that you are listening, take notes, and communicate back your findings. Find ways to connect with the tribal elders, youth, cultural leaders, and other community members every chance you get (see figure 2). This rapport will grow you as a tribal administrator. Don't just show up when there is a tribal meeting or big event. Learn how to always be around without being overbearing.

A holistic approach to connecting will build relationships between community and government and will empower your community. When you empower people, they become powerful allies. Ultimately, you will gain trust and respect.

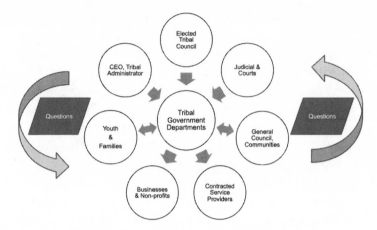

Figure 2. Tribal administrators should humbly and inquisitively circulate questions among formal and informal governance participants and structures.

SOURCE: A. GOULD, "TRIBAL GOVERNMENT IS PUBLIC ADMINISTRATION," PRESENTATION, MPA PROGRAM, EVERGREEN STATE COLLEGE, 2019.

THIRD LEADERSHIP LENS: ROLES AND ABILITIES

Governments have formal structures and processes. This is the operating environment. However, governing is comprised of relational actions and decisions based on our authority and ability to act within formal and informal power sources. This is our authorizing environment. In turn, tribal governance culminates within both environments: relational processes to structure the ability and authority to act. This is self-governing; this is the meaning of our authority.

However, dominant models assume "authority is the right to give commands, orders and get the things done."[4] This is based on a hierarchical model of authority based on position (see figure 3). Giving commands as an act of authority assumes authority is simply legitimized power. However, such a Western view of authority is limited to dominant understandings of formal power without regard to the informal ways we govern as administrators within tribal communities and governments—how power is distributed and shared relationally in community (see figure 3).

The hierarchical-authority model argues that authority depends on accepting the obligation of an administrator to give directives based on sources

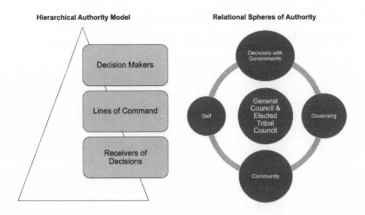

Figure 3. A hierarchical model of authority cannot account for the often relational nature of authority in tribal governance contexts.

SOURCE: A. GOULD, "TRIBAL GOVERNMENT IS PUBLIC ADMINISTRATION," PRESENTATION, MPA PROGRAM, EVERGREEN STATE COLLEGE, 2019.

of legitimized power (e.g., John Locke's consent of the governed). For example, Max Weber wrote about authority in three ways:[5]

- Traditional authority: power legitimized by respect for long-term patterns
- Charismatic authority: power legitimized by personality that inspires others
- Rational-legal authority: (bureaucratic) power legitimized by governments

However, within tribal administration, authority is not solely about legitimized position power. More often than not, authority in tribal administration is about redefining our authorizing environments through our many roles within various relational spheres. These relational spheres of authority to act in tribal administration are based on the values in Kenny and Fraser's *Living Indigenous Leadership*.[6]

- Roles in family and community
- Roles for what is needed in time and place
- Informal systems holding power
- Distributed decision-making based on who has skills

- Noncoercive and nonhierarchical
- Mutual inquiry and understanding: deliberative, discourse, oral traditions, decide based on multiple perspectives

Real authority to act as a tribal administrator is about acting in a good way (see figure 4). This involves skillfully resonating like a drum beat in and out, back and forth, across our levels of governing: individuals, communities, and systems. This comes from personal authority, relational authority, and professional authority.

Scenario

Working for a tribe can be very different than working for most other organizations. It is not uncommon to have a council member or a family member as an employee. What if one of these individuals is a difficult employee? What if your family is on Council? How do you navigate this in a good way? Working in tribal country can present you with potential conflicts of interest and complaints of nepotism. It is imperative to maintain your integrity at all times. Perception can be worse than reality, especially in today's world of social media. Be conscious of this; be willing to recuse yourself from certain situations that call for it.

Working with your relatives at a tribe, especially a small one, can be unavoidable at times. Indigenous people (since time immemorial) have always lived, worked, learned, and survived with each other. Tribes have never been a singular people but a collective. You do not need to abandon this way of thinking. You can continue to find ways to work together as a family, and as a tribe. Your current system may have family work in close proximity and even work for each other. It gets dysfunctional when you or another give special treatment to someone because they are family. You have to be disciplined enough to stay consistent and transparent in everything you do. Strong policies and a disciplined and empowered human resources department will go a long way in helping your organization in this. Your family, coworkers, and community will respect you more in the long run if you communicate clearly with sincerity and are consistent in your decision-making.

Another aspect of knowing your roles and abilities is in your relationship with outside entities. Find that fine line of building healthy working relationships with outside entities while maintaining your sovereignty, self-determination,

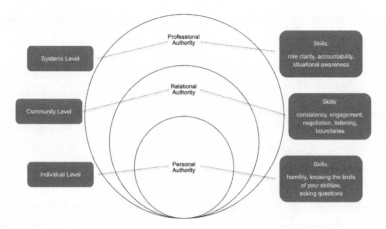

Figure 4. Tribal administration involves skillfully navigating individual, community, and systems levels of governance based on personal authority, relational authority, and professional authority.

SOURCE: A. GOULD, "TRIBAL GOVERNMENT IS PUBLIC ADMINISTRATION," PRESENTATION, MPA PROGRAM, EVERGREEN STATE COLLEGE, 2019.

and practicing self-governance. You may have to bring people to the table, be patient, listen, and be willing to educate. Sometimes it all starts with inviting them out, sharing bread, telling them your story and what you are looking to accomplish, and how it might even help them as an entity. This approach as a sovereign to another sovereign can be very effective.

Best Practice (Part 1): Know Your Role, Not Just Your Position

It is important to recognize where you stand with the people around you, know your role, and stay in your lane. You have a relationship with your directors, managers, employees, Council, community, county officials, state and federal government. You are at least partly responsible for how good those relationships are. You need to understand emotions, recognize people's values, and be able to make connections with others.

Being in a position of leadership in itself does not make you a leader, and now that you are in this position as a tribal administrator, it does not mean you will be a successful one. Take into account the history between tribal families and the experiences of the elders, and recognize the long-standing hierarchies that exist within the tribe. You may have to earn some trust and credibility among your new coworkers and the community in which you serve. Do not just assume because you have this title as the leader of the government on paper that you are actually in charge. There are some authorizing environments that must be navigated before you are accepted beyond the title as a leader.

There are times when you should consult with elders, cultural or spiritual leaders, or other community members. How will your decisions affect one or more of these groups? But beyond the importance of consulting with these individuals, it is important to have strong, respectful relationships with them throughout your tenure in tribal government.

An important piece of the puzzle in learning how to relate to the people around you is your ability to recognize your inner self. Emotional intelligence is something that should be constantly worked on. Learn how to balance your cognitive and emotional abilities. Managing your emotions requires control over emotions and impulses. Be aware of how your personal qualities influence others. After you have control over yourself, then you can more effectively manage your relationships. Learn how to recognize and be empathetic to other people's emotions. Recognizing the emotional needs of others, the ability to deal with difficult situations, and having the ability to build meaningful relationships with those around you will instill trust and respect towards you in the community.

To maintain positive relationships with those around you, remember to be yourself, and never stop communicating. Handle things in a consistent way and be honest, respectful, and compassionate towards the needs of others.

Best Practice (Part 2): Know Your Ability

It is very important to understand your limitations in your role and ability. Do not make promises you can't keep. You do not have the authority to get someone a job, award someone a contract, fix someone's utility bill, create a position or program, or do really anything on your own. Nor do you want that power. You have policies and procedures in place for a reason. Consistency and fairness is essential and you have surrounded yourself with smart, capable employees who know how to do their jobs. Put the system in place and trust it. It may make people feel good to hear you say "yes," but it may not be good for the tribe or your job to always say "yes."

Your Council will come to you with a lot of ideas for the tribe. Some are really good and some are not good at all. Some are good in theory and may have worked at another tribe, but may not work for your tribe. Be careful about promising to make something happen. Do not be quick to say "no" either. Do the research, then make a recommendation based on that research.

Employees will try to get their way with you as well. You can't give employees, directors, and programs everything they want. You as a good boss will do everything you can to make their jobs easier, comfortable, and safe. Give them all the tools they need to do the job. And you want them to be happy. But sometimes employees will ask for things they do not actually need or that might not be a fiscally responsible purchase. Some employees will try to jump the chain of command and ask you for something instead of talking to their direct supervisor. Send them back to their supervisor. Directors can always justify why their budgets should be increased, why they need more employees, upgraded equipment, more office space, and on and on. But the tribe does not have an unlimited budget. Be consistent and fair with all of your departments and directors.

Individual community members may come to you with requests, or tell you how they believe the tribe should do things. Some even have the ear of a council member or two. Some are even noisy and outspoken. But they may not be right. Remember as the administrator, when something fails, it is going to be on you, especially if it ends up costing a lot of money. You are the one with the resources to do the research, and are the one whom the tribe has hired to make some of these decisions. Don't get beaten into submission and make a bad decision for the tribe. And quite frankly, some things are not your decision. Some things require Council to decide on. Do not promise something just to have Council turn around and shoot it down. Make sure decisions are good for the entire community and not just one or a few. Sometimes you will need to consult with the entire community on a decision.

There are also many times when you might have the authority to say yes, but you probably shouldn't. Because it might not stand up to the "making decisions with Grandma" test. If it isn't something you can look your Grandma in the eye after doing, then don't do it. Your family and community are important; it has to feel right for your people.

Practitioner Perspective

If you are not sincere in your word, people will stop believing in you. Stay away from placation. Work on empathy and be humble.

Don't forget where you came from and remember where you work. It is great if you have achieved successes in life, work, and education. There is a time and place to celebrate those and feed off of those experiences. But refrain from acting smarter or better than others. The community does not want its leadership holding itself on a pedestal. This could create barriers, and give you a "holier than thou" aura that makes it hard to connect with you. If people cannot connect with their leadership, then they will lose trust in you.

Brian Cladoosby, a former longtime chairman of the Swinomish Tribe in Washington State and former president of the National Congress of American Indians (NCAI), once stated in a speech:

> Often leaders think they have reached the top. That they are above everyone else and the people are looking up to them. Some believe this so much that they look down on their people. Reaching the top indicates our work is done and we have made it to the destination. The reality is, as leaders we are not at the top. The hard work has just now begun when you become a leader. You carry the weight of your Tribe on your back and work every day for your people. True leaders are not at the top. They are at the bottom holding up their people.[7]

You are in public service as a tribal administrator. You work for the community in which you serve. The mindset of not being above everyone but instead being below the people you serve is a way to keep you grounded and humble.

Try to surround yourself with good, smart people who are willing to work together. As a leader, don't be intimidated or insecure about hiring smart, accomplished employees. Relish it. Take care of those people, give them credit, reward them. In turn they will work hard, solve problems, and work together. Programs will run smoothly and services will be administered to your people. That is success.

Treat your employees and community members well. Show them respect. Never stop being kind and humble.

NOTES

1. Matt Andrews, Lant Pritchett, and Michael Woolcock, *Building State Capability: Evidence, Analysis, Action*, 2017, Oxford Scholarship Online, https://oxford. universitypressscholarship.com.

2. "Authorizing," Thesaurus.com, https://www.thesaurus.com/browse/authorizing?s=t.

3. M. Moore, *Creating Public Value: Strategic Management in Government* (Cambridge, MA: Harvard University Press, 1995).

4. "Delegation of Authority—Meaning, Importance and Its Principles," Management Study Guide, https://www.managementstudyguide.com/delegation_of_authority.htm.

5. Richard M. Ebeling, "Max Weber on Politics as a Vocation," American Institute for Economic Research, October 28, 2019, https://www.aier.org/article/max-weber-on-politics-as-a-vocation/.

6. C. Kenny and T. Ngaroimata Fraser, eds., *Living Indigenous Leadership: Native Narratives on Building Strong Communities* (Vancouver: University of British Columbia Press, 2013).

7. Brian Cladoosby, "Tribal Leaders on Education," keynote speaker, Tribal Leaders on Education Summit, Swinomish Casino and Lodge, Anacortes, Washington, November 2019.

GLOSSARY

Authorizing environment. The personal, communal, and workplace shared understandings that allow all of us to invest in getting things done for our people. This is the essence of governing as our relational actions and decisions are based on our authority and ability to act within formal and informal power sources.

Humility. If you are not sincere in your word people will stop believing in you. Don't forget where you came from; remember where you work, and who you work for.

Operating environment. The day-to-day functions of administration in governments through formal structures and processes.

Seven generations mindset. Respect, honor, and carry on the ways of our ancestors; teach our youth and protect and ensure a healthy environment; maintaining our culture for future generations.

Relationality. Tribes have never been a singular people but a collective. With consistent communication, tribal administrators maintain relationships with coworkers, family, community, self, and outside governments—all of whom may overlap across categories.

Leadership and Ethics in Higher Education

Laural Ballew, ses yehomia/tsi kuts bat soot

THIS CHAPTER DISCUSSES LEADERSHIP AND ETHICS FOR TRIBAL LEADERS THAT are influenced by cultural values and tribal responsibilities. Since all American Indian tribes have their own distinct method of leadership customs, the author recognizes the challenge of oversimplifying the outline of tribal leadership practice for training purposes. There is no definitive model of leadership that fits all tribal governments; therefore, this chapter will identify the commonalities of leadership that are rooted in tribal cultures.

Most management practices are written for a Western model through a westernized lens. For the sake of this chapter, I will emphasize the principles of tribal leadership that are foundational through place-based Indigenous knowledge in higher education practice. These Native concepts are presented through the tribal lens when pertaining to leadership and capacity building to motivate community influencers without using authoritative law. A tribal leader is recognized for their strength in cultural traditions, practices, and the ability to guide their people through a sustainable and healthy future.

BEST PRACTICES

- Prioritize cultural concepts of leadership.
- Emphasize place-based Indigenous knowledge.
- Seek out and develop relevant frameworks for resolution.

INTRODUCTION

As I prepared to write a chapter for leadership and ethics, I reflected on my own journey in education and academia throughout the years. A colleague of mine suggested I write my personal story to represent a journey that influenced years of work experiences with leadership and principles as it relates to being a traditional mother/grandmother. As a Native American woman, ethics from my lens is viewed as the beliefs and principles through oral traditions that were modeled by my elders. For me, the first recognition of leadership and ethics is how you care for people, which becomes immersed in your everyday actions as a tribal member.

My Lummi name is Ses yehomia, which means "she cares for." I also carry the female version of my father's name, tsi kuts bat soot, and I recognize that in our culture I am carrying on his legacy by keeping his name alive. My English name is Laural Wilbur-Ballew. I am a member of the Swinomish Tribe located on Puget Sound, on the southeast side of Fidalgo Island in Skagit County, Washington. I currently live on the Lummi reservation with my husband Timothy Ballew Sr. and we have two sons, Timothy II and Raymond, and two grandsons, Hunter and Tandy.

As Native people we are recognized by our family ties. In the honor of tradition, I will explain mine here. I have always considered myself an intertribal-Native woman as I descend from the Upper Skagit, Nooksack, Sauk-Suiattle, Suquamish, and Aleut people. My family settled on the Swinomish reservation, which is where I am a tribal member. I am the fourth of five children to Claude Wilbur Sr. and Marie Charles. My paternal grandparents are Tandy Wilbur Sr. and Laura Waun-Wilbur; my maternal grandparents are Raymond Charles and Agnes Smith-Charles.

I descend from a family of tribal leaders; my great-great-grandfather, Charles Wilbur, was a signer of the Point Elliott Treaty of 1855. It is his leadership role that encouraged my grandparents to continue working in support of the Swinomish community. My grandparents were active leaders in tribal government by organizing the Swinomish Tribe through the Indian Reorganization Act and the Termination Era. My grandfather, Tandy Wilbur Sr., was a founder of the current Native Congress of American Indians. Both my grandparents, Tandy and Laura, represented Swinomish in regional, state, and national legislation for the sake of tribal development for the tribe. These were my role models of tribal leaders as I grew into adulthood.

My own personal beliefs in the concepts of leadership have led me to understand the commitment of educating future tribal leaders. I was encouraged by my parents and grandparents to pursue education in order to best serve my tribal community. Tribal nations are pursuing educational opportunities for their members; therefore, it is important to prepare tribal members with academic and foundational knowledge to become the future leaders of their respective communities. These ideals have inspired me to support higher education in developing curriculum to prepare Native students with the skills and knowledge to become tribal leaders.

CASE STUDY: NORTHWEST INDIAN COLLEGE

This case study examines Indigenous knowledge within the higher education curriculum of Northwest Indian College (Washington State) to ascertain how traditional knowledge is factored into tribal institutions as a means to promote leadership and governance in the visions and philosophies of institutions. The research identifies the related principles that are developed to prepare future tribal leaders as the frontrunners for their Native communities. As stated by Greg Cajete at the American Indian Higher Education Consortium 40th Anniversary Conference in 2013, "The Indigenous mind is rising."[1]

NORTHWEST INDIAN COLLEGE

Northwest Indian College (NWIC), a baccalaureate-level tribal college chartered by the Lummi Nation located in Bellingham, Washington, which is devoted to upholding the vision of the ancestors, has as its goal to provide quality Indigenous educational opportunities for students to support their personal growth and tribal identity. Therefore, the primary purpose of NWIC is to provide access for the higher education needs of tribal communities in the Pacific Northwest. The college's mission statement is as follows: "Through education, Northwest Indian College promotes indigenous self-determination and knowledge."[2] Northwest Indian College evolved from the former Lummi Indian School of Aquaculture (LISA), which was founded in 1974. LISA offered fish and shellfish hatchery training for Indigenous people from all over the world. During the early 1980s, LISA evolved into Lummi Community College, a tribally chartered postsecondary institution.

The courses offered through the college eventually multiplied and expanded its service area to include tribes from throughout the Pacific Northwest. In acknowledgment of the progress due to the growth and development of the college, in 1989, Lummi Indian Community College became Northwest Indian College. In providing that access, the college currently has six extended campus sites located at the tribal reservations of Muckleshoot, Nez Perce, Nisqually, Port Gamble S'Klallam, Swinomish, and Tulalip.

Following several years of research and development, NWIC proposed to offer a unique Indigenous-based program on Native nation-building and business management at the baccalaureate level. This proposal was established for NWIC in Tribal Governance and Business Management (TGBM) based on extensive research of other similar four-year degree programs, consultations with other colleges and universities, and input from faculty and administration. The program offers students the fundamental knowledge and experience necessary to succeed in the areas of leadership, sovereignty, economic development, entrepreneurship, and management. These themes helped inform the curriculum and context for the program of study.

The TGBM vision, mission, and program outcomes below provide the overarching framework for the program and serve to guide the program structure and content.[3]

> Vision: To provide students with the skills, knowledge, and experience to be effective and successful in leading tribal governments and business organizations with respect to sovereignty and cultural values.
>
> Mission: To provide the opportunity for Native American students who are engaged in support of improving the wellbeing of indigenous people through

academic achievement, community service, and self-determination. By recognizing the current and future economic needs of Native American communities, the Tribal Governance and Business Management program provides students with tribal government and business education, leadership skills, and the fundamental qualities needed to successfully manage community organizations. The program of study offers the essential accounting, legal, economic, and management skills to immediately function successfully in tribal government or business organizations.

The foundation for the TGBM program curriculum is built upon five program outcomes as follows:

PROGRAM OUTCOME 1—SOVEREIGNTY

Native American (Indian) tribes are inherently sovereign nations, who possess both the inherent and acquired rights to govern themselves, their traditional homelands and their natural resources. Contemporarily, tribes find themselves in the position to provide a broader range of culturally specific, social and economic programs, to their respective citizens. Upon successful completion of the program, students will be able to (A) articulate and apply knowledge of inherent and acquired rights and (B) analyze the sovereign rights of tribal nation status with regard to the purpose of governing authority.[4]

PROGRAM OUTCOME 2—LEADERSHIP

The TGBM program aspires to train future tribal leaders and managers of Native American (Indian) communities through the pursuit of coursework specific to the exploration of the traditional, historic, and contemporary importance of sovereignty, ethics, administration, management, economic development and leadership. The cultural elements of service-learning components will be interwoven throughout TGBM coursework. Upon successful completion of the program students will be able to (A) Practice culturally competent leadership in decision making, organizational development and human resource management, (B) Act as community change agents toward improving the quality of life in tribal communities, (C) Contribute to the restoration of tribal knowledge.[5]

PROGRAM OUTCOME 3—MANAGEMENT AND ADMINISTRATION

Although management and administration are implicitly western terms, they are ideologies by which tribal people have governed themselves throughout their respective and/or collective, inherent tribal histories. Therefore, it stands to reason that contemporary tribal communities regularly engage in the effective implementation of organizational and administrative structures, business management and financial decision making. Upon successful completion of the program students will be able to (A) Develop and implement organizational structures to meet the needs for tribal, community, and personal development, (B) Utilize broad knowledge of management and administration to support tribal organizational goals including the evaluation and use of financial statements, decision making and leadership models, and (C) Demonstrate effective use of business and project management technology.[6]

PROGRAM OUTCOME 4—ENTREPRENEURSHIP

The entrepreneur has always served as the catalyst for economic development and subsequently the economic stimulation of a given community. Nowhere is the aforementioned statement more accurate than within a given tribal community. Entrepreneurship is a pathway to not only self-sufficiency, but perhaps more importantly to economic stimulation. Upon successful completion of the program students will be able to (A) Integrate physical, social, and human capital regarding healthy tribal economies, and (B) Utilize, implement, and organize resources to meet community needs in creative ways.[7]

The TGBM degree will provide students with the fundamental knowledge, skills, and organizational concepts in order to effectively perform as self-governed and culturally prepared administrators or business managers with an emphasis on tribal context. Given the college's culture-based mission, offering a bachelor of arts degree in tribal governance and business management is an extension of NWIC's efforts to promote Indigenous self-determination and knowledge through the teaching of tribal histories, culture, and organizational concepts in a postsecondary context.

With more tribal nations seeking higher education opportunities for their members, it becomes relevant to prepare students with the academic and foundational knowledge to guide them to become empowering leaders within their communities. As Dr. Cheryl Crazy Bull stated, "there has been an educational movement within tribal colleges throughout the United States."[8] Part of this movement includes thirty-two fully accredited tribal colleges that are grounded in traditions and place-based knowledge to serve the needs of tribal nations.

There is currently a lack of experiential information related to tribal leadership in higher education academia within westernized curricula.[9] The intention of preparing tribal leaders includes research of leadership in all community roles with the foundational knowledge for capacity. It should be recognized that there are hundreds of tribal nations within the United States and each nation is constitutionally diverse as a separate sovereign nation. Therefore, American Indian tribes require and find it necessary to work with Western governments that impact our communities, while protecting our tribal sovereignty. Historically, tribal nations have struggled with the oppression of Western laws and policies at the local, state, and national levels. Currently, most tribal nations are developing independent governing infrastructures to uphold sovereignty and collaborating with non-tribal rural local, state, and federal agencies.

An article written by Steven E. Aufrecht titled "Missing: Native American Governance in American Public Administration Literature" is the recognition of the absence of literature regarding tribal governance with his own interpretation for this phenomenon.[10] In his article, his reasoning and acknowledgment of information that is "missing" calls for the inclusion of Native American governance issues in public administration literature. With more Native Americans researching and writing literature in this field of study, Native people's viewpoint regarding tribal governance will be brought to the forefront.

Another article by John C. Ronquillo, titled "American Indian Tribal Governance and Management: Public Administration Promise or Pretense?" is written with a rather simple general principle.[11] The context of tribal governance in American public administrations is not completely missing, but rather it is merely unrecognizable by certain groups of scholars. I found this to be true with my research for the Tribal Governance and Business Management program of study for NWIC. I found it difficult to categorize research topics to support the curriculum for tribal governance in a higher education institution.

These are two thought-provoking and contrasting readings, which at the same time provide parallel reasons for the requirement of scholarly significance in the field of tribal governance. These principles are motivation for higher education institutions to recommend the inclusion of this case study in order to benefit tribal communities. This will support Native students to continue their academic progress with the knowledge in tribal governance to serve at the local, state, and national levels as future leaders.

It is the purpose of tribal colleges' culture-based mission to promote histories and organizational concepts in a postsecondary context to honor tribal sovereignty. This recognizes that Indian tribes are sovereign nations with the right to govern themselves and their territories. A westernized concept has been a "one size fits all" approach that does not acknowledge tribal sovereignty.

PRINCIPAL CONCEPTS

The concept of leadership and ethics within tribal organizations can be characterized as broad and diverse in accordance with the cultural traditions and practices of each tribal nation. There is no formal model of leadership since each tribal nation is unique in its traditions, beliefs, and principles. The theory of leadership is foundational and place-based in connection to each tribal nation. Tribal beliefs and principles are held up by oral traditions for most tribes, and the leadership skills of tradition and practice are fundamental qualifications for their leadership.

Tribal communities have structured leadership and governance, but it may be important to further develop the infrastructures currently in place. The objective of contemporary education is to promote nation-building for tribal government institutions and prepare succeeding tribal leadership to continue to meet the needs of their people. This method of capacity building can benefit tribal institutions with resources pertaining to tribal governance and leadership training.

The following leadership skills can best identify, in general terms, the ideals for tribal leadership:

- Practice culturally competent leadership in decision-making, organizational development, and human resource management
- Act as community change agents toward improving the quality of life in tribal communities
- Contribute to the restoration of tribal knowledge

These concepts provide leadership qualities that are essential in tribal governance relevant to current tribal communities' needs. The skills of capacity building can be useful to tribal communities that require culturally based workforce training. Through a cultural lens, a tribal leader can be described by one's ability to incorporate physical, social, and human capital to work toward healthy tribal economies. A tribal leader has the ability to utilize, implement, and organize resources for building a strong and sustaining tribal nation.

A pathway to self-sufficiency from a cultural lens should be defined by one's leadership skills to integrate physical, social, and human capital regarding healthy tribal economies. In addition, the ability to utilize, implement, and organize resources to meet tribal community needs can prove to be beneficial for tribal nations. As the future of tribal workforce training is continually analyzed, there is an expectation for mentoring and developing training for grooming culturally immersed tribal leaders. The ability to analyze and determine the impacts that lead towards solutions, therefore, meets the needs of a tribal nation's success.

The main characteristic of a tribal leader is the ability to understand a vision and emphasize a mission, including the ability to work in collaboration with tribal members and governments. This would be defined as a role model for leaders who have a vision and mission to support tribal culture and encourage tribal members to work uniformly toward the best equitable resolution.

Relevant to this chapter are the leadership roles of Native American women, which are as different as the tribes they represent. Historically, Native women held the matriarchal role and were the knowledge holders for their families. Today, if you search Native American women leaders, you are likely to find examples such as Elizabeth Peratrovich (Tlingit), Wilma Man Killer (Cherokee), Winona LaDuke (Ojibwe), LaDonna Harris (Comanche), Ramona Bennett (Puyallup), Debra Haaland (Laguna Pueblo), and Sharice Davids (Ho-Chunk). There is no distinctive leadership model to compare Native women leaders. The commonality is that these Native women have stepped forward to guide and manage their tribal communities as models of Native leadership. Native American women leaders are natural caregivers, respectful, and hold the wisdom of knowledge for their families and tribal communities. As leaders they have the ability to serve as facilitators to highlight and emphasize cultural knowledge for unity and stability of their tribal nations.[12]

Practitioner Perspective

I am a Native woman who began my education at NWIC with an associate of arts and sciences degree in business administration.[13] I then completed a bachelor of arts in American cultural studies from Western Washington University (WWU). Subsequently, I received a master's of public administration with a concentration in tribal governance from The Evergreen State College. As I have continued my educational and professional leadership path, the vision of a doctoral degree is an organic fit. I began the Doctor of Indigenous Development and Advancement program at Te Whare Wananga o Awanuiarangi—Maori Indigenous University in March 2013.

Early on, I realized that my academic and personal experiences allowed me to serve as an example of success for tribal communities within the Pacific Northwest. In order to fulfill my desire to be a role model for Native American students, I returned to the institution that inspired my success—NWIC. With over forty years of experience working in tribal administrative and financial management roles, I gained a unique perspective regarding the social, economic, and academic progress within the tribal communities. My deep involvement with family and community combined with a background in leadership and management skills have inspired me to continue serving tribal communities within academia. My experiences are an example of practicing culturally competent leadership and contributing to the restoration of tribal knowledge.

My current position as WWU's first executive director of American Indian/Alaska Native and First Nations Relations and tribal liaison is a testament of my life experiences that have prepared me for an educational pathway as a Native woman scholar. My commitment to professional development has always been the inspiration of what I can give back to my tribal community. This illustrates my competence in leadership skills for decision-making and organizational development.

The Office of Tribal Relations advises the president of WWU on legislative and policy matters of concern to tribes and First Nations. The office functions as support for fostering working relationships with the twenty-nine federally recognized tribes across the State of Washington. The office recognizes the partnership opportunities with tribal communities as a way to enhance the support and success of Native students. The office works to encourage the development of programs, events, and activities designed to educate the campus community and increase capacity to serve American Indian, Alaska Native, and First Nation communities. These are the elements of best practices in cultural leadership and Indigenous knowledge.

The Tribal Relations Office functions as support for establishing working relationships with tribal communities as a way to sustain the success of Native American/Alaska Native and First Nation students at WWU. The tribal liaison has formed an advisory committee that offers interdepartmental collaboration with students, faculty, staff, academics, and student services to ensure students' needs are met holistically, and to ensure community-based collaboration occurs when developing programming for Native students at WWU. These functions are examples of the skills needed for competent leadership decision-making, organizational development, and human resource management.

Leadership training in higher education can be evident with the organizational opportunities made available for Native students. These opportunities are ideal for students to practice their leadership training. A case study of Native student leadership is the WWU's Native American Student Union (NASU). On May 16, 2016, NASU sent a formal request advocating for action by the university president and Board of Trustees. The first request was to implement a tribal liaison position. The second request was for a traditional Coast Salish longhouse. The final three requests have been met through the support of the tribal liaison: certification of Native tribal enrollment or descendance at WWU in order to ascertain an accurate count of our Native student population; funding for NASU's annual powwow; and government-to-government training. By the power and actions of the NASU group leaders, along with support from Native faculty and staff at WWU, the inaugural first Tribal Relations Department and tribal liaison position was appointed by the WWU Board of Trustees in 2019.

The NASU students recognize that the inclusion of a Coast Salish–style longhouse on the WWU campus would honor the traditional Lhaq'temish (people of the sea) Lummi territory the campus currently occupies. A facility to respectfully honor a gathering space will have a powerful impact on the retention of Native students, but more importantly would promote cultural sovereignty and a sense of belonging for Native students, faculty, staff, and the tribal communities. The longhouse will amplify the actions of WWU's land acknowledgment statement for the campus and tribal communities who serve Native students. A longhouse model honors lived experiences and cultural values of Native people. This model promotes student leadership that is built on cultural elements significant to

Native people. Most importantly, it is a principal model of leadership that is relevant for students to view themselves as strong tribal leaders.

There is an opportunity for students to learn from the benefit of educating faculty and staff as positive role models in higher education. As positive change agents for Native nation-building, students are empowered to share their stories. The longhouse model is an opportunity to share generational cultural practices and ceremonies as well as Western academic knowledge to navigate a contemporary world. These opportunities will not only enhance the life of an individual, but they also bring opportunities for the institution to demonstrate how to "grow our own."

This example of the NASU students requesting a longhouse on the WWU campus illustrates successful student leadership training enacted in solidarity with a clear focus and mission by Native students supported and guided by Native faculty and staff. This is a powerful and triumphant model of presenting students with a voice and a space in order to develop a clear vision with a purpose to succeed. This involved perseverance and devotion to follow through with the conclusion of their mission. This is clearly evidence of the best practice of identifying and developing an appropriate framework toward a resolution.

The principle of leadership training was taught to me at a young age and I sustain these values with my children and grandchildren. I see myself as a leader for my family and for the Native students whom I support on a daily basis. I consider my work in higher education as an opportunity to prepare students to become successful leaders within their tribal communities.

NOTES

1. Cajete, Greg (2013), Statement at American Indian Higher Education Consortium 40th Anniversary Conference, Santa Fe, New Mexico, August 2013, "Forty Years of Nation Building," www.AIHEC.org.
2. *Northwest Indian College Catalog* (2015–17), 3.
3. *Northwest Indian College Catalog* (2015–17), 49.
4. *Northwest Indian College Catalog* (2015–17), 52.
5. *Northwest Indian College Catalog* (2015–17), 52.
6. *Northwest Indian College Catalog* (2015–17), 52.
7. *Northwest Indian College Catalog* (2015–17), 52.
8. Cheryl Crazy Bull, "Journey to Freedom: Reflecting on our Responsibilities, Renewing Our

Promises," *Tribal College Journal*, November 6, 2012.

9. Steven E. Aufrecht, "Missing: Native American Governance in American Public Administration Literature," *American Review of Public Administration* 29, no. 4 (1999): 370–90.

10. Aufrecht, "Missing," 370–90.

11. John C. Ronquillo, "American Indian Tribal Governance and Management: Public Administration Promise or Pretense?," University of Georgia, *Public Administration Review*, 2011.

12. S. L. Black, and C. Birmingham, "American Indian Leadership Practices," in *American Indian Business: Principles and Practices*, edited by Deanna M. Kennedy, Charles F. Harrington, Amy Klemm Verbos, Daniel Stewart, Joseph Scott Gladstone, and Gavin Clarkson (Seattle: University of Washington Press, 2017).

13. Laural Ballew, tribal liaison, Western Washington University.

GLOSSARY

Aleut. The earliest people of the Aleutian Islands, also known as Unanganin in southwest Alaska.

Change agent. A person from inside or outside a community who is empowered to help promote, champion, enable, and support positive changes in the development of an improved nation.

Coast Salish longhouse. A structure for gathering and ceremonial space to promote cultural exchange and understanding of place-based learning.

Indigenous-based. Using the skills, knowledge, and experiences of place-based knowledge as cultural values for leadership.

Lummi. Lhaq`temish, original inhabitants of Washington's northernmost coast and southern British Columbia, Canada.

National Congress of American Indians. Founded in 1944, NCAI is the oldest, largest, and most representative association to serve American Indian and Alaska Nation tribal governments and communities.

Native American Student Union (NASU). Western Washington University in Bellingham, Washington, first coordinated in 1969 by a group of Native students for the awareness, inclusion, and support of Native students at WWU.

Native nation-building. The process by which Native nations strengthen their capacity for effective and culturally appropriate self-governance and addressing the nation's challenges.

Nooksack. Located in Deming, the northwest corner of Washington State, 15 miles east of Bellingham, Washington, and 12 miles south of the Canadian border.

Place-based knowledge. The pedagogy approach that emphasizes the characteristics and meaning of place as a foundation of learning.

Point Elliott Treaty of 1855. Land settlement treaty between the U.S. government and the Native American tribes of the Puget Sound region in Washington Territory.

Reorganization Act of 1939. Public Law 76-1953 Stat. 561, enacted April 3, 1939, which gave the President of the United States authority to reorganize the executive branch, which created a new Cabinet agency, the Federal Security Agency, and placed the Social Security board under its jurisdiction.

Self-determination. The process for tribal governments to act upon their own political standing on behalf of their community.

Ses yehomia. Traditional name in Lummi language, which means, "she cares for . . ."

Sovereignty. The inherent and acquired rights as an independent nation.

Suak-Suiattle. The region of Sauk is located near Darrington, Marblemount, and Rockport, Washington, earlier known as the Sah-ku-me-hu, in the foothills of the North Cascades.

Suquamish. Located on the Port Madison Indian Reservation in Central Puget Sound Region of Washington State on the Kitsap Peninsula.

Termination Era. The 1950s federal Indian policy, Public Law 280 aimed to terminate federal obligations to tribes, under which over one hundred tribes were terminated under this policy, and over a million acres were removed from trust status.

Tsi kuts bat soot. Traditional name kuts bat soot from the Suquamish Tribe carried by my father, Claude Wilbur Sr., which was given to me in the female version, Tsi kuts bat soot.

Upper Skagit. The Upper Skagit people descended from a tribe that inhabited ten villages on the Upper Skagit River Valley, east of Sedro-Woolley in Skagit County, Washington.

RECOMMENDED RESOURCES

Hill, M., and M. A. K. Hoss. (2018). "Reclaiming American Indian Women Leadership: Indigenous Pathway to Leadership." *Open Journal of Leadership* 7: 225–36.

Krumm, B. L., and W. Johnson. (2011). "Tribal Colleges: Cultural Support for Women." In *Women of Color in Higher Education.* Emerald Group Publishing.

Mcleod, M. (2002). "Keeping the Circle Strong." *Tribal College Journal* 13, no. 4: 10–13.

Miller, D. L. (1978). "Native American Women: Leadership Images." *Integrated Education* 91, no. 15 (January–February): 37–39

Strategic Management

Implementing Culturally Appropriate Planning Methods in a Contemporary World

Rebecca M. Webster and Julie Clark

THIS CHAPTER DISCUSSES THE ABILITY OF TRIBAL NATIONS AND OUR RESPECTIVE communities to use strategic planning tools in a culturally appropriate manner to bring about positive changes for the community. It walks us through a general planning process that consists of preparing, planning, implementing, and evaluating the strategic plan. We use specific examples from the Oneida Cannery's portion of the Oneida Nation's strategic plan. Examples include mission, vision, values from the Oneida Nation and SWOT analysis, goals, and objectives from the Oneida Cannery.[1]

BEST PRACTICES

- Get buy-in and commitment from key leadership.
- Find an effective facilitator for planning meetings and work sessions.
- Include voices and input from your community, including youth, elders, and cultural leaders.
- Make sure your planning team contains diverse perspectives.
- Take the time to complete each step of the planning process.
- Don't put your plan on a shelf and forget about it.
- Communicate your progress and results.
- Strategy models need to provide clear direction to your community.

INTRODUCTION

People throughout North and South America have been engaged in strategic planning since before European contact. Take the Haudenosaunee for example. Prior to European contact, the Peacemaker and his partner traveled throughout what is now the State of New York to unite warring villages under one figurative longhouse with the foundational principles of *kanikuliyo*, *skaʌna*, and *katsas-tʌnsla* (peace of mind, peace, and power). They buried their weapons under a tree of peace and committed to extending the longhouse rafters over any other tribes that wanted to join and seek protection. Unquestionably, uniting these people was no small task. This process took years to complete and involved countless conversations. Although the Peacemaker had his original principles in place from the beginning, those encounters and conversations throughout his travels ultimately shaped the roles and responsibilities for people that would become faithkeepers, clan mothers, and chiefs. They shaped condolence protocols for mourning, replacing chiefs and clan mothers. They also shaped consensus-based decision-making processes. The Peacemaker and his partner's travels throughout the villages comprise the story of what would later be known as the Kayanla? Kówa (Great Law). Despite the impacts of colonialism, genocide, forced assimilation, and removal, the Kayanla? Kówa and the Haudenosaunee Confederacy still stand today.

PURPOSE OF STRATEGIC PLANNING

Communities engage in strategic planning for a number of reasons. Primarily, it helps identify where the community wants to be in the future and sets the direction for staff and community to follow in order to get there. We created the visual of traveling down a river. Before strategic planning, everyone is off doing their own thing, and everyone is headed in the direction they think they should be headed in. Strategic planning is a way to get input from a lot of people and build consensus about what direction the entire community should be heading in. After strategic planning, everyone is going in the same general direction down the river together, as in figure 1.

In addition to getting everyone moving in the same direction, strategic planning also helps elected officials and staff make decisions, because the plan,

Before   **After**

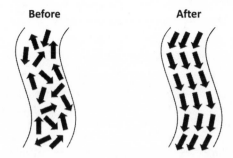

Figure 1. Traveling Down the River: Before and After Strategic Planning

once developed, sets forth the community's direction and priorities. The plan will define everyone's roles and responsibilities to help move the community forward. Strategic planning also increases accountability. After the tribal nation completes a strategic plan and begins to implement it, elected officials and staff need to monitor their progress and report on their outcomes. The results of a strategic planning initiative in various tribal communities revealed that the planning process brings consistency, predictability, and credibility.[2] These results are embodied in figure 1, where we travel down the river in a purposeful, coordinated manner.

UNIQUE CHARACTERISTICS OF TRIBAL NATIONS

In countless ways, tribal nations are unique. Most notably, we generally don't take advantage of a tax base to fund our government operations. Rather, we rely on a variety of sources: gaming, retail, other economic development initiatives, grants, etc. When we engage in strategic planning, we carry on a bit like other governments, but also a bit like other businesses. During the strategic planning process, the community needs to balance economic development with traditional values.[3]

When we engage in strategic planning, we also must keep in mind the history of how our community came to be.[4] Our tribal nations are often located on reservations. Rarely does the tribe own all the land on the reservations. Other governments own land, including schools and municipal buildings. Non-tribal members own land. Also, the tribal nation is not the only government asserting authority on the reservation. Often, the federal government, state government, and local governments are carrying out responsibilities within that shared space.[5] This can impact the strategic planning process. Even on land the tribe owns, we often have non-tribal family members residing there. We also employ non-tribal members in our tribal operations. Our communities are diverse, and we need to keep our uniqueness in mind when we use strategic planning models off the shelf. We will likely need to modify them to fit our individual community needs.[6]

Lastly, and perhaps most importantly, our culture is integral to all aspects of who we are as a people. It is crucial to be able to celebrate our history, language, and culture in our plans for the future.

STRATEGIC PLANNING OVERVIEW

There are many models for strategic planning with varying stages and labels. For the purposes of this chapter, we broke the strategic planning stage into four main steps: prepare, conduct, implement, and evaluate. A common Haudenosaunee silver brooch generally referred to as a council square or council fire inspired our illustration of the cycle of strategic planning (see figure 2). Historically, this brooch represented a meeting. The outside logs represent the chiefs and clan mothers, and the inside logs represent the firekeepers. The clan mothers and the chiefs received input from the community before making decisions. As we will see, input from the community is key in successful strategic planning.

An additional item to note about our illustration is that it runs counter-clockwise. This direction represents the cycle of life. In our creation story, that is the direction that Sky Woman walked to expand the earth on the back of Turtle Island. In the longhouses, we dance in that direction, serve our food in that direction, and offer tobacco in that direction.

STEP 1: PREPARE FOR THE STRATEGIC PLANNING PROCESS

Before anyone even starts to talk about developing a vision, mission, and goals, there is a lot of work that needs to be done. Primarily, you will need to determine if your community is ready for the strategic planning process. There are

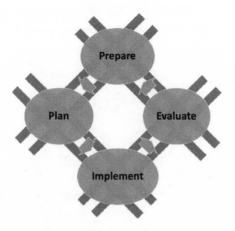

Figure 2. Haudenosaunee Council Square Strategic Planning Cycle

many considerations to determine readiness, the primary consideration being whether elected and appointed leadership buy into the process. If you do not have support from the leadership, the planning process is unlikely to succeed. If you have buy-in from leadership, they will also need to commit to participate in the process. They will need to ensure staff and community members have the time and resources to engage in the process. You will need a facilitator, and you will need to determine whether to employ an internal or external facilitator. An internal facilitator will already be familiar with the community, but may come in with his or her own bias about the direction the community should be going in. An external facilitator might have a larger learning curve to become familiar with the community, but he/she might be less biased about the direction he/she feels the community should go in.

During the process, everyone involved will need to remain committed, yet flexible in order to adapt to changes along the process. During that process, your community needs must still be met while staff dedicate time to participate in the planning process. Preparing for and engaging in the planning process requires a lot of staff time. If your community is understaffed and overworked, it might be difficult to justify giving them more work on a project that will take a while before the community sees the results.

Once you determine that your community is ready for strategic planning, reflect on your community's past experiences with planning. Consider whether your community was successful and contributed to successes and shortcomings. Also consider how tribal leaders can help address foreseeable challenges to the process.

Community Members as Stakeholders

The strategic planning field often refers to internal and external stakeholders. Internal stakeholders can include community members, elected tribal council members, advisory boards and committee members, tribal administration, tribal program managers, administrative staff, frontline staff, and other special target populations. These will likely be unique to each tribe and may consist of youth groups, elder groups, and cultural leaders. External stakeholders can include federal agencies, partner organizations, state and local agency representatives, grant funders, customers, and non-tribal members. Their role in the strategic planning process includes helping to develop the mission, vision, and values; staying informed of the process; participating in surveys, interviews, and focus groups; helping make decisions about the process and outcomes; serving on the planning committee; providing resources, data, and information; and helping set priorities. For the purpose of this chapter, we refer to them simply as community members. For each step in the strategic planning process, it is up to those driving the process to determine which community members need to participate at which stage of the process, always keeping in mind that in order for this process to be successful, you will need to have adequate representation and buy-in from the community. A strategic planning initiative in various tribal communities reported that "Telling the stories of the process of community involvement . . . and the struggles to involve key stakeholders, while initially undervalued, was ultimately understood to be as valuable as the task of producing the model."[7] This reaffirms that gaining the support from community is essential in the planning process.

Form the Strategic Planning Committee

The strategic planning team will vary based on the community's size and needs. Smaller communities may have an elected leader and a couple of employees develop their strategy. Others may have a team of elected officials along with executives, professionals, department heads, or even an office of strategy management. The team members should be available to meet in the initial development of the strategy and be active participants in regularly scheduled strategy reviews. Each community, regardless of size, should decide everyone's role upfront to ensure everyone involved is clear on their roles and team expectations.

Regardless of size, a strategy team needs a champion. A champion is a person in a leadership role who is engaged in the strategy process and supports the strategy team. A champion should be a decision-maker with authority to delegate work to be done. A champion's role is to participate in establishing the vision, mission, and values. Another major role for the champion is to clear a path for the strategy team to execute the strategy. They help ensure that resources such as time, money, personnel, technology, and space are available to achieve any required actions or initiatives. A designated facilitator will help the champion keep the group focused and moving. They spend time coordinating the strategy development and may schedule and facilitate regular strategy reviews.

Gather Background Information

Gathering relevant background information about your community will help you to develop goals, objectives, and SWOTs. Different planning processes call this step fact-finding or an environmental scan. The information should be about the past, present, and future of your community. It can include organizational charts, lists of services offered, community statistics, etc. Identify what information is available and what information you will need to obtain. When compiling this information, you will need to find a balance between presenting too little information and too much information. The compiled information you gather should provide an overall picture of your community while ensuring that it encompasses a variety of community interests.

Determine the Strategic Planning Approach

There are many approaches to strategic planning.[8] The key is to find a process that meets the needs of your community. A strategic plan may be very complex depending on the size and structure of your tribal government. The key is to customize your approach as you go to fit the needs of your community. This is especially important when using models or approaches intended for businesses or state/federal governments.

Develop a Timeline

It is important to develop a timeline to keep moving with the process and to keep each other accountable. It is equally important to be flexible and cognizant of the fact that unexpected issues may come up during the planning process and the process may take longer than anticipated. The key is to keep moving and adjusting timelines as necessary.

STEP 2: CONDUCT STRATEGIC PLANNING

After you determine that your tribal nation is ready for strategic planning and you have gathered all the background information, you are now set to engage in the planning. This step is often the most time-consuming part of strategic planning because it requires input from so many community members.

Develop Mission, Vision, and Values Statements

Mission statements describe what the purpose of the community is. It explains what the community does and why. It also should guide the overall direction the community wants to go in. Vision statements lay out an ideal image of the future, mention how we will get there, and describe how the community will benefit. Values are sets of deeply held beliefs, principles, and underlying assumptions that influence the community.

Table 1. Oneida Nation Mission, Vision, and Values

MISSION: To strengthen and protect our people, reclaim our land, and enhance the environment by exercising our sovereignty.
VISION: A Nation of strong families built on Tsi? niyukwaliho t^ (our ways) and a strong economy.
VALUES: • Kahletsyatlúsla: The heartfelt encouragement of the best in each of us • Kanolukhwásla: Compassion, caring identity, and joy of being • Ka?nikuhli·yo: The openness of the good spirit and mind • Ka?tshatstʌsla: The strength of belief and vision as a People • Kalihwíyo: The use of the good words about ourselves, our Nation, and our future • Twahwahtsílayʌ: All of us are Family • Yukwatsistayʌ: Our fire, our spirit within each one of us

When engaged in strategic planning, it is important to review any current mission, vision, and values. If you have existing ones, consider if they are still relevant or if they are missing anything. The next step is to brainstorm ideas with community members. A facilitator can help consolidate and wordsmith ideas into statements. Once you have adopted the mission, vision, and values, the next step is to communicate them to the larger community. Even though the strategic planning process is still underway, the community should have a vested interest in the progress made toward developing the plan.

To help illustrate the different components of a strategic plan, we have provided some examples throughout this chapter. To reaffirm our assertion that we can use available tools in a culturally appropriate way, we chose to use examples from the Oneida Nation. Table 1 includes the Nation's mission, vision, and values statements.[9]

Complete a SWOT Analysis

A SWOT analysis can help assess your community's current situation to help decide on what strategies to implement.[10] SWOT stands for Strengths, Weaknesses, Opportunities, and Threats. Strengths and weaknesses are internal to your community. They can include things like your organizational culture, capacity to deliver government and community services, policies, decision-making authority, internal resources. Opportunities and threats are external. They can include technology, funding sources, government regulations, state of the economy, and competition for resources. A SWOT analysis can help identify what weaknesses can be turned into strengths and what threats can be turned into opportunities.

Table 2 provides an example of a swot analysis from the Oneida Cannery. The Cannery has been processing foods including heirloom, indigenous white corn for the Oneida community for over forty years. They have a state-of-the-art facility with commercial-grade equipment where they process foods for sale at the Oneida Market, for use throughout the tribal organization, and for community members. They also hold classes for the community in the Cannery.

Identify Strategic Priorities

With so many interests within a tribal community, it can be challenging to decide which priorities to pursue.[11] The information the team assembled in preparation for planning and the SWOT analysis can help identify strategic priorities. Relying on those sources of information to develop priorities can help ensure they are done objectively and based on data rather than opinion or personal interests.

Goals and Objectives

When developing goals, think of them as destinations that you want to see your community reach. They should be aligned with the mission, vision, and values. That alignment will help guide the community's provision of government services. Objectives serve as a way to measure change in your community as you try to reach your goals. Together, your goals and objectives should be SMART.[12] Table 3 outlines the acronyms that help ensure that your objectives are clear, measurable, and related to mission and vision. Table 4 provides an example of a goal and objective from the Oneida Cannery tied to food sovereignty initiatives. To measure their success, the Cannery will use the numbers of outreach events, people who participate, and participant education hours. Those numbers will help determine whether they met their goal. After establishing goals and objectives, you should also establish a set of action steps to accomplish those goals and objectives.

Table 2. Example SWOT Analysis from the Oneida Nation Cannery

	HELPFUL	HARMFUL
INTERNAL	Strengths: • White corn processing experts • Affordable products and services • Equipment allows for bulk processing and a variety of processing methods • Safety in food production and kitchen environment • Food program development	Weaknesses: • Community and client access to the Cannery can be limited • Mentorship for succession and program sustainability • Integrated marketing with internal partners and resources and program financial sustainability • Unable to meet demand for white corn • Staff availability
EXTERNAL	Opportunities: • Ensure white corn availability and product development • Create new cultural food resources and partnerships • Relevant cultural teachings related to food • Relevant Indigenous food policy • Extend availability to community processors and small entrepreneurs	Threats: • Availability of raw white corn is limited • Dissatisfied customers • Different services and products need the same space and equipment at the same time • GTC (tribal membership) decisions • Losing specialized staff with specialized training

Compiling the Strategic Plan Document

After going through the process to conduct strategic planning, you should compile all your information into one place so you can share it easily and have ready access to it. What follows is a sample table of contents for a strategic plan:

- Letter or Introduction
- Executive Summary
- Strategic Planning Process Summary
- Vision, Mission, and Values
- SWOT
- Strategic Priorities
- Goals and Objectives
- Appendices

Table 3. Defining What Makes SMART Objectives

S	Specific	Specify what, how much, and when you want to achieve
M	Measurable	You need to be able to measure the objective and have data to measure your progress
A	Achievable	Achievement of the objective needs to be within reach
R	Relevant	The objective should align with the mission and vision
T	Time-Oriented	Establish a time frame for reaching the objective

Table 4. Example of a Goal and SMART Objective from the Oneida Nation Cannery

GOAL	By 2021, the Oneida Cannery will increase the Oneida communities' knowledge of traditional and conventional food processing by engaging 10,000 people through educational opportunities that create skills and raise awareness.
OBJECTIVE	Oneida families and community members will have the skills and abilities to prepare and store traditional food in their own home or process their own products at the Oneida Cannery. They will be able to share what they learn and create healthy food culture for our nation. They will view the Oneida Cannery as a leader in the food system because of their knowledge, teaching, and innovation.

STEP 3: IMPLEMENTING THE STRATEGIC PLAN

Implementing strategic plans is often where it all falls apart. Too often, tribal nations spend countless hours and substantial staff resources on developing elaborate and well-intentioned strategic plans only to put them on a bookshelf and forget about them. There are four main keys to achieve your objectives: focus on the wildly important, act on the lead measures, keep a compelling scoreboard, and create a cadence of accountability.[13] First, if we focus on doing too much, we will not be very successful. We need to set priorities and focus on those first. Down the road, we can revisit other issues that didn't make the first cut. Second, we should start by acting on those goals that will result in the largest impact on our community. They also measure the behaviors that will drive overall success. Third, communicating clear results will drive the highest levels of engagement with your team and your community. Fourth, having regular, brief update meetings helps team members to remain accountable for the tasks they are responsible for. Regular meetings are also an opportunity to quickly adapt to challenges and opportunities that come up.

One challenge our communities often face is the change throughout our tribal organizations when new elected officials take office. Previous elected officials, staff, and community members dedicate a lot of hard work and time to plan and develop strategic plans. New elections can bring new priorities and new methods to achieve those priorities. However, a strong strategy should not change with a change in leadership. If it was developed through extensive community input, it should be able to stand the test of time.

STEP 4: MONITOR AND EVALUATE THE PROGRESS

After you have successfully implemented your strategic plan, it is time to measure your progress to see how successful you were, and to see whether you need to make changes to your programming. There are a number of questions to ask during this time. Did you accomplish what you set out to accomplish? Did you meet specified timelines and budgets? How efficient was your work? How did your efforts impact the community? What should you change moving forward?

When it comes time to communicate the results, be sure to cast your message far and wide. You could write up a story for the tribal newspaper and newsletters. Include it in your annual report to the tribal membership. Put it on your tribal website. Bring it up at board meetings, staff meetings, and community meetings. Remember, this is not the end of the process. It starts over as soon as you are ready to start making more positive changes in your community.

PRACTITIONER PERSPECTIVE

My experience with the Oneida Nation has allowed me to work with various tribal operations and services.[14] Our casino provides financial resources for the nation and provides jobs for tribal members. My role in the gaming operation is as an organizational development specialist. I have an active role in helping facilitate our gaming management team review and assess our gaming strategies. During my work with Oneida, I learned that it is important to be flexible with schedules since the professionals I'm dealing with are the top senior managers in the gaming division. Although I must be flexible, I'm diligent in ensuring they meet to conduct the quarterly and annual reviews. It's also important to revisit the goals and action items to ensure we're doing the right things to achieve our vision. During the quarterly strategy review meetings, we spend time looking at progress made toward our goals.

During our annual review meetings, we look back over the past year and identify overall effectiveness of the goals set. We decide if we have any new goals or priorities that need focus over the next year or beyond. When reviewing our activity progress and challenges, we check the pulse of the world around us and keep our destination in clear sight.

NOTES

1. SWOT: Strengths, Weaknesses, Opportunities, and Threats.

2. Brenda Freeman, Ethleen Iron Cloud-Two Dogs, Douglas K. Novins, and Pamela L. LeMaster, "Contextual Issues for Strategic Planning and Evaluation of Systems of Care for American Indian and Alaska Native Communities: An Introduction to Circles of Care," *American Indian and Alaska Native Mental Health Research: The Journal of the National Center* 11, no. 2 (2004): 1–29, 24.

3. Benjamin J. Broome and Irene L. Cromer, "Strategic Planning for Tribal Economic Development: A Culturally Appropriate Model for Consensus Building," *International Journal of Conflict Management* 2, no. 3 (1991): 217–33.

4. Rebecca M. Webster, "This Land Can Sustain Us: Cooperative Land Use Planning on the Oneida Reservation." *Planning Theory & Practice* 17, no. 1 (2016): 9–34.

5. Nicholas Christos Zaferatos, "Planning the Native American Tribal Community: Understanding the Basis of Power Controlling the Reservation Territory," *Journal of the American Planning Association* 64, no. 4 (1998): 395–410.

6. Freeman, Iron Cloud-Two Dogs, Novins, and LeMaster, "Contextual Issues."

7. Freeman, Iron Cloud-Two Dogs, Novins, and LeMaster, "Contextual Issues," 24.

8. Rachel Smith, "16 Strategic Planning Models to Consider," Clear Point Strategy, 2019, https://www.clearpointstrategy.com/strategic-planning-models/.

9. "Vision, Mission, and Values," Oneida Nation of Wisconsin, https://oneida-nsn.gov/government/business-committee/members/#Vision-Mission-and-Values.

10. Nicholas Christos Zaferatos, "Developing an Effective Approach to Strategic Planning for Native American Indian Reservations," *Space and Polity* 8, no. 1 (2004): 87–104.

11. Joseph S. Anderson, and Dean Howard Smith, "Managing Tribal Assets: Developing Long-Term Strategic Plans," *American Indian Culture and Research Journal* 22, no. 3 (1998): 139–56.

12. George T. Doran, "There's a SMART Way to Write Management's Goals and Objectives," *Management Review* 70, no. 11 (1981): 35–36.

13. Chris McChesney, Sean Covey, and Jim Huling, *The 4 Disciplines of Execution: Achieving Your Wildly Important Goals* (New York: Simon and Schuster, 2012).

14. Julie Clark, organizational development specialist, Oneida Nation.

GLOSSARY

Environmental scan. Survey of relevant background information about the organization's past, present, and future.

Goals. Destinations that you want to see your community reach.

Mission statement. Brief description of an organization's fundamental purpose.

Objectives. Serve as a way to measure change in your community as you try to reach your goals.

SMART goals and objectives. SMART stands for Specific, Measurable, Achievable, Relevant, and Time-Oriented. This helps ensure your goals and objectives are clear, measurable, and related to mission and vision.

Stakeholders. Anyone that has an interest in the decisions or activities of the organization.

SWOT. SWOT stands for Strengths, Weaknesses, Opportunities, and Threats. SWOT is a tool to analyze your current situation. Strengths and weaknesses are internal to your community. Opportunities and threats are external.

Values statement. Conveys the values and priorities of the organization and signals what is important to the organization.

Vision statement. States the future objectives of an organization. It helps guide the organization to make decisions that align with its philosophy and declared set of goals.

Project Management

From Idea to Implementation

Joseph Bauerkemper and Jason Hollinday

THIS CHAPTER SETS OUT TO DEMYSTIFY THE PRACTICES OF PROJECT MANAGEMENT and offers tools for pursuing successful initiatives in tribal governance contexts. With an emphasis on planning and documentation, we explain the key components of a project portfolio approach and situate those components in applied relation to one another. Our aim is to underscore stakeholder relations and cultural resonance as matters of paramount importance to effective tribal project management.

BEST PRACTICES

- Collaboratively develop a comprehensive articulation of the project's purpose, and orient all activities to it.
- Ensure that cultural insight, relevance, and humility shape all aspects of the project.
- Identify the core objectives and associated deliverables necessary for the project to fulfill its purpose.
- Delineate all tasks and resources required for success.
- Schedule tasks in strategic relation to one another.
- Anticipate risks, mitigate them, and prepare contingency plans.
- Attend to the dynamic complexity of tribal governance contexts.

Peanutty Chocolate Cookies

If you happen to have a cookbook handy, take a moment to flip through it and skim-read one of the recipes. I'll wait . . .

Okay, thanks. It is quite likely that you were just now looking at a thorough project plan. It delineated a detailed accounting of required resources. It chronicled a carefully sequenced list of tasks. It noted important benchmarks you would achieve along the way. And it might have even provided guidance for when and how to serve the results to those lucky enough to dine with you. And look again, back up top. Does the recipe indicate the total amount of time it will take to prepare? Does it perhaps even break down that total time into active and passive phases?

During a recent session of a course I teach for the Master of Tribal Administration and Governance program at the University of Minnesota Duluth, we pursued this very activity. A student in the class just so happened to have *The Best Little Cookbook in Minnesota* close by. Published by the Leech Lake Band of Ojibwe's White Oak Casino ("The Best Little Casino in Minnesota"), the cookbook includes a recipe for "Peanutty Chocolate Cookies" that sounded tasty to our class that day.[1] As anticipated, the recipe presented us with a fine-tuned roster of necessary materials and a sequenced to-do list with key status checks along the way. We were also made aware that we would naturally spend active time prepping the dough and 14 minutes awaiting the bake, and that we could expect to provide cookies to two dozen lucky eaters—if we could convince them to eat only one each. Indeed, a thorough project-management plan.

What I am getting at here is that *you are already a project manager.* There. That is perhaps all you need from this chapter. Indeed, this is its primary point—to underscore that all of us are already doing the work of project management. Whether baking a humble loaf of bread, getting dressed in the morning, or tending to a garden, we are constantly managing projects. By demystifying the realm of project management, this chapter sets out to illuminate and build upon various knowledges and strategies that you already have and deploy, even if you are not actively aware of them.

Project management may seem to be the purview of exclusive professional networks and self-proclaimed credentialing organizations, rife with jargon, hierarchies, and secret handshakes. All of this is to some extent the case. More importantly, however, project management is simply what organized people with a lot on their plate do. Much of project management is intuitive, rarely given direct attention and consideration. By slowing down to think through how we go about things and by gaining new tools and techniques, we can all better appreciate and significantly enhance the value we bring to our communities and organizations.

The hallmarks of project management are communication, responsibility, risk management, accountability, and the efficient and effective use of resources. Aside from relatively rare solo projects, it takes a team to get things done. Moreover, projects are nearly always taken up at someone's or some entity's behest. It is crucial that clear and ongoing communication take place within a project team and between that team and the person or entity that asked for the project to be pursued. Deliberate project planning and documentation make effective communication possible and vastly improve project processes and outcomes. Good project management clearly establishes where responsibility for particular tasks lies, ensuring that team members know what they need to be doing. Through reliable communication, clear assignment of duties, and comprehensive awareness of project status and trajectory, risks can be anticipated, averted, and mitigated. Far less will slip through the cracks. When things nevertheless slip and when duties are not adequately fulfilled, project management protocols reveal where accountability resides and indicate what corrective action is required. Finally, careful planning allows for informed anticipation of what and who will be needed for project success and how those resources can be best deployed.

This chapter will set about an exploration and explanation of these hallmarks—communication, responsibility, risk management, accountability, and the efficient and effective use of resources—by presenting an overview of a project-management model developed with tribal governance contexts in mind. The model emphasizes a procedure for creating comprehensive project plans. We will then consider factors that are particularly resonant with tribal governance contexts. Finally, an accomplished manager with a broad and deep record in tribal project planning will share insights earned through that wealth of experience.

PROJECT PLANNING PORTFOLIOS

I feel I should admit: things are about to get a bit tedious. I point this out to call attention to an ever-present temptation within the day-to-day of project management to set aside deliberate procedures and instead lean on intuition and instincts. Please resist this temptation. Intuition and instinct, especially as developed over time and through multiple encounters with success and failure, are certainly vital to good project management. Intuition and instinct are not to be discounted, yet they are also not to be our only orientations. Coupling intuition and instinct with careful adherence to reliable procedures—even while that can mean grappling with tedium—ensures that we are consistently addressing the hallmarks of project management mentioned above.

The project management model under consideration here entails the creation of several documents that make up a project planning portfolio. Though it has been adapted and reshaped through experience in and study of tribal governance contexts, this model is largely drawn from insights curated and generated by Anthony T. Cobb, a management-studies faculty member within Virginia Tech's Pamplin College of Business. Cobb's book *Leading Project Teams* has beneficially served many students pursuing graduate and undergraduate degrees in tribal administration, and it likewise serves as a key resource for this chapter.[2] The model presented here departs in some significant ways from that advanced by Cobb, but it remains deeply indebted to him.

A project planning portfolio consists of eight distinct yet interrelated components. Each of these should be documented both for use by the project manager and as primary tools for communication with members of the project team and key stakeholders. A project arises out of a need or opportunity. The purpose of the project is to address that need or leverage that opportunity. The project begins, then, with the articulation of its purpose. Some might view this articulation as a mission statement. In order to avoid confusion in relation to organizational contexts, we will refer to this as the project's statement of purpose. The statement of purpose does just what it says; it delineates the reasons the project exists and what it is fundamentally doing or creating. The project's purpose should be relevant to the broader mission of the organization within which or for which the project is being pursued, and the statement of purpose should serve as a consistent reference providing orientation and discipline for the project. If the project has no apparent connection with the relevant organization's mission, that apparent lack of connection should be explored before moving forward. As the project proceeds, if certain project activities lack apparent connection to the project's statement of purpose, those activities should be carefully reconsidered and/or the statement of purpose itself should be reassessed.

When crafting a project's statement of purpose, use direct language. It is often productive to simply begin by stating, "The purpose of this project is to . . ." Make sure to develop the statement of purpose in collaboration with the decision-makers who are originating and authorizing the project. It is crucial for those providing a project's mandate to be invested in the operative articulation of its purpose. A functional statement of purpose provides the project team with their fundamental mandate for action. It is the original and most important "page" of a project planning portfolio. When project teams and key stakeholders talk of "being on the same page," the statement of purpose is that all-important place. These considerations are exponentially important and exceptionally challenging in tribal governance contexts, where the core organizational mission is ultimately the effective practice of sovereign nationhood. Complex and always-changing networks of decision-making and constituencies make it all the more vital that project mandates are clear and solid. More on this crucial matter of stakeholder management in a moment.

In order for a project to fulfill its stated purpose, the project team must identify core objectives and create the conditions in which those objectives will be realized. These are the outcomes that need to take place in order for the project's purpose to be fulfilled. For example, if a project's purpose involves holding a community event, among the objectives might be collecting thirty RSVPs in advance of the event date. When identifying and articulating objectives, have in mind the clever acronym SMART. This reminds us that project objectives should generally be specific, measurable, achievable, relevant, and time-oriented. The simple example just mentioned hits each of these characteristics: It is an outcome specifically pertaining to tracking attendees. It sets forth a readily measurable target. The outcome can be reasonably achieved. It is relevant to the overall success of the project. And it is associated with a moment in time within the project.

There are several versions and interpretations of the SMART acronym, and each project manager should adapt the tool for their practice and projects. In addition to flexibility when it comes to the characteristics that make an objective SMART, project managers, team members, and stakeholders should also recognize that effective objectives don't always need to cover every component of the SMART model. Moreover, these characteristics should not distract the team away from emphasizing what is of primary importance to the effort at hand. For example, not everything worth pursuing can be readily and reliably measured, and just because something can be finely measured does not mean it is worth pursuing. As sociologist William Bruce Cameron observed, "Not everything that can be counted counts, and not everything that counts can be counted."[3]

In order to cultivate the conditions in which project objectives will be realized, project teams need to create and deliver the necessary products, services, input, and outputs. These vital project building blocks are referred to as "deliverables" in that they are whatever it is that project teams need to deliver. Deliverables can be interim or culminating in nature. Interim deliverables are those that are necessary for ultimately allowing culminating deliverables to be realized. When identifying project deliverables during the project planning phase, it is important to maintain continued collaboration with the decision-makers who initiated and authorized the project. If a project team has ideas about appropriate deliverables that differ from the ideas held by the people or entity that mandated the project, tension will surely arise. For example, if officials who provided the mandate for a community event assume that appropriate refreshments—a key project deliverable—would entail a multicourse meal, while the project team assumes a tray of Peanutty Chocolate Cookies will suffice, this will at the very least lead to disappointment (until they try those cookies). It is therefore vital that project managers seek and facilitate deliberate and clear communication and documentation regarding deliverable expectations. Not only should all relevant parties agree on what the deliverables should be, but also what qualities and characteristics those deliverables should have.

Even when we have established a statement of purpose, identified core objectives, and determined what interim and culminating deliverables the project requires, we still are not ready to dig into the guts of our project. Before diving into the work at hand, we need to thoroughly consider and document precisely what that work will be. We need a to-do list. This entails documenting all project tasks that need to be undertaken in order to create and carry out our project deliverables. Each deliverable should be broken down into the things that need to be done in order for that deliverable to be achieved. Tasks will often involve subtasks, which should be considered and documented.

Taking on project tasks requires resources. We need budgets, materials, information, equipment, facilities, time, and labor to engage in project work, and we need to carefully and strategically allocate these resources across the various tasks associated with a project. Experience and data make it possible to engage in informed speculation about what resources we need and when we need them. The more accurate and reliable that speculation, the more efficient our project will be. As we consider a project's constellation of tasks in relation to available resources, we can begin mapping a pathway toward the deliverables that will enable the objectives we need to realize in order to fulfill the project's purpose. This mapping is our project schedule, which documents the strategic sequencing of project tasks and represents key resources needed for each, especially time. Project schedules help managers and teams communicate and track who should be doing what, with what resources, when. They also represent vital relationships between tasks, which only very rarely are independent of one another. Far more often, project tasks are connected and even reliant upon one another. It is quite common for one task to have to wait until another is completed. For example, we cannot create and deliver invitations for a community event until the event date has been established. The task of creating and delivering invitations (themselves an interim project deliverable) is dependent on the task of establishing an event date. An effective project schedule accounts for the time each individual task and subtask will take, while also accounting for the dependent relationships between tasks. If it is going to take one day to gather information and establish our event date, and if it is going to take two days to create invitations, we cannot schedule both tasks for the same days. Our schedule needs to reflect this dependency and allocate adequate time for the necessary sequencing of work. The following example of a project schedule is about as simple as such a schedule can get. As you can imagine, projects and associated schedules can be (and typically are) exponentially more complex. Yet even in its simplicity the following example in table 1 reflects many of the core contours of project scheduling.

A well-composed project schedule allows project managers to ascertain the most direct path toward project completion. Tasks can be strategically sequenced to account for both dependencies and efficient use of resources.

For example, while we need to know our event date before we can finalize and deliver invitations, we could (and likely should) simultaneously develop our decoration theme and invitation design. These tasks are dependent yet can overlap. In addition to involving tasks that necessarily take place before, with, or after other tasks, projects also often include tasks that are more independent and therefore can be scheduled with some flexibility. There are several options for when we might schedule the two days' worth of work that it would likely take to create decorations for the event. This slack allows us to think strategically, delegating the decor task to team members and days that are available, perhaps while those team members are waiting to start other tasks that cannot begin until other tightly sequenced tasks have been completed. Having this slack and managing it strategically achieves enhanced project efficiency.

But what about when (not if, always when) things go wrong? Risk assessment and contingency planning are crucial to project management. Even if we develop what seems like an air-tight plan, leaks can emerge, team members can drop the ball, efforts can fail, resources can be unavailable, etc. It is neither reasonable nor possible to pursue a project without any risk. In light of this reality, project managers assess their projects, looking for what can go wrong. When a potential risk seems relatively unlikely to occur and not all that devastating if it were to happen, a project manager might reasonably decide to accept the risk as is and move on to focus on other aspects of the project. If, however, a risk seems more likely to occur and/or would significantly impact the timeline, quality, or budget of the project, a project manager would work to address the risk in advance. This might involve reconfiguring relevant aspects of the project to avoid the risk altogether. Or it might mean taking steps to decrease the likelihood of the risk happening. Another related approach would be taking steps to decrease the impact of a risk if it were to occur, perhaps by buffering aspects of the project in relation to each other. In addition to avoiding and decreasing risks, they can sometimes be externalized. This can be arranged through purchasing insurance on select project components, insisting that suppliers take on risk associated with materials and equipment, and even outsourcing some project tasks and deliverables. Externalizing risks does not ensure they won't happen, nor does it completely remove negative project impact if problems occur. It also comes at increased project cost. Nevertheless, this may serve as a viable and appropriate approach. When it comes to assessing and planning in relation to project risk, project managers strive to recognize potential trouble before

Table 1. Simple Project Schedule Example: Community Event

PROJECT TASKS	BUDGET	TASK TIME	STAFF	DAY 1	D 2	D 3	D 4	D 5	D 6	D 7	D 8	D 9
select event date		1 day	Pat, Sam	x								
announce save-the-date		1 day	Bob	x								
reserve location		1 day	Pat	x								
plan refreshments		1 day	Sam	x								
plan decorations		1 day	Pat, Ned		x							
create invitations		2 days	Pat, Sam		x	x						
print invitations	$80	1 day	vendor				x					
mail invitations	$30	2 days	Bob					x	x			
create decorations		2 days	Ned, Sam			x	x					
receive RSVPs		2 days	Bob							x	x	
create guest list		1 day	Bob									x
finalize refreshments	$220	1 day	Sam									x
decorate	$40	1 day	Pat, Ned									x

it occurs, they document perceived risks by identifying them by type (time, quality, or budget) and likelihood of occurrence, and they draft contingency plans ready to implement if need arises.

Compiled together, the multiple pieces of documentation mentioned above serve as a project manager's planning portfolio. We have the statement of purpose, core objectives, delineated deliverables, list of tasks and subtasks, account of needed resources, project schedule, and the risk assessment. A project manager who works with key decision-makers and team members to develop a thorough project planning portfolio exponentially increases the likelihood of success. Yet in addition to these seven items, there is an eighth project management component that happens to be exceptionally important within tribal governance contexts.

THE XIEST OF X FACTORS

When considering a typical project, it is typically rather easy to identify primary stakeholders. These include the members of a project team, the decision-makers who provide the mandate for pursuing the project, and the people or entities that will make use of the project. It should come as no surprise that projects in tribal governance contexts tend not to be typical. For this reason, project managers working in tribal governance contexts need to be particularly mindful of the interwoven network of stakeholders that will impact and often fundamentally determine success or failure.[4]

Tribal governments are diverse. There are hundreds of them, and each is unique. There are patterns shared across many, but no uniformity. One thing that perhaps all tribal governance contexts do share is dynamic complexity. Both of these terms and the reality they describe should not be neglected by project managers. Tribal governance contexts are dynamic. They are always in flux. There are significant rates of turnover in elected, appointed, and civil service roles, and programs are always one election and one funding cycle away from major shifts. Tribal governance contexts are also complex. There are multiple sources of authority and influence, and these rarely align to push in a common direction. Tribal governments are invested with the sovereign authority of Native nations, which means—among many other things—that projects are always inherently politicized. Elected officials, career administrators, and tribal citizens all wield simultaneous authority and influence. Federal factors are also always close at hand, and relations with state governments increasingly impact tribal initiatives. Of course, federal and state structures are themselves dynamic and complex, and therefore their influence is as well.

Effective project management in tribal governance contexts demands incisive analyses of stakeholders and attentive management of them. Stakeholders are the multifaceted x-factor of tribal project management. They assert—whether actively or passively, directly or indirectly—determinate influence both from and toward multiple directions. This poses a formidable challenge for project managers, but it is also potentially empowering. Navigating this dynamic complexity, and channeling it into the workings of projects to enhance them, necessitates nuanced analysis of the contributions and influence that varying stakeholders will bring into the fray. This means anticipating what persons and entities will have, or perceive themselves to have, a stake in a project, and thinking through how those factors might translate into influential action. It also means managing that influence through proactive communication, delegation, and consultation, as well as reactive responses to critiques, shifting conditions, and emerging opportunities.

Finally, and most importantly, the effectiveness and relevance of project management in tribal governance contexts deeply depends on cultural resonance and influences. Managers and project teams must recognize, honor, and align with the cultural milieu in which they are immersed. Community norms and practices are paramount. They must be neither essentialized, romanticized, nor neglected. The development and exercise of the insight, humility, and care required to ensure cultural propriety and cultural match may seem, and may very well be, daunting. For many projects, this can be productively addressed by deliberately and explicitly seeking—through appropriate protocol, of course—participation from stakeholders who are trusted by the community for their own well-established cultural insight, humility, and care. Do not mistake this as a quick fix to be checked off a list. Rather, it is a sustained ethic and orientation.

PRACTITIONER PERSPECTIVE

Experience and knowledge in project management will move your project from an idea to reality.[5] All projects, regardless of size or expense, will have a similar structure. These projects can be completed by an individual or a group of people depending on your particular situation. The project management style used at Fond du Lac is adapted from an American Planning Association model and has multiple steps or layers to it, each mentioned below. Along with identifying each step, I've included illustrative examples drawn from one of our major projects, development of the Fond du Lac Fiber to the Home broadband network.

- *Define a problem or opportunity*: For the Fond du Lac Fiber to the Home Project, the Band secured grant funds for community outreach and education on potential uses of high speed internet and what it can mean for the future of the tribe. A bonus to this is that project staff incorporated this data into the Fond du Lac Band's Strategic Plan.
- *Setting project goals and objectives*: Information gathered from community meetings informed project goals and objectives for the overall Fiber to the Home project (i.e., speeds, fiber vs. wireless, potential uses, and types of user packages: internet, video, and phone).
- *Research alternate strategies*: In particular, the strategy chosen was based on the primary objective to get high speed internet to every

home on the Fond du Lac Reservation. The Fond du Lac IT Division had studies done to compare wireless vs. fiber pros and cons.

- *Select the preferred strategy*: Once the alternate strategies were analyzed by project staff a recommendation was selected. The recommended option was brought to the Fond du Lac Tribal Council for discussion and approval.
- *Implement the preferred strategy*: After the project staff was given the permission to proceed, work began immediately to pursue grants, begin engineering and design, hire staff, and to communicate with other divisions and partners.
- *Monitor and evaluate performance*: Tracking performance measures, which are often required by funders, helps keep your project on task and on time. Depending on the project, you may want to have weekly or biweekly meetings with the project group to keep everyone on schedule and on the same page, and to see if problems have arisen.
- *Time management—Gantt charts*: Time management is always important. The use of Gantt charts, a basic example of which is given in table 1, can assist in the management of project activities measured against time. For the Fiber to the Home project there are a total of six grants for specific parts of the reservation. All these grants have different goals, locations, and terms to be completed. The use of Gantt charts helps keep the process organized and moving smoothly.
- *Open communication*: Keep in contact with project staff, funders (reporting), vendors, tribal council, and the community. More communication will always make a project move more effectively.
- *Don't give up too soon*: It is 2021 as I write this, and the Fond du Lac Fiber to the Home project is still being constructed and is also operational with over 525 customers. This is a long ways from 2006 when there was just an idea. There were five grant submissions that were not funded, and multiple potential versions of the network plan were dismissed for various issues. It took ten years before all the right pieces were put together and the Band received the first two grants for construction. It was important enough to pursue, and we kept at it and eventually figured it out.

Strategic planning is vital to an organization when developing community goals and objectives. If your organization has a solid strategic plan, you can use your project management skills to pursue that plan's goals. If your organization does not have a strategic plan, your project management skills and knowledge can help by providing the basis to create strategic paths forward. Using project management skills, you can create a strategic approach where you can work with your community directly through public meetings and surveys, conduct research on other local communities, and work with other tribal departments in addition to the Tribal Council.

Once created, your community's strategic plan will have a list of ideas, projects, and recommendations on what the community wants; the plan can assist in buy-in from staff and provide guidance on how it is implemented. In a sense a community strategic plan established your initial steps in project management. It can set the table for you by defining a problem or opportunity and setting project goals and objectives. The plan provides early traction and momentum for the project, enabling you to convince community stakeholders and potential funders, which are crucial to getting projects to completion.

NOTES

1. White Oak Casino, *The Best Little Cookbook in Minnesota* (Kearney, NE: Morris Press), 84–86. Chi miigwech to Jody O'Connor for being a good sport during this in-class exercise.
2. Anthony T. Cobb, *Leading Project Teams: The Basics of Project Management and Team Leadership*, 2nd ed. (Los Angeles: Sage, 2012).
3. William Bruce Cameron, *Informal Sociology* (New York: Random House, 1963), 13.
4. When engaging in intergovernmental relations with settler governments, tribal nations are often mischaracterized as "stakeholders" rather than regarded as sovereign nations pursuing diplomacy. The use of the term "stakeholders" in this chapter, however, refers to individuals and groups engaging with and impacting tribal governance processes.
5. Jason Hollinday, planning director, Fond du Lac Band of Lake Superior Chippewa.

GLOSSARY

Dependencies. The relationships between two project tasks that rely upon one another. The finish-to-start dependency is the most common, referring to a circumstance in which one task cannot begin until another task has been completed. The start-to-start dependency refers to circumstances in which two tasks must start at the same time. Similarly, the finish-to-finish dependency refers to circumstances in which two tasks must be brought to completion at the same time. Finally, the relatively rare start-to-finish dependency refers to circumstances in which one task cannot be brought to completion until another task has begun.

Gantt chart. A widely used format for project scheduling emphasizing the timing of project tasks and how they relate to one another. The schedule example in this chapter is a basic Gantt chart.

Project deliverables. The products, services, input, and outputs that make up the necessary building blocks of the project. Deliverables can be interim or culminating in nature. Interim deliverables are those that are necessary for ultimately allowing culminating deliverables to be realized.

Project planning portfolio. The comprehensive collection of documents that project managers use to oversee a project. A complete portfolio would include a statement of purpose, core objectives, delineated deliverables, list of tasks and subtasks, account of needed resources, project schedule, and risk assessment. A project manager works with key decision-makers, stakeholders, and team members to develop the project planning portfolio.

Slack. A characteristic of some project tasks when strict dependencies don't apply. This means that tasks with slack provide some scheduling flexibility, which in turn may provide opportunities for resources to be strategically deployed for increased efficiency.

SMART objectives. The targeted outcomes that need to be achieved in order for a project to fulfill its purpose. Generally speaking, these objectives should be Specific, Measurable, Achievable, Relevant, and Time-Oriented.

RECOMMENDED RESOURCES

Anthony T. Cobb. *Leading Project Teams: The Basics of Project Management and Team Leadership*, 2nd ed. (Los Angeles: Sage, 2012).

Brett Harned. *Project Management for Humans: Helping People Get Things Done* (New York: Rosenfeld Media, 2017).

Duncan Haughey. "A Brief History of SMART Goals," https://www.projectsmart.co.uk/brief-history-of-smart-goals.php.

Joseph Heagney. *Fundamentals of Project Management*, 5th ed. (New York: AMACOM, 2016).

Kory Kogon, Suzette Blakemore, and James Wood. *Project Management for the Unofficial Project Manager* (Dallas: BenBella Books, 2015).

"Project Planning and Development Toolkit." Administration for Native Americans (https://www.acf.hhs.gov/sites/default/files/documents/ana/2020_ppd_toolkit_508_compliant.pdf).

Tribal Government Human Resources

Rebecca M. Webster, Paul Ninham, and Michael J. Poitra

TRIBAL NATIONS RELY ON TRIBAL HUMAN RESOURCES DEPARTMENTS FOR A number of essential functions involving job analysis, job design, recruitment, staffing, development, compensation, benefits, safety, health, training, development, employee relations, and labor relations. This chapter helps navigate through the complex, and occasionally competing application of tribal, state, and federal employment laws; explains the importance of having codified tribal employment ordinances and well-tested employee handbooks in place; describes Indian preference and the Tribal Employment Rights Office (TERO); walks through the hiring process; explains the need for training and retention efforts; and explains the importance of following the process for disciplinary procedures while providing a mechanism for employees to have their disputes resolved.

BEST PRACTICES

- Adopt a sound tribal employment ordinance and accompanying employee handbook.
- Establish explicit Indian preference goals.
- Communicate job performance, wage scales, and employment rules.

- Provide clear methods for recruitment, retention, training, discipline, and termination.
- Provide a forum to hear employment disputes.

INTRODUCTION

Human resources can be defined as a system of activities and strategies that focus on successfully managing employees at all levels of an organization to achieve organizational goals.[1] Tribal human resource departments support the success of tribal employees as they support and staff tribal government operations, businesses, and enterprises. They hold significant responsibilities to the workforce, as well as the tribal organization as a whole. They are responsible for

- Drafting and reviewing personnel policies, procedures, and employment agreements
- Identifying and hiring candidates
- Assisting with employee terminations or layoffs
- Managing benefits and perks programs
- Ensuring internal and external compensation equity
- Handling nepotism and conflicts of interest

NAVIGATING THE JURISDICTIONAL LANDSCAPE OF FEDERAL, STATE, AND TRIBAL EMPLOYMENT LAWS

While much of this chapter is dedicated to providing guidance for tribes to make positive changes to their human resource practices, understanding the convergence and interactions of federal, state, and tribal employment laws can have an impact on tribal efforts to make their own laws and to be governed by them. After all, the ability to make our own laws and be governed by them is the foundation of tribal sovereignty.[2] This can be difficult when federal and state employment laws find their way into the tribal employment sphere. Navigating which laws, and to what extent tribes need to comply, can be a complex task.

With respect to federal laws, an analysis based on the landmark *Tuscarora* and *Donovan* court cases can be helpful to determine which federal employment laws may apply to tribal government operations.[3] This analysis recognizes that federal statutes of general applicability apply to tribes,[4] but if the statute interferes with tribal self-governance or treaty rights, or the congressional intent to exclude tribes is clear, then the statute will not apply to tribes.[5] Many courts and federal agencies have adopted a distinction between Indian tribes as employers in purely governmental functions and Indian tribes as enterprises engaged in commercial activities. Courts have been more willing to find that Indian tribes or tribal enterprises engaged in commercial activities are subject to federal labor and employment statutes of general applicability. This is one of the reasons why it is important to memorialize government goals to clarify that funds generated from economic development initiatives fund essential governmental services.

Tribes would be best served if there were a neat and tidy chart clearly outlining what parts of federal laws apply to them. There is no such a chart because the analysis of whether a federal law applies to tribes is often complex, with different courts often reaching disparate conclusions. In light of these uncertainties, tribes have options that lead to varying levels of asserting tribal sovereignty and autonomy, as well as the litigation risks associated with pushing the limits of tribal sovereignty. Below are four basic options for tribes to pursue, beginning with the most conservative approach and ending with the most assertive (and risky) approach. Individual tribes need to decide for themselves which option is the best fit for their community.

1. Follow the federal employment laws.
2. Promulgate tribal employment laws that meet the minimum requirements of federal employment laws.
3. Promulgate tribal employment laws that reflect the tribe's values and some of the federal government's good ideas.
4. The tribe does what it wants, when it wants, and federal employment laws are not considered relevant to the discussion.

With respect to state employment laws, we start with the general rule that state laws do not apply to tribes. The exceptions to this are where Congress grants states jurisdiction, if not applying the law would violate state public policy, or if tribes agree to be bound by the state laws. One of the most common examples of a situation where Congress granted states authority they did not previously have was through the enactment of PL-280. Consider the nature of state employment laws. They are not criminal prohibitory, meaning state laws do not automatically apply on Indian reservations. Some may be considered civil regulatory, which should also mean they do not apply to tribal employment situations. The last type of law addressed in PL-280 are civil causes of action. Under PL-280, Congress opened up state courts for tribal members to resolve their disputes. This action is most notable when individuals attempt to get their employment grievances heard in state courts instead of tribal courts. They may also try to get their dispute resolved in accordance with state contract laws instead of tribal employment laws.[6]

Despite the inapplicability of state employment laws to tribes, tribes often agree to be bound by those laws through compacts, agreements, and grants. Tribal-state gaming compacts can be an avenue where states have negotiated to include application of state employment laws to tribal gaming operations. Examples include human rights laws, workers' compensation, unemployment compensation, as well as health, safety, and even traffic laws. When considering compacts, agreements, and grants, tribes should address the applicability of laws as a point of negotiation, instead of an automatic requirement. Oftentimes, external entities rely on standard forms and past practices to enter into these contracts and are unaware of the unique political and legal situation of tribal governments.

On the flip side of navigating the applicability of federal and state employment laws to tribal governments is the applicability of tribal employment laws to non-Indian tribal employees.[7] Ostensibly, it appears obvious that if a non-Indian voluntarily works for an Indian tribe, that individual should also be bound by tribal employment laws. However, tribes often need to take steps to ensure the employee has consented to tribal jurisdiction, including the application of tribal laws and resolving disputes in a tribal judicial forum. To this end, we present some sample language tribes may consider having their employees sign during their orientation process:

> As an employee of ____, a wholly owned enterprise of the ____ (the "____"), I consent to the exclusive jurisdiction of the Nation's Court for any and all disputes in connection with my employment with the ____. I also consent to the application of the Nation's law, both substantive and procedural, regarding any and all proceedings or matters relating to my employment relationship with the ____.

In addition to this language, consider anticipating modifications to employee rules over time. Here is some sample language: "Employers reserve the right to revise, supplement, modify and rescind any policies or portion of this Manual from time to time as it deems appropriate, in its sole discretion."

Navigating the complex and confusing arena of federal, state, and tribal employment laws can be a daunting task. Relying on the expertise of tribal attorneys is paramount. It is requisite for tribal human-resources staff, tribal attorneys, and the tribal elected officials to work together in a cohesive and collaborative manner to assure that purposeful decision-making protocols are executed while moving forward in this employment landscape.

EMPLOYMENT ORDINANCES AND HANDBOOKS

Switching focus back to how tribes can bolster their employment practices, one of the key factors to success is adopting a sound tribal employment ordinance and employee handbook. This can reduce the uncertainty of leadership decisions by providing the legislative intent, and increase an employer's objectivity and impartiality, provide due process for employees, and define employer expectations. Any time a tribe affirmatively enacts law, tribal sovereignty is exerted and exercised. Having a solid law codified can result in more predictable outcomes from the courts. Where tribes do not have laws, codes, and ordinances in place, some state courts have filled the gaps with state laws that would otherwise not apply.[8] It is critical for tribes to enact ordinances so they have a voice in how employment issues are handled. Employment handbooks that either include or refer to employment policies and procedures enhance and strengthen the tribal law by providing more details and further guidance on tribal employment-related matters.

Conflicts of interest can be a concern in close-knit tribal communities. Conflicts of interest are generally situations where an employee (or applicant or his/her family) has a relationship with an external business, or has investments that may potentially sway an employee's decisions at work that could financially benefit them personally. This could occur with family-owned businesses and employees responsible for entering into contracts with businesses to perform work for the tribe. Tribes need to find a way to balance encouraging tribal-member entrepreneurs with preventing actual or perceived conflicts of interest.

Another type of conflict of interest that arises in close-knit communities is nepotism. Nepotism is a type of favoritism based on familial relationships where a person with decision-making authority accords special treatment to an individual based on family relationship instead of merit indicators such as performance, achievements, or qualifications. Tribal ordinances should draw clear and absolute lines to ensure familial ties do not influence hiring, promotions, job assignments, wages, or other employment decisions.

In addition to conflict of interest and nepotism, tribal employment ordinances should address a wide array of topics to ensure consistency in employment matters. Table 1 contains the ordinances that are included in Title 2 of the Oneida Nation's Code of Laws:[9]

A tribe can have laws, policies, handbooks, and standard operating procedures addressing all aspects of tribal employment matters, but if it doesn't communicate with the employee base, the employees will not fully understand their expectations, duties, responsibilities, or standards. Employees need to be aware of and have access to those delineated requirements. The documents should be readily available in paper and electronic format for the entire tribal employee base. The orientation of new hires is a great venue to inform employees how to access that information. Additionally, documenting that communication eases the enforcement of all employee rules and regulations.

In addition to communicating the expectations and standards, employers should directly inform and convey to the employees information regarding job performance, wages, and benefits. Employers should also explain how employees can attain success while performing their job duties for the tribe. Temporary setbacks can be transformed into success if the employee periodically revisits their handbook, job descriptions, annual reviews, and attends the required employee meetings. Defining rewards for exceeding expectations, as well as consequences for poor performance, can strengthen a tribe's employee base. With respect to wages, tribal employers need to provide a reasonable salary to their employees while communicating the methodology used to determine the tribal pay scale. Also, illustrating the benefits of working for the tribe needs to be conveyed to the employee base. Some of the benefits that may be offered are health insurance, vision, dental, emergency insurance, 401(k), Christmas savings, life insurance, short-term disability benefits, long-term benefits, tuition reimbursement, childcare benefits, time off for ceremonies, and employee wellness programs.

Table 1. Oneida Nation Employment Ordinances

Chapter 202	Drug and Alcohol Free Workplace
Chapter 203	Oneida Worker's Compensation Law
Chapter 204	Garnishment
Chapter 205	Furlough
Chapter 206	Back Pay
Chapter 207	Layoff Policy
Chapter 208	Investigative Leave
Chapter 209	Early Return to Work
Chapter 210	Vehicle Driver Certification and Fleet Management
Chapter 211	Whistleblower Protection
Chapter 213	Military Service Employee Protection Act
Chapter 214	Oneida Policy on Reporting Child Abuse and Neglect
Chapter 215	Computer Resources Ordinance
Chapter 216	Attorney Contract Policy
Chapter 217	Conflict of Interest
Chapter 218	Social Media Policy
Chapter 219	Oneida Travel and Expense Policy
Chapter 220	Paper Reduction Policy
Chapter 221	Oneida Early Childhood Program—Internal Investigation of Complaints
Chapter 223	Workplace Violence

INDIAN PREFERENCE AND TERO

One basic element of tribal employment practices is to establish explicit Indian preference goals in hiring and contracting. This can be done through a tribal employment ordinance that specifies Indian preference in hiring. It can also be accomplished through a Tribal Employment Rights Ordinance (TERO) that requires employers who are engaged in operating a business to give preference to qualified Indians in all aspects of employment, contracting, and other business activities. Together, Indian preference and TERO provide access to more employment and training opportunities for Indians, and provide more business and economic opportunities for businesses owned by Indians.

These preferences in hiring and contracting are permitted under federal laws. In *Morton v. Mancari*, the U.S. Supreme Court laid the foundation for the principle that an individual's status as a tribal member is a political classification, not a racial classification.[10] The issue in this case was an Indian preference in hiring at the Bureau of Indian Affairs. The Court reasoned that such a preference gave Indians a greater participation in their own self-government, furthered the government's trust obligation toward the Indian tribes, and reduced the negative effect of having non-Indians administer matters that affect Indian tribal life. Similarly, Title VII of the Civil Rights Act specifically prohibits discrimination against a person because of a person's race, color, religion, gender, or national origin, thus protecting Indian tribes from employers' potential bias.[11]

Indian preference for hiring should ideally be memorialized in a tribal employment ordinance. When considering how to implement Indian preference goals, different tribes utilize different methods. In varying weights, priorities, and rankings, tribes generally include these categories for Indian preference:

- Enrollment in the tribe
- Enrollment in another federally recognized tribe
- Married to an enrolled member
- Descendant of an enrolled member

Some tribes use a point system, others implement a ranking system, while others include in the job description that certain positions are required to be filled by an enrolled tribal member. Whatever means the tribe ends up deciding on, once again, it should be clearly and concisely delineated.

With respect to TERO, Indian preference requirements can reach beyond tribal governments to other employers contracting with tribes and conducting business on Indian reservations. TERO has two main elements, conceptual and programmatic.[12] Conceptual TERO is a sovereignty-based, self-help, and systematic approach to Indian and economic self-reliance or self-determination. Programmatic TERO is also a tribal enforcement and compliance program that monitors employers to ensure optimal benefits are attained from federal and tribal employment laws, regulations, policies, and procedures. Combined, Indian preference and TERO can help ensure that Indians gain a more proportional share of employment, training, contracting, subcontracting, and business opportunities on their reservations.

HIRING PROCESS

The basic components to hiring, firing, retaining, and training employees can be summarized as follows:

- Identifying the need for a position
- Creating job descriptions with qualifications
- Recruiting qualified candidates
- Selecting and hiring the most qualified applicant
- Offering training opportunities
- Engaging in retention efforts
- Following disciplinary procedures

The process to recruit, hire, and retain new staff commences with determining what the needs of the tribal organization are, what the budget will allow, and what type of qualifications and expertise a new employee is required to possess. Once these are determined, a clear and concise job description will be crafted. Even if human resources is posting for an existing position, they should review the existing description to determine if there are any updates or revisions that are warranted. Once HR has gone through this initial process, they can begin recruitment efforts.

Recruitment

The recruitment process is a critical component for any organization's success. Tribes are continually seeking and recruiting the most talented individuals to fit into the tribal organizational structure. There are two types of recruitment actions: internal recruitment and external recruitment. Internal recruitment is hiring an existing employee for a new, targeted position, while external recruitment consists of recruiting potential candidates outside of the organization. Securing the right internal or external candidate that possesses the educational qualifications, experience, abilities, and skills can be a great challenge.

Tribal advertising and marketing departments can help attract qualified prospective candidates that will meet the needs of the tribe. A clear and aesthetic advertisement, accompanied with a job description that includes a program history, pay scale, career opportunities, as well as minimum and preferred qualifications can be key factors to successfully recruit candidates. Social media and job-seeking platforms will further help target specific pools of applicants seeking employment.

Screening and Interviewing Applicants

After tribes advertise for a position and receive applications, the next step in the process is to shortlist the pool of applicants through a screening process. A completed application should have all the components required to properly screen the applicants, including all the relevant job-description-related information, as well as information that will allow the human resources staff to complete an employment verification, complete a background check, and contact any listed references.

Depending on the size of the pool of applications, the tribe may decide to interview all the qualified individuals or the top tier of applicants. Depending how the interview process is organized, and taking into consideration the position being interviewed for, different individuals may be included in the interview panel or selection committee. The immediate supervisor, along with other human resources staff and elected officials, may sit on the panel and assist with the decision-making process for hiring.

Prior to the interview, it is incumbent upon everyone on the interview panel to thoroughly review the job description and position requirements, and to complete a review of the applicant's file. During the interview, limit questions to those that are job-related, including their goals, career objectives, problem-solving experiences, and salary expectations. Don't ask personal questions, medically related questions, or questions regarding gender, religion, or age. Ultimately, the interview should supplement the application.

Selecting the Applicant

Following the interviews, the selection committee will rank the applicants. In addition to factors such as Indian preference and veterans' preference, there are different options available for scoring an applicant. Most methods involve a numerical process with points associated with and awarded to various job-related requirements. Implementing a numerical scoring system helps remove ambiguity in the hiring process. To further its goals of transparency and accountability, the Leech Lake Band of Ojibwe requires the selection committee to forward the following information to the human resources department:

- Interview panel information
- All scoring methods cited and identified
- Names of all candidates that are qualified and were listed on the interview schedule, or all candidates that made the top positions to be voted on
- Full legal name of candidate that was recommended for hire and tribal enrollment affiliations (if applicable)
- Complete application and associated documents
- Copies of letters to all candidates invited to interview
- Each interview panel member's questionnaire sheet on each candidate interviewed, along with written detailed documentation of candidate's responses to questions and score for each candidate[13]

TRAINING AND RETAINING EMPLOYEES

Tribal training has evolved in the past decade due to available funding and applying the very latest in technology. Many tribes have progressed by training employees to develop the needed skill set to succeed in a plethora of positions for tribal governments and within the tribal organization. The development of the human resource department is also evolving so that the tribal government will meet the current and future challenges of training. Training presents innovative ways for people to think outside of the box, and helps develop the abilities of individual employees to satisfy the current and future needs of the tribe.

There are several different ways that tribal governments train their employees. There is on-the-job training, which is planned, structured, and executed at the workplace. It involves onsite training with managers, directors, colleagues, and key personnel who are intimately familiar with the job duties, function, and responsibilities. Another form of on-the-job training is mentoring, a more prolonged and sustained method of teaching. Some departments in tribal governments and operations have employed directors and managers for multiple decades. When they retire, if no succession plan is existent, they leave critical positions without guidance for the new employee, a detriment to the tribe regarding institutional knowledge. A well-crafted policy designed for directors and managers to implement a succession plan, to include an extended orientation phase, could make the transition substantially smoother and more efficient.

Other types of training include off-the-job training, which can involve group discussions, one-on-one tutorials, lectures, reading, training courses, and workshops. These types of training techniques enable employees to learn and apply new skills and knowledge in a safe working context. A new approach tribal governments have been utilizing in training is through e-learning.[14] E-Learning refers to the use of information technology to enhance and support education and learning, which in part provides a variety of learning strategies and presentations to exchange information and acquire skills. E-Learning is normally less costly than other forms of training. It is self-paced; the content is consistent; it can be used anywhere at any time; it is easy to update, manage, and control for large numbers of people; and it can assist organizations in enhancing performance.

Retaining employees can be a challenging aspect for any organization. In recent decades, tribal governments have become a more promising employment opportunity for younger generations. Many tribal governments have incorporated health-insurance options such as individual health insurance, dental, eye, accident, short- and long-term disability insurance, a 401(k) savings plan, and life insurance. They also may provide the employee with options to improve and maintain their quality of life. Many tribes recognize the correlation between holistically healthy employees and overall job performance. If a tribe does not own a health and fitness center for community members and employees to utilize, alternatives are generally offered, in the form of passes, to local, non-tribal health and wellness facilities. Many of the full-time tribal government positions also have the option of annual and sick leave. Other factors that may help retain employees include positive employer/employee relationships, open communication, advancement opportunities, training opportunities, and lifelong learning.

DISCIPLINARY ACTIONS AND APPEALS

Human resource departments should ensure management is trained to effectively carry out disciplinary processes. Supervisors need to vigilantly follow disciplinary procedures for a variety of infractions, including failure to report to the worksite on time, failure to call the supervisor, calling in too often, theft, destruction of tribal property, working while intoxicated, possession of drugs or weapons, fighting, sexual harassment, using excessively abusive language, intimidation, or sabotaging another's work. Failure to follow established policies and procedures can result in an employee effectively having their disciplinary action overturned due to a technicality. In general, the following steps make up the progressive disciplinary process:

- Informal warning
- Formal, written warning
- Suspension with or without pay
- Probation
- Termination or demotion

To begin, each action should be placed in the employee's file with a notation of how long it should remain there. Some actions are removed after a set period of time while other actions are permanently kept in the file. When supervisors meet with employees about disciplinary actions, the primary discussion should focus on ways the employee can improve their performance. Here are some key points to consider when meeting with an employee:

- Reiterate performance expectations
- Have all the facts and documentation
- Focus on behaviors, not feelings
- Develop a plan and timetable for improvement with a review date

There are many instances other than disciplinary actions that an employee may want to challenge and address with their supervisors. For example, an employee may raise a concern about nepotism, conflict of interest, unfavorable performance evaluation, or title reassignments. In these instances, it is important to provide a forum for employees to resolve those disputes. In those situations, the tribe should ensure that the hearing body or court's scope of review is clearly defined, as well as the employee's rights to such judicial oversight. Providing such a forum to resolve disputes increases due process afforded to tribal employees, limits the arguments for unions to form in the first place, limits state and federal court review, and permits the tribe to develop employment common law.

Practitioner Perspective

Even in instances where tribes met all the best practices for human resource departments, the current global pandemic proved that many tribes were unprepared. Tribes with strong employment ordinances, readily available employee handbooks, great communication with the employee base, clear employment procedures, and a reliable forum to hear disputes may have been in a better position. Human resource departments must establish a respectful partnership with tribal top management and their respective councils to assure sound action plans are drafted. These plans must reflect flexible policies and protocols to adjust to the rapidly changing market and needs of the tribes. No one was prepared to lay off or furlough huge percentages of their tribal workforces, effectively cutting off services to tribal members.

In response, many organizations implemented new policies for remaining employees to follow so they could work comfortably and safely from home. To prevent the spread of the COVID-19 virus, many tribes switched to a remote work model at a rate and scale they've never experienced. Many tribes used email and video conferencing rather than the traditional face-to-face contact to collaborate on work projects. Supervisors are finding new ways to ensure employees are accountable, productive, motivated, engaged, and connected. Virtual communication and working remotely must be embraced, as trust among the employees and tribal citizenry is requisite. The pandemic will also serve as an opportunity to evaluate tribal policies beyond those impacting tribal human resources.

NOTES

1. Byars, Lloyd L., and Leslie W. Rue. *Human Resource Management.* New York: McGraw-Hill, 1997.
2. Williams v. Lee, 358 U.S. 217 (1959).
3. McGee, Richard G. *A Guide to Tribal Employment: An Employment Guide for Tribal Council, Human resources, and Enterprise Officials.* Bloomington, IN: Xlibris Corporation, 2008.
4. Fed. Power Comm'n. v. Tuscarora Indian Nation, 362 U.S. 99 (1960).
5. Donovan v. Coeur d'Alene Tribal Farm, 751 F.2d 1113 (9th Cir. 1985).
6. Kroner v. Oneida Seven Generations Corp. Wisconsin Supreme Court, 2010AP2533, unpublished slip opinion.
7. See Dollar General Corp. v. Mississippi Band of Choctaw Indians, 135 S. Ct. 2833 (2015).
8. County of Vilas v. Chapman, 122 Wis. 2d 211 (1985), 361 N.W.2d 699. The Court allowed the imposition of traffic laws on a tribal member on the reservation because the tribe did not have a longstanding history of regulating traffic.
9. https://oneida-nsn.gov/government_trashed/register/laws/#TITLE-2-EMPLOYMENT.
10. 417 U.S. 535 (1974).
11. 42 U.S.C.§ 2000e(b).
12. Pawnee Nation of Oklahoma, "Pawnee Nation of Oklahoma Tribal Employment Rights Ordinance." Tribal Employment Rights Ordinance (2018): 1–30.
13. Leech Lake Band of Chippewa, General Administration Personnel Policies (2008), https://www.llojibwe.org/employee/hr/gapp6-23-08.pdf.
14. Bratton, J., and J. Gold (eds.). *Human Resources Management Theory and Practice* (4th ed.). Houndmills, UK: Macmillan, 2007.

GLOSSARY

Conflict of interest. Situations where an employee (or applicant or his/her family) has a relationship with an external business, or has investments that may potentially sway an employee's decisions at work that could financially benefit them personally.

Due process. Recognizing the employee's right to be informed of unsatisfactory performance and to have a chance to defend him/herself and improve before an adverse employment action is taken. It also recognizes the employee's right to consistent and predictable employer responses when employees violate rules.

Employee handbook. A document that communicates an organization's mission, policies, and expectations. Employers give this to employees to clarify their rights and responsibilities while they're employed with the organization.

Nepotism. Type of favoritism based on familial relationships where a person with decision-making authority accords special treatment to an individual based on family relationship instead of merit indicators such as performance, achievements, or qualifications.

Personnel policies. Rules that govern how to deal with a human-resources or personnel-related situation. They are guidelines to decision-making that help keep the system as fair and unbiased as possible.

TERO. Stands for Tribal Employment Rights Ordinance. It requires employers who are engaged in operating a business to give preference to qualified Indians in all aspects of employment, contracting, and other business activities.

PART 2

Funding and Delivery of Core Services

Our tribal communities have been determining how to acquire and allocate resources since time immemorial. We faced decisions such as whether to eat the seeds coming from a poor harvest or save them all to plant the following spring. During wartime, we had to consider where we sent our people who would otherwise be out hunting, fishing, or trading. How many should stay behind to protect the most vulnerable people in our community, and how many should go on the offensive? We made decisions on how to allocate those limited resources. Today, unlike federal, state, and local governments, tribal governments generally do not have a tax base to raise financial resources. Instead, tribes often engage in economic development to fund their government programs and services. Like seeds and human capital, money is generally a limited resource. We need to carefully consider how to allocate it in ways that best meet the physical and spiritual needs of our people and our land base.

Tribal Finance

Eric S. Trevan and Jon Panamaroff

ACCESS TO CAPITAL IS CRITICAL TO THE ONGOING PROGRESS OF TRIBAL ECONO-
mies, economic wealth, and overall quality of life for tribes and tribal citizens.
No matter if we are working within the boundaries of our Native lands, be it a
tribal reservation or a village in Alaska, or operating a business in a standard
metropolitan city, Native Americans have begun the transformation of our
communities. To continue this progress and ensure that we maintain success
for the next seven generations, all Native communities should adhere to the
development of financial policies and practices to guide Native American
commerce's success. These policies are critical not only to generate revenue
on a specific project but also to support the entire tribal economy to realize
optimal returns. With the appropriate regulatory environment, a financial
strategy will allow access to capital, business and political alignment, and
overall maximation of leverage for transactions, credit, competitive advantages,
and economic sustainability. Understanding the market's overall conditions,
consumer demand, economic leakages, and GDP drive the finance strategy and
individual project finance for a tribal nation.

Tribes look to their leaders to leverage all tools to support tribal economies
and access to capital. Finance tools are broad and expansive, and tribes have
worked hard to decolonize finance constructs and restrictions. This reform
opened the opportunity to develop solutions for tribal nations and their citizens

to make sovereign decisions and acquire access to capital opportunities. Finance is critical to the future success of tribes, and understanding the necessary components of finance are outlined in this discussion. In this chapter we will introduce financial concepts that will allow a tribal nation to set forth policies and implement a business activity that will make Native communities more self-sufficient and practice economic self-determination.

BEST PRACTICES

- Understand the fundamental structure of finance through the five C's of Credit.
- Identify tribal financial frameworks that support economic activity.
- Follow the processes of better practices of tribal economic and community development.
- Use key indicators, financial ratios, and banking/debt structures to orient economic and community development approaches.
- Focus on policies that will develop a competitive advantage.

INTRODUCTION

Finance can be complicated, but fundamentally when thinking about finance, bank or debt, and business or enterprise development, start by understanding the Five C's of Credit. The five C framework is the basis for most credit decisions, including a credit card, a home mortgage, to a multimillion-dollar credit facility. The fundamentals in this framework give tribal leadership the core understanding of how to evaluate opportunities that need to be financed to ensure that they assess the proper level of risk with the nation's assets.

The Five C's of Credit (or Investment) Analysis

The following Five C's of Credit will provide a baseline for the primary platform on which finance and capital markets are structured. Capacity is the first and most critical of five key factors for the tribe to consider. Banks and investors want to know precisely how they will be repaid. Investors or lending organizations will look at cash flow, the timing of repayment, the probability of repayment, and if there is a contingent source of repayment when assessing tribal capacity to manage debt. The second factor is capital, the money the organization has also invested in the business. Investment is an indication of how much the tribe has at risk should the business fail. Investors and lenders will expect a contribution to the project. The question will be asked: does the borrower have skin in the game? Thirds is collateral, a type of guarantee that secures loans or investment. Giving a lender collateral or having fixed assets in the company for an investor means that there is a way for a group to provide liquidity for a project or organization to recoup some of their investment back if the organization closes. Loan guarantees are essential in Indian Country and will be covered in greater detail later in the chapter.

The fourth factor is the collective conditions in which financing might occur. The focus here would be on the intended purpose of the loan or investment and on the economic climate in which it would take place. Lenders and investors will seek to understand if the money will be used for working capital, additional equipment, inventory, etc., and they will consider the prevailing economic conditions within the specific industries at hand and related industries that could affect a business. The final factor is the general organizational or institutional character as perceived by prospective lenders and investors. Is the organization mature and is management professional and trustworthy? Is there stability in the government, leadership, and community backing? Does personnel have relevant and adequate education and experience in the field of business.

In parallel with these concepts, Native American economic development is not uncomplicated, and traditional financial models and capital markets are not designed to follow federal Indian law. The national financial system is not designed with the Marshall Trilogy in mind, does not understand post-traumatic stress related to poverty, nor does it understand our cultural values with an emphasis on the community above the individual. However, even with this foundation, tribal communities that follow financial practices rooted in the fundamental theories of financial management will succeed in creating long-term financial stability for their people.

Risk mitigation is at the forefront of financial planning and access to capital. Leaders must look to provide an understanding to the provider of capital that their investment is secure. Proper financial management looks beyond the traditional payment term's extension. It discusses receivables strategies, risk mitigation, and ways for financially secure companies or governments to leverage their position to grow revenue and market share.[1] The foundational information provided in this chapter will give leadership tools to allow for more significant growth within a community's financial viability.

Understanding Different Financial Frameworks

Native leaders who provide oversight and management of our governments' financial well-being, villages, and business operations have immense responsibilities to guide overall finance policy. To understand what is included in financial statements, the leader must first understand different frameworks for how financial information is presented. "An accounting framework is a set of criteria used to measure, recognize, present, and disclose the information appearing in an entity's financial statements."[2] Recognized frameworks include, but are not limited to:

- GASB: Governmental Accounting Standards Board
- FASB: Financial Accounting Standards Board
- IFRS: International Financial Reporting Standards (IFRS)
- FASAB: Federal Accounting Standards Advisory Board
- Non-GAAP: Special purpose frameworks
  - Cash, tax, regulatory
  - AICPA small and medium size entity

These frameworks provide the financial manager information to look for when evaluating the tribal community operation's financial health. These frameworks set the criteria used to determine measurement, recognition, presentation, and disclosure of items in financial statements.

The selection of the applicable framework is the responsibility of management and those charged with governance, and allows for organizations and nations to select the proper auditing service to provide the proper oversight for operations. Auditor selection is a critical step as auditors are obligated to review the appropriateness of the selected framework.[3]

For a tribal community—really for all communities—to remain forward-thinking, communication must be clear, to the point, and put in a way that people who do not have an advanced degree in finance can understand the overall financial health of the tribe. Knowing who is receiving the information is vital for allowing the community to become part of the success within the tribal nation's business and is a vital part of advancing financial well-being for a tribal nation. Communication should be shared with all stakeholders as it shows proper governance and allows for accountability in leadership.

Key Indicators/Financial Ratios

To monitor the progress of transactions or to analyze possible transactions, there are standard benchmarks used in various industries. These scores are transferrable among industry sectors and provide a range of possibilities when understanding the transaction. There are key indicators to monitor as a leader with fiduciary responsibility and allow for better planning. These indicators are:

SOLVENCY RATIOS

1. Current

   Current ratio measures a company's ability to pay short-term obligations or those due within one year. It tells investors and analysts how a company can maximize the current assets on its balance sheet to satisfy its current debt and other payables.

$$\frac{\text{Current Assets}}{\text{Current Liabilities}}$$

2. Quick

   The quick ratio indicates a company's capacity to pay its current liabilities without selling its inventory or getting additional financing.

$$\frac{\text{Cash + Accts. Receivable}}{\text{Current Liabilities}}$$

3. Debt Service Coverage

   (DSCR) measures the cash flow a company has available to pay current debts. The ratio states net operating income as a multiple of debt obligations due within one year, including interest, principal, sinking-fund, and lease payments.

$$\frac{\text{Net Income + Int. + Non-Cash Exp.}}{\text{CPLTD + Interest}}$$

SAFETY RATIO

4. Debt to Equity

Figuring out your company's debt-to-equity ratio is a straightforward calculation. You take your company's total liabilities (what it owes others) and divide it by equity (this is the company's book value or its assets minus its liabilities). Both of these numbers come from your company's balance sheet.[4]

$$\frac{\text{Total Liabilities}}{\text{Equity}}$$

PROFITABILITY RATIOS

5. Gross Profit Margin (%)

$$\frac{\text{Gross Profit}}{\text{Sales}}$$

6. Net Profit Margin (%)

$$\frac{\text{Net Profit before Tax}}{\text{Sales}}$$

The profitability ratios help to show how much income a company is making based on its sales. A company can have gross sales but still not be making money. Traditionally one would like to see high profitability ratios. However, it is essential to note that these need to be compared to other companies within their industry to ensure they are making the type of return that an investor should expect.

ASSET MANAGEMENT RATIOS

7. Sales to Assets

$$\frac{\text{Sales}}{\text{Total Assets}}$$

8. Inventory (days)

$$365/ \frac{\text{Cost of Goods Sold}}{\text{Inventory}}$$

9. Accounts Receivable (days)

$$365/ \frac{\text{Sales}}{\text{Accts. Receivable}}$$

10. Accounts Payable (days)

$$365/ \frac{\text{Cost of Goods Sold}}{\text{Acct. Payable}}$$

Asset management ratios (turnover ratios or efficiency ratios) show how quickly the company's assets are turning over or being sold. An investor wants to see high asset turnover ratios because it sells its product and brings much-needed cash flow into the company.

These key indicators will not only allow for Native leaders to analyze the current operations, but it will also give operations a foundation to understand what financial institutions are looking for and how to evaluate potential business targets.

FINANCIAL POLICIES

Finance theory identifies three types of policies that corporate or tribal managers have to optimize the firm's value, including investment, financing, and dividend/payout policies.[5] However, before developing tribal corporate policies, start with assessing the community's economy by obtaining baseline financial information regarding unemployment, underemployment, and labor participation rates. For example, determine how many tribal members work in the community and how many must travel outside of it for jobs, identify the largest employers in the community and their prospects for growth, and learn about what types of services are offered in the community and what services tribal members must leave the community to obtain.[6] The information should be utilized for an overall comprehensive economic development strategy or master plan for tribal and business development to track critical indicators in the value matrix.

After this is complete, look at the tribe's investment policy. Investment policies involve smart money managers, and leadership will create an investment policy that allows for proper growth while staying within the tribal organization's risk tolerance. Creating a policy will allow for investments to be made, but allowing the tribe or company to make sure it is appropriately diversified will allow for up- and downturns in investments. Financing policies guide a methodology to allow the tribe or company to ensure that they are not overleveraged and make sure that they can keep proper cash flow for operations. Finally, dividend policies represent the distribution of funds outside the tribal business entity, be it a traditional dividend, like the Alaskan Native corporations, payable to their Native shareholders or a per capita payment from the tribe. It is vital that the right balance of payment to membership, payment for tribal government needs, and future investment into the businesses should be achieved. Financing policies development is not a one-size-fits-all decision and needs to be considered carefully as leadership sets priorities, as we think seven generations ahead.

BANKING AND DEBT STRUCTURING

Traditional financing is not designed to work on tribal trust lands. Due to the trust land statutes, many of the traditional debt models do not work due to the burden that is put on the company, as they are unable to leverage land assets. Most tribal corporations and tribal member-owned businesses need both startup and expansion capital, yet Indian Country is the most underbanked territory.[7] Due to these challenges, several programs are designed to assist tribes and their members in obtaining much-needed financing.

There are two significant considerations in obtaining credit through conventional lending. First, the lenders need to enforce an agreement, and second, they need to protect their investment in the event of a default. A tribe operating an enterprise as an arm of the tribal government may have difficulty obtaining conventional financing.[8] To work in a collaborative but distinct separation that allows for better protections for the tribal government and the business enterprise to obtain financing, many tribes will create either a Federally Chartered Section 17 Corporation or a Tribal Limited Liability Corporation. These structures will allow the company to operate within the laws of the tribal nation and allow for the business to operate nimbly and efficiently.

Additionally, the ability to enforce agreements due to federal Indian law is one of the primary reasons proper structure is vital. The establishment of the legal framework by tribal leadership for the laws that will govern all business transactions on tribal land is the first step before tribal finance can provide access to capital. This core concept has been covered in earlier chapters more extensively. However, it must be highlighted again here as it will guide financial planning and the community's ability to develop commerce. From the establishment or acceptance of a uniform commercial code (UCC) to the utilization of limited waiver of sovereign immunity, these practices must be agreed upon before any financial transaction can be executed at a level that the investor feels comfortable with to develop commerce within the boundaries of the tribal nation. Without knowing the rules of the road, lending institutions and investors will be reluctant to do business with or in the tribal community. In addition to sovereign immunity concerns, a conventional lender will also want collateral or security interest to protect its investment in case there is a default or the enterprise is not successful.[9] Several programs are designed to allow lenders to conduct business on trust land to mitigate these lending challenges.

LOAN GUARANTY PROGRAMS AND BONDING

There are various credit enhancement programs developed to identify barriers to tribal access to credit, and to support tribes and related entities in finalizing financial transactions to support overall tribal services and economies. Here are some of the programs more commonly used by our tribal nations.

Indian Affairs Loan Guaranty, Insurance, and Interest Subsidy Program

Contact Information

MIB-4138, 1849 C Street, NW
Mail Stop 4132
Washington, DC 20240
Phone Number: 202-219-0749
Website: https://www.bia.gov/service/loans/ilgp

Program Established: 1974

Guaranty Percentage: 90%

Nature of Loans

- Operating capital
- Equipment purchases
- Acquisition and refinancing
- Building construction
- Lines of credit

Eligibility Information from the Agency

Through ILGP, our Division of Capital Investment (DCI) helps American Indian/ Alaska Native (AI/AN) tribes and individuals overcome barriers to conventional financing and secure reasonable interest rates while also reducing the risk to lenders by providing financial backing from the federal government. Since its inception, the Indian Affairs Loan Guaranty program has supported more than $2 billion in loan guarantees to tribal business enterprises.

To qualify for a loan through the program, one must be

- an individual who is an enrolled member of a federally recognized American Indian/Alaska Native (AI/AN) tribe or group;
- a federally recognized AI/AN group;

- a corporation, limited liability company, or other business entity with no less than 51 percent ownership by federally recognized AI/AN individuals.

Borrowers must have at least 20 percent equity in the project being financed, and the project must benefit the economy of a reservation or tribal service area.

U.S. Department of Agriculture (USDA) Business & Industry (B&I) Loan Guarantee Program

Contact Information

Rural Housing Service
1400 Independence Ave., SW, Rm 5014, STOP 0701
Washington, DC 20250-0701
Phone Number: 202-692-0268
Website: https://www.rd.usda.gov/programs-services/business-industry-loan-guarantees

Guaranty Percentage: 80%–60% depending on the loan size

Nature of Loans

- Business conversion, enlargement, repair, modernization, or development
- Purchase and development of land
- Purchase and installation of machinery and equipment
- Debt refinancing
- Business and industrial acquisitions

Eligibility Information from the Agency

The B&I program provides guarantees for loans made to businesses that save or create jobs in rural areas. Borrowers may be individuals, partnerships, cooperatives, for-profit or nonprofit corporations, Indian tribes, or public bodies. Individual borrowers must be citizens of the United States or reside in the United States after being legally admitted for permanent residence. Private entity borrowers must demonstrate that loan funds will remain in the United States. The facility being financed will primarily create new jobs or save existing jobs for rural U.S. residents.

The program is open to new and existing businesses. Eligible business activities include manufacturing, sales (retail and wholesale), providing services, and other activities to provide employment and improve the economic or environmental climate. Existing businesses must have a minimum of 10 percent tangible balance sheet equity. For new businesses, a minimum of 20 percent tangible balance sheet equity is required. For energy projects, the minimum tangible balance sheet equity requirement ranges from 25 percent to 40 percent. There are no size standards for businesses and no minimum occupancy requirements for borrowers acquiring or refinancing real estate.

Generally, projects being financed must be located in eligible rural areas. A rural area is generally defined as any area other than a city or town with a population of greater than fifty thousand inhabitants, or any urbanized area contiguous and adjacent to such a city or town.

Small Business Administration (SBA) 7(a) Program

Contact Information

409 3rd St, SW
Washington, DC 20416
Phone Number: 800-827-5722

Website: https://www.sba.gov/partners/lenders/7a-loan-program/types-7a-loans

Guaranty Percentage: 90%–50% depending on the 7(a) programs

Nature of Loans: The program accepts all traditional loans and lines of credit.

Eligibility Information from the Agency

There are several different 7(a) loans, such as the Standard 7(a) Loan, 7(a) Small Loan, SBA Express, Export Express, Export Working Capital, International Trade, and CAPLines. These range from $350,000 to $5 million. We will highlight the structure for a Standard 7(a) Loan program in this chapter, but for more information, please visit the SBA website listed above.

A Standard 7(a) loan has a maximum of about $5 million, and the maximum SBA guarantee is 85% for loans up to $150,000 and 75% for loans greater than $150,000. Lenders and borrowers can negotiate the interest rate, but it may not exceed the SBA maximum. Eligibility and credit decisions are made by the SBA, though qualified lenders may be granted delegated authority (PLP) to make eligibility determinations and/or credit decisions without SBA review. The SBA turnaround time is typically 5–10 business days. Mandatory forms required for every loan are SBA Form 1919 and SBA Form 1920, and other SBA forms may be required. Lenders are not required to take collateral for loans up to $25,000. For loans over $350,000, the SBA requires that the lender collateralize the loan to the maximum extent possible up to the loan amount. If business fixed assets do not "fully secure" the loan, the lender may include trading assets (using 10%

of current book value for the calculation) and must take available equity in the personal real estate (residential and investment) of the principals as collateral.

Federally recognized Indian tribal governments can also issue tax-exempt bonds for specific governmental and qualified purposes. Section 7871(a)(4) of the U.S. Internal Revenue Code (Title 26) provides that, subject to additional requirements, tribal governments are treated as states for purposes of issuing valid debt obligations under Section 103 of the same Title. However, tribal governments that issue taxable bonds do not have to comply with the requirements applicable to the issuance of tax-exempt bonds. Section 7871(c) further provides that tribal governments may issue tax-exempt bonds to finance both the provision of "essential governmental functions" and the construction of certain qualified manufacturing facilities. Section 7871(c)(1) states that "subsection (a) of section 103 shall apply to any obligation issued by an Indian tribal government (or subdivision thereof) only if such obligation is part of an issue substantially all of the proceeds of which are to be used in the exercise of any essential governmental function." [10] Section 7871(c)(3)(B) provides that tax-exempt bonds can be issued to finance the acquisition, construction, reconstruction, or improvement of property that is of a character subject to the allowance for depreciation and that is part of a manufacturing facility (as defined in Section 144(a)(12)(C) provided that specific use, location, ownership, and employment requirements are satisfied. For further detail consult the IRS "FAQs for Indian Tribal Governments regarding Tax Exempt Bonds." [11]

Tribes, TBEs, and native entrepreneurs must consider their financing needs and how these components fit within their financial planning decision-making process. Although Indian Country is still an emerging domestic economy, entrepreneurs and tribal ventures have more opportunities and better tools to pursue those opportunities than ever before. Although access to capital remains a significant challenge, more Indian Country entrepreneurs succeed, and more capital will flow into Indian Country. [12]

Many tribes have invested in Native-owned banks to accelerate this process, and created Native Community Development Finance Institutions (CDFI) and Community Development Entities (CDE). Their unique programs and services are designed to build financial assets in the low-income populations they serve and provide access to economic opportunities by offering a New Market Tax Credit (NMTC). CDFIs that can obtain an NMTC allocation can then use those tax credits to attract outside investment. [13]

Practitioner Perspective

Although Indian Country is still an emerging domestic economy, entrepreneurs and tribal ventures have more opportunities and better tools to pursue those opportunities than ever before.[14] As tribal finance is more challenging due to structural norms unique to tribal trust land, the solution is still based on the fundamental theories of finance, auditing, and economics. The chapter gives the tribal enterprise and Native business a starting point when deciding how they will successfully implement economic change through sound financial practices, and give them a resource guide on some of the programs and competitive advantages that we have as Native Americans. No matter if we are leaders within our tribal government or tribal business enterprise, or if we are Native American entrepreneurs, sound financial practices and basic understanding of how finance works will make our organization secure for the generations to come.

Modern financial transactions are based on financial performance rooted in risk mitigation, and identification of areas of return on investment (ROI) to benefit the original investor, be that in the form of a loan or a capital investment. The system has always been counter to our cultural norms and beliefs. However, in the last twenty-five years, we see ways that financing and how we monetize returns are changing to align with our traditional values. John Elkington coined the term "triple bottom line" in 1994, focusing on return on investment by profit, social and environmental. It was initially intended as a genetic code, a triple helix of change for tomorrow's capitalism, focusing on breakthrough change, disruption, asymmetric growth (with unsustainable sectors actively sidelined), and scaling next-generation market solutions.[15] Although some movement towards our traditional values has occurred and pockets of investors are taking this very seriously, it has not replaced the purely profit-driven model. As tribal leaders, we must know the value of modern finance. However, it finds partners looking for sustainable, long-term economic growth as the nation is looking forward to many generations to come.

NOTES

1. B. Dyckman, "Supply Chain Finance: Risk Mitigation and Revenue Growth," *Journal of Corporate Treasury Management* 4, no. 2 (May 2011): 168–73.

2. Native American Financial Officers Association (NAFOA), Orange Book, *Financial Reporting and Information Guide for Tribal Governments and Enterprises* (Washington, DC: NAFOA, 2018).

3. Native American Financial Officers Association (NAFOA), Orange Book, *Financial Reporting and Information Guide for Tribal Governments and Enterprises* (Washington, DC: NAFOA 2018).

4. A. Gallo, "A Refresher on Debt-to-Equity Ratio," *Harvard Business Review*, July 13, 2015.

5. G. Cohen and J. Yagl, *Corporate Financial Policies: An International Survey*, European Financial Management Association (EFMA) presentation (2007).

6. K. Atkinson and M. Niles, *Tribal Business Structure Handbook*, Tribal Self-Governance Project of the Tulalip Tribes (Office of the Assistant Secretary–Indian Affairs, 2008).

7. G. Clarkson, "Tribal Bonds: Statutory Shackles and Regulatory Restraints on Tribal Economic Development," *North Carolina Law Review* 85, no. 4 (2007): 1009.

8. Atkinson and Niles, *Tribal Business Structure Handbook.*

9. Atkinson and Niles, *Tribal Business Structure Handbook.*

10. Definition of Essential Governmental Function under Section 7871, 71 Fed.Reg.45474 (Aug. 9, 2006).

11. https://www.irs.gov/government-entities/indian-tribal-governments/faqs-for-indian-tribal-governments-regarding-tax-exempt-bonds.

12. D. M. Kennedy, C. F. Harrington, A. Klemm Verbos, D. Stewart, J. S. Gladstone, and G. Clarkson, *American Indian Business: Principles and Practices* (Seattle: University of Washington Press, 2017).

13. Kennedy et al., *American Indian Business.*

14. Kennedy et al., *American Indian Business.*

15. J. Elkington, "25 Years Ago I Coined the Phrase 'Triple Bottom Line.' Here's Why It's Time to Rethink It," *Harvard Business Review* (May–June 2018).

GLOSSARY

AICPA. American Institute of Certified Public Accountants

Cash flow. Cash flow is the net amount of cash and cash equivalents being transferred into and out of a business. Cash received represents inflows, while money spent represents outflows.

Competitive advantage. Refers to factors that allow a company to produce goods or services better or more cheaply than its rivals. These factors allow the productive entity to generate more sales or superior margins compared to its market rivals.

Consumer demand. Willingness and ability of consumers to purchase a quantity of goods and services in a given period of time, or at a given point in time.

Current portion of long-term debt (CPLTD). The section of a company's balance sheet that records the total amount of long-term debt that must be paid within the current year.

Debt. An obligation that requires one party, the debtor, to pay money or other agreed-upon value to another party, the creditor.

Economic leakages. Diversion of funds from some iterative process.

Economic sustainability. Refers to practices that support long-term economic growth without negatively impacting social, environmental, and cultural aspects of the community.

Gross domestic product (GDP). A monetary measure of the market value of all the final goods and services produced in a specific time period.

ILGP. Indian Loan Guaranty Program.

Leverage. The ratio of a company's loan capital (debt) to the value of its common stock (equity).

Marshall Trilogy. A set of three Supreme Court decisions in the early nineteenth century affirming the legal and political standing of Indian nations, *Johnson v. M'Intosh* (1823) holding that private citizens could not purchase lands from Native Americans.

Maximization of leverage for transactions. To maximize leverage and make a gain, you need to make more money than you borrow plus the interest on the debt.

NAFOA. Native American Financial Officers Association.

Per capita. Relating or applied to each person.

Return on investment (ROI). A ratio between net income and investment. A high ROI means the investment's gains compare favorably to its cost. As a performance measure, ROI is used to evaluate the efficiency of an investment or to compare the efficiencies of several different investments.

TBE. Tribal business enterprise.

Uniform Commercial Code (UCC). A set of laws that provide legal rules and regulations governing commercial or business dealings and transactions.

Building Tribal Economies through Economic Development

Eric S. Trevan and Jon Panamaroff

ECONOMIC DEVELOPMENT IS A TERM THAT EXPLAINS PUBLIC POLICIES AND administration of programs that support increased economic activity. The result of these activities leads to increased employment, business revenue, tax revenue, and entrepreneurship. Tribal economic development embraces these concepts toward building a functioning economy. This is similar to domestic U.S. economic policy; however, there are critical differences between tribal nations exercising their sovereignty.

This chapter addresses foundational principles of economics and economic development for generating revenue for tribal businesses and building systems necessary for functional tribal economies. Understanding the fundamental components of tribal economies, deploying effective strategy, and emphasizing intersections with community development are vital to effective and sustainable tribal economic development.

BEST PRACTICES

- Develop processes and policies that support economic growth.
- Identify tribal economic development frameworks that support economic activity.

- Follow the processes of better practices of tribal economic and community development.
- Understand fundamental structures that define economic and community development approaches.
- Focus on three economic development components (waves).
- Explain strategies around four key points of competitive advantages.
- Shift economic progress from revenue to tribal GDP.

TRIBAL ECONOMICS OVERVIEW

Public administrators who work with tribal nations—including elected and appointed leadership and consultants—serve in trade associations, cultural programs, as advocates, and as other governmental liaisons; all play a role in a successful economic development program. Successful policy development focuses on implementing a strategy that concentrates on current economic assets, specific components of economic development applications of competitive advantages, and final execution.

Since time immemorial, sovereign tribal nations have had functioning economies that expand beyond individual profit motives, including markets, trade, mediums of exchange, and economic processes and principles.[1] These markets include food, clothing, raw materials, precious minerals, and highly valued ceremonial items. The focus of activity relies on the specialization of tribes. These activities vary depending on the tribe's available resources, geography, skills of tribal citizens, and long-term planning in balance with nature. There are conflicts of influence (between sovereign tribal nations and other nations), outside influence, disease, and struggles of intergovernmental trust (social capital and the ability to form relationships with multiple stakeholders). These tribal economies are no different from today's domestic economies. Understanding economic development and its relation to tribal economies is instrumental in understanding the foundational components of the economy. Tribes as sovereign nations continue to exercise their political and business strategies to improve their economies, increase economic wealth, and improve the overall quality of life for the tribe and tribal citizens.[2]

Economics emphasizes the trade of goods and services and the measurement of the medium of exchange for related goods and services.[3] Economic

Summary of Economic Principles of the Economy and GDP = I + G + C + (X-M)

Investment (I)	18%
Government (G)	17%
Consumption (C)	70%
Net Exports (X-M)	-5% (Imports are greater than exports)

development focuses on the relationship of trade, not just profits, and is measured by gross domestic product (GDP). These four economic principles include government expenditures (G), overall investment (I), consumption (C), and exports (X) minus imports (M) and are the major components of a functioning economy. GDP is an evaluative measure of the economy's overall wealth, not simply stating the revenue estimates of businesses in the economy. The overall formula results in GDP = I + G + C + (X-M).

Reservation-Related Economies

Tribal economies embrace many of these principles, and economic development concepts should include emphasis on these principles. Drivers of economic activities are not solely transferred payments between the government and tribal citizens or investing in another nation's stock market, but rather a strong foundation of trade supported by multiple economic actors, focusing on increased consumption and exporting goods and services. Yes, many tribal governments are instrumental in providing economic activity on the reservation; however, comparable to the overall relationships within a wholly functioning economy, this is just the beginning.[4] Success measured by only profits results in suboptimal returns to the tribal economy as a whole. Tribal economies are healthy when there is an intentional focus on increasing consumption from consumers regularly, and exporting goods and/or services beyond the reservation economies.[5] Since consumption (compared to other economic output measures) is the key driver of GDP, policy focused on increasing expenditures by consumers will provide the highest financial stimulus to tribal economies.

Tribal populations make up approximately 1.7 percent of the U.S. population. However, there is not parity with other populations and leading indicators of economic wealth and quality of life throughout the country.[6] Tribes and tribal citizens have lagged behind in many indicators (including, but not limited to, lower incomes, higher levels of poverty, and lower levels of health) that support higher levels of economic wealth and quality of life.[7] Reservation-related economies (economic areas that intersect tribal lands) make up approximately 20 percent of all U.S. economic activity.[8] Even though tribal populations make up less than 2 percent of the overall population, tribal lands intersect with economic geographies making up one fifth of the United States!

Community Capital and Assets

Many systems are involved with an economy's strength with positive and sometimes negative impacts on the community. Community capitals represent a measurement of systems that serve to provide values to the overall progress within communities. These can range from economic, cultural, environmental, social (the measurement of relationships), human (the measurement of knowledge, skills, and abilities), and other activities that are critical to community.[9] Public administrators are responsible for identifying these capitals and ensuring that these assets are utilized in an overall economic development strategy. To develop a robust tribal economy, policymakers and business leaders focus on strengthening all related systems, not just systems for profit.[10] When all systems are not functioning, consumers cannot buy goods, banks cannot provide capital, governments cannot provide public services, and ultimately, there is a collapse in the overall quality of life. There are many types of community capitals, representing assets in the community. Their influence on economic outcomes drives overall strategy, the sustainability of the tribal economy, and the creation of opportunities. Economic capital closely aligns with the economy. Community's capacity, as measured by human capital, includes the skills, education, and experience of individuals and social capital, which measures individuals' trust, bridging, and bonding.[11] Additionally, other capitals provide a deep understanding of the economy of a tribe. Environmental capitals, cultural capitals, and political capitals all influence economic outcomes.

With dollars leaking outside reservation boundaries and into other economies, there is evidence of opportunity for additional consumers, investment, and the need to build strong tribal governance and find ways to participate in related economies.[12] By stopping economic leakages from tribal economies, tribes and related economic actors can realize additional financial benefits

Software Packages Used for Economic Development

IMPLAN	Economic Impact
REMI	Economic Impact and Trade Flows
aLocal	Market Demand for Industry and Housing
ESRI	Geographic Information Systems (GIS) and Spatial Data

and translate these payments to build vital components of tribal economies.[13] To achieve an optimal economy, economic policy should focus on a balance of business with the amount of consumer demand to support businesses. A variety of analytical software packages can help identify economic demand, impact, and tax implications.

Software packages enable data collection and analysis that explain surrounding economies and possible retail opportunities. Using the aLocal software, for example, provides heat maps that help identify high-demand areas for retail activity and compare them to the surrounding communities. This helps administrators determine strategy and economic development focus. The maps include information and analysis, which provide a lens to understand economic actors in and outside tribal lands.

ECONOMIC DEVELOPMENT FOCUS AND STRATEGY

Economic Development and Tribes

Economic development is a functional policy approach to stimulate positive economic growth, ultimately leading to improved economic wealth and quality of life.[14] Whereas economic development experts, practitioners, and researchers have transitioned this definition to focus on a narrow interpretation of solely increasing revenue and jobs, the etymology of the term development is based on the definition to simplify or un-mess the economy.[15] Based on this definition and focus on the original principles of the economy (investment, government, consumption, and net exports), tribes can use decolonized approaches to build functioning economies and generate resources that lead to increased levels of wealth and improved quality of life.

Since time immemorial, tribes have focused on improving their economies. However, since European contact, colonial constructs have created economic conditions that do not meet overall priorities and strategies conducive to the well-being of tribal nations.[16] It is difficult for tribes to seek additional revenue through current colonial economic structures while addressing new sovereign structures. Over the past five hundred plus years, economic development has been initiated by colonizing governments at a cost to the tribes that cannot be recovered. Public policy has evolved over the past century, centering on the inherent focus of tribes as sovereign governments, relations with the U.S. government, and the ability to foster a tribal economy through specific business and political strategies. Recently, successful tribes have found opportunities with gaming, federal contracting, lending, cannabis, real estate, and other economic actors that support standard-day economic necessities. This leads to multiple tribes who exercise their sovereignty, such as Winnebago Tribe of Nebraska (Ho-Chunk Incorporated) diversifying on and off tribal lands, Pokagon Band of Potawatomi (Mno-Bmadsen) specializing with multiple industries not dependent on gaming, and Salt River Pima Maricopa Indian Community using a variety of businesses with gaming as a catalyst, as well as leveraging the Phoenix urban area and thousands of cars of daily traffic from AZ 101. Specifically, in most cases, tribes separate their business and political focuses to have overall priorities that support economic outcomes from their various perspectives.[17] Recent U.S. Supreme Court decisions such as *McGirt v. Oklahoma* and *Nebraska v. Parker* build on existing case law and affirm that the United States and its subordinate governments (i.e., cities, counties, states) should continue to find opportunities of intergovernmental agreements working cooperatively with the tribal government, other tribes, and consortiums of tribes.[18] These court decisions acknowledge that previously executed treaties between tribes and the United States represent the supreme law of the land.

Components of Economic Development

Specific functions vary according to different political boundaries, geographies, and strategies. A focus on economic development policy is cross-sectional with the overall approach and components sometimes referred to as waves.[19] Based on economic development research, three overall economic development components improve the overall economy.[20] By utilizing different policy levers, strategies can influence economic actors, including businesses, industries,

Tribal Periods of Economic Policy

PRE-COLUMBIAN, PRE-1492

Indians planned their own organized societies
No European colonial influence on land decisions

COLONIAL PERIOD, 1492–1828

European colonization acquired and managed Indian lands
under Discovery Doctrine
Colonial governments treated Indians as governments
Post-Revolutionary War—U.S. worked with tribes as
governments
Focused on land control and management for colonization
purposes

REMOVAL, RESERVATION, AND TREATY PERIOD, 1828–1887

U.S. population/military grew—needed land—forced
migration
Military campaign—Indians located to the reservation
Traded land for rights of self-governance
Land management was forcibly removed from tribes

ALLOTMENT AND ASSIMILATION PERIOD, 1887–1934

U.S. wanted to Americanize Indians
Dawes Act/General Allotment Act 1887—separated
communal land into separated tribal land
90,000,000 acres taken from tribes—most without
compensation
Without land, tribes limited on culturally appropriate
planning for their nations' futures

INDIAN REORGANIZATION ACT, 1934–1945

Ended allotment policy
Created constitutional guidelines to frame tribal planning
Federal programs/projects to help tribes
Tribes began planning efforts, but still restricted due to IRA
constitution guidelines

TERMINATION PERIOD, 1945–1968

Terminated federal recognition of more than 100 tribes
The U.S. realized the ongoing opportunity and progress of
Indian people
Public Act 2880 (1935)
Imposed state and criminal jurisdiction
Loss of millions of acres—tax forfeitures
Policy attempted to move Indians to urban areas

SELF-DETERMINATION PERIOD, 1968–1992

Self-determination and self-governance
Policies favored tribal control and planning
Tribes managed federal programs
Tribal Gaming Supreme Court Decision
California v. Cabazon Band of Mission Indians (480 US 202
[1987])
Gaming supported tribal planning for the future allocation of
land and resources
U.S. policy found progress with tribal planning and
management of land

NATION TO NATION PERIOD, 1992–2009

President Clinton executive order required consultation
President Obama reaffirmed Clinton executive order
White House Tribal Nations Summit convened
Reconciliation of Nation to Nation relationships
Strengthened tribal nations to plan appropriately for their
culture and vision of the future

ECONOMIC EMPOWERMENT ERA, 2009–PRESENT

Small Business Jobs Act (2010)
Business and Economic Development Policy Agenda (2011)
HEARTH Act (2012)
General Welfare Exclusion Act of 2014
Gun Lake Trust Land Reaffirmation Act (2017)
MI Partial Settlement Agreement Gun Lake Tribe
Tribes referred to as emerging domestic markets
Economic progress strengthened the need and desire of
tribes to plan for multiple generations

individuals, tourists, experts, investors, elected leaders, researchers, consumers, and other nations.[21]

- *Recruit Businesses*: First, a focus on attracting economic actors to a specific economy helps recruit economic activity to the tribe. This identifies potential economic businesses and actors who can support the economy's overall improvement.
- *Retain Businesses*: Second, a focus on the current economic actors and surrounding businesses is critical to ensure that they remain a central part of the economy.

- *Create New Businesses and Entrepreneurs*: Finally, the focus of the community and entrepreneurs is to develop new innovative opportunities within the economy. Using existing community capitals in the economy, balancing new economic opportunities, capturing revenues leaking from the economy, and creating increased economic multipliers from additional dollars spent within tribes stimulate growth across all GDP principles.

The Tulalip Indian Tribe, located north of Seattle, Washington, embraces an economic development focus of all three economic development components throughout Quil Ceda Village. Exercising their sovereignty, they operate a federated city charter to strategically leverage competitive economic advantages along Interstate 5 (I-5) north of the Seattle metropolitan area. They recruit new businesses to develop property along the I-5 corridor, which has resulted in tax revenue for the tribe. The policy focus is on reducing overall input costs to keep businesses operating. Tulalip developed new opportunities through gaming known as Tulalip Casino and Resort. Previous economic development strategies have only focused on a profit margin. Using economic policy to concentrate on the implementation of all economic components (recruit, retain, and develop new businesses/entrepreneurs), the economy is functioning as a whole, ultimately optimizing the tribal economy. Understanding the market conditions, competitive advantages, combined with different economic development components has positioned Tulalip as a tribal economic development model.

Competitive Advantages and Strategy

Economic strategy is based on the implementation of specific economic, social, and political policy that influences economic behavior of individual and collective businesses (referred to as businesses, organizations, and/or firms). The strategy is essential when utilizing different economic development components, ultimately finding competitive advantages for building strong tribal economies.[22] The Otoe-Missouria Tribe implemented competitive advantages within the lending space and can now reach out successfully to consumers and provide access to capital in new markets. Creating different laws and a regulatory framework, and a new business entity, the tribe can expand with technology, finance, and other related industries. Through the development of businesses on-reservation and implementation of a technology platform, they realize benefits to the tribal economy through net exports, additional consumption, and additional support to their tribal government and related investments.[23]

While alignment between public policy and business is critical, embracing a specific approach to strengthening the economy is essential. Aligning with the culture of the tribe is critical, and understanding different strategies to improve the economy leads to developing a balance of economic activity. There are four approaches to firm strategy, and it is important that tribes understand the four approaches and how they may align with their approach to improve tribal economies.[24]

FACTOR (INPUT) CONDITIONS

First, tribes should understand the overall conditions that are associated with factors and/or inputs and related costs. This may include the quality of the input, the cost, and the specialization of the factor (such as labor or raw materials). In economic development literature, the overall cost of inputs is a typical strategy specifically addressing taxation. When economic actors work with the tribe and tribal business entities (TBE), the tax liability is reduced (if not eliminated), and based on the tribal nation, tax revenue is captured to support governmental operations and future economic efforts. Many states still try to capture taxes on goods and services. However, due to the inherent sovereign ability of the tribes to tax, often states and tribes develop tax agreements that can provide clear outlines on how taxation applies to each government.

CONTEXT FOR FIRM STRATEGY AND RIVALRY

The second competitive advantage concerns the firm's strategy and rival businesses/economies. The strategy of the operation of economic activities and its relation to rivals is critical to overall success of the tribe. Some of the strategies employed are reaching out to different market segments, different amenities, and overall offerings. Focusing on the overall market conditions and how economic strategies can capture dollars leaking outside the tribal economy can significantly impact the economy.

Related and Supporting Industries

Third, related and supporting industries provide integration into the economy through two integrative horizontal and vertical approaches: first, horizontally with related industries, suppliers, experts, and clusters of industries; second, using vertical integrative aspects, such as logistics, materials, professional services, and retail establishments. Some tribes have focused on expertise to utilize specialization with particular economic focuses to stimulate all GDP components. The expanded knowledge of different industries has led to many tribes taking this experience and beginning to support the federal government with goods and services, through federal contracting opportunities for tribes and tribal business entities, a nearly $14 billion industry for tribes. The diversification of federal contracting for goods and services has allowed a tribe to expand their revenue base and allow for outside revenue to be imported to the tribal economy, reversing reservation leakage trends in tribal communities.

DEMAND CONDITIONS

Finally, a focus on overall demand is critical, with the alignment of increasing consumption within tribal economies. Finding ways to increase wages, expenditures on needed purchases, and providing critical industries are all ways to improve demand conditions. Demand runs in parallel with consumption, which represents the largest share of GDP.

Gaming

One of the most significant impacts on tribal economies is gaming. The Cabazon and Morongo Band of Mission Indians' victory in *California v. Cabazon Band of Mission Indians*, 480 U.S. 202, in 1987 affirms case law supporting tribal gaming and opened the doors for tribes to develop regulatory environments for gaming enterprises). This has evolved to over a $33 billion industry in 2020, with approximately one third of all sovereign tribal nations participating in the industry. This has had significant impacts on many community capitals within the tribal economy, including economic, cultural, human, social, political, environmental, and other related systems.[25]

Economic Geography

The overall clustering of economic activity and geography is critical to building a tribal economy. Many tribes, albeit connected to other reservation-related economies, are often in remote areas with few resources, as intentionally designed by previous U.S. Indian policy. As a leading indicator of the economy's strength, the clustering of activities within an economy realizes agglomerative advantages (benefits when activity is closely clustered) when economic actors are working together. The overall proximity of this clustering activity has influences that are exogenous (influences from outside the economy) and naturally occurring endogenous impacts (influences from within the economy). Economies are more robust when there are higher-performing clusters of consumers and industries. Therefore, using policy levers to help guide consumers to live, shop, and entertain within the tribal economy are essential.

An example of a tribe implementing this strategy is the Winnebago Tribe of Nebraska, through their TBE Ho-Chunk Incorporated (HCI). They have invested outside their original reservation, but now are concentrating efforts to improve multiple capitals. With a focus on housing and retail within proximity, they realize agglomerative benefits from combining consumers and industry investments. Additionally, HCI has invested in the immediate surrounding economies with other businesses, housing, and real estate. Understanding the proximity, applying a strategy of competitive advantages, and agglomerative benefits from developing a critical mass of activity is truly understanding how to move from a revenue priority to a GDP focus strategy.

COMMUNITY DEVELOPMENT

Community development is not only improving a common destination and location, but also a common set of ideals and values.[26] Tribes are connected to their community, culture, and environment, and policies that improve the community develop stronger economies. Optimal economies rely on sound economic development and core community development fundamentals. These fundamentals must be kept at the forefront when identifying strategies that improve the community and economy. Economic development is not able to be separated from community development. They are intricately tied together; however, they are different approaches, and both (economic and community development) need to be successful to support a system-wide functioning economy that improves both economic wealth and quality of life. Recent research over the past ten years has shown that economic growth alone does not support increases in economic wealth and improve measures of quality of life; rather, a balance of economic businesses positively impacts

GDP and innovation. Additionally, community involvement has positive impacts improving all economic systems.[27]

Community development, concerning economic development, uses three predominant approaches that align with economic development.

Needs-based community development: First, an approach of needs-based development identifies needs in the community and where there are deficiencies of economic actors and other damaging components of the community.

Community economic development: Second, a focus on community economic development is a tangential approach to asset-based community development (ABCD), which narrows the policy objectives to find development activities that support the overall economy's foundation.

Asset-based community development: Finally, evolving from this approach is an ABCD approach that focuses on identifying community assets and employing successful strategies embracing and elevating the assets.[28] The ABCD approach aligns with the recent report *Reclaiming Native Truth*, which focuses on tribal assets and how to utilize these assets to develop competitive advantages.[29]

Community and Local Small Business

When finding the intersections between community development and economic development, there is a connection between ABCD and community economic development with local development: community and local small business. Three connections exist weaving together community and economic development.[30] First, community capacity and economic capital, which focuses on assets, intersect with community and economic systems. Second, community solidarity, collaboration, and partnership show the benefits of social capital, trust, and relationship bonds working together. Tribal nations have always attempted to work with other groups, immigrants, and other tribes since time immemorial. Finally, the third component connecting community and economic development includes structure and market/nonmarket systems. This relates to the overall culture and structures of the tribal nation, assets of the tribe, and the multiple intersectional systems and how they impact the overall economy.

Community and Economic Development Process

It is important to work with community stakeholders who are making decisions in the community's best interest. The community optimizes all economic decisions and builds a more robust tribal economy. Many times, a group of stakeholders will assemble and make decisions, not based on data, but on personal preferences and what they feel is right. There is a better way! Tribes can evolve from solely reviewing individual projects for feasibility to understanding and analyzing all economic and housing conditions. This analysis truly optimizes the entire tribe's economy. As represented in a pyramid, there are four steps toward successful tribal economic development. Compared with an upside-down pyramid of the wrong approach toward economic development projects, this builds a sound foundation. First, identify market data and trends. Where are dollars leaking outside the tribal economy, and how does this fit into an overall economy. Second, develop a strategy based on where the tribe has competitive advantages. Review the four components and identify the economic assets and how they can leverage these advantages. Third, execute the strategy. As public administrators, one can encourage policy, develop programs, and deploy resources for this execution. Finally, evaluate the outcomes and adjust any new strategies. Narrow investment diligence embraces the upside-down pyramid approach to only review single projects in contrast to the wide foundation of the pyramid, which shows how it's critical for a tribe to understand all economic conditions and opportunities. The intersection between the two pyramids explains that the better approach is to understand the entire economy before selecting individual investment and development projects.

Building from data and analysis of data, and understanding economic and housing conditions, decision-makers in tribes use this information to guide decision-making and then judge the feasibility of economic decisions—instead of picking a project and dedicating all resources and time to the project. Suppose tribes use data, deconstruct simple linear choices of only seeking returns from one project without consideration for other opportunities, and select economic decisions in the tribe's best interest. In that case, the focus is organized and planned, and leadership moves from a single focus to how the tribe plans for its economy and impacts from other surrounding economies.

PRACTITIONER PERSPECTIVE

We can find new opportunities that exist in the ever-evolving space of economic development strategies moving from project feasibility to understanding the entire market, leveraging competitive advantages, and understanding how to optimize returns to the tribe (jobs, tax revenue, multiplier effects, GDP) through a focus on the four principles of the economy (government, investment, consumption, net exports). Tribes are sovereign nations with economies that are not necessarily tied to one geography; however, by increasing overall economic activity, the tribe is inherently part of the regional and international economy. Currently recognizing tribes as an emerging domestic economy, tribes are finding ways to guide investment strategies, understand how to leverage government and outside consumers, and develop lucrative export strategies for goods, services, technology, lending, and entertainment. It is our responsibility to use the economy for positive change throughout Indian Country.

Tribes are now exploring banking and possible development funds and sovereign wealth funds to move away from other investment vehicles. A focus on multiple regulatory environments has built on the success of gaming and transitioned into finance, cannabis, entertainment, and even distilling and brewing in a joint partnership between Chehalis Tribal Enterprises (CTE), a tribal business entity, and Heritage Distilling, a for-profit U.S. domestic corporation. Using the expertise of the tribe to develop a commercial area off of Interstate 5, consisting of gas stations, a hotel, a Great Wolf Lodge water park, and other restaurants, CTE worked with a U.S. domestic company to change laws, develop financial plans, and successfully launch their venture. An abundance of tribes are moving beyond the popularity contest of merely a good idea with a feasibility study to understand market analytics, economic principles, and the multiple systems that impact the economy.

Tribes are an entertainment destination, from the Skywalk over the Grand Canyon (Hualapai Tribe); Talking Stick Resort Arena (Salt River Pima Maricopa Indian Community) and Gila River Arena (Gila River Indian Community), both in the metropolitan Phoenix area; to the Hard Rock owned by the Seminole Tribe of Florida. Additionally, tribes are working together with ownership, such as the McKay Tower in Grand Rapids, Michigan, which is owned by Gun Lake Investments (Match-E-Be-Nash-She-Wish Band of Pottawatomi Indians) and Waséyabek Development Company (Nottawaseppi Huron Band of Potawatomi Indians), and ilani Casino, owned by the Cowlitz Indian Tribe and developed/managed by Mohegan Gaming and Entertainment.[31]

Building the entire tribal economy is the future of economic wealth and overall quality of life for tribal citizens, the tribal government, and innovative solutions to address society's challenges and use opportunities to find ways to balance the community and the economy. It is time to use economic knowledge gained over the past few decades and build strong tribal economies. Moving from revenue priorities to overall GDP is the focus of economic development, and the only way to optimize returns to the tribe for the benefit of the tribe is to embrace long-term policies that support this trajectory.

There are three components of economic development that summarize strategies toward tribal economic development. These components include policies that recruit new businesses, retain current businesses, focus on the community, and develop new and innovative opportunities internally within the tribal economy. Balanced with developing competitive advantages, overall approaches improve input conditions, business strategy, and competition; have related industries and suppliers; and finally focus on demand conditions, which align with the most considerable GDP focus that is represented by consumption.

Many community capitals impact the economy, and understanding all the capitals, assets, and capacity of the community shows how the economy is optimized. A balance of economic capital and community capacity (human and social capital) guides workforce, relationships, knowledge, and leadership with economic decisions. These systems impact economies in different ways through external exogenous impacts and internal endogenous influences within the tribal economy. By working together and strategically aligning different economic actors, tribal economies can achieve agglomerative benefits and ultimately have higher economic multipliers to move from suboptimal returns towards highly functioning economies.

In respect to the formation of tribal business entities (TBE), there are formalized processes through the United States (such as Section 17 and tribal limited liability corporation codes) and the inherent sovereign right of tribes to develop their laws, rules, and regulation of business formation. This includes the opportunity to develop other relationships, operate businesses anywhere globally, and partner across lines of other businesses, governments, tribes, and respective teaming arrangements.

Focus on the tribal economy promotes the improvement of economic wealth and overall quality of life. Economic returns are optimized in shorter time periods, and benefits have higher economic impacts when all systems are considered. Revenues alone provide short-term suboptimal gains, while a focus on the actual tribal economy provides the highest level of progress in the best interests of the community, the tribe, and tribal citizens. Through thoughtful integration into overall tribal administration, tribal economies provide resources and wealth, and improve quality of life that supports progress throughout Indian Country.

NOTES

1. R. J. Miller, *Reservation "Capitalism": Economic Development in Indian Country* (ABC-CLIO, 2012).

2. M. Jorgensen, ed., *Rebuilding Native Nations: Strategies for Governance and Development* (Tucson: University of Arizona Press, 2007); Miller, *Reservation "Capitalism".*

3. P. Krugman, *Arguing with Zombies: Economics, Politics, and the Fight for a Better Future* (New York: W. W. Norton & Co., 2020).

4. R. J. Miller, M. Jorgensen, and D. Stewart, eds., *Creating Private Sector Economies in Native America: Sustainable Development through Entrepreneurship* (Cambridge: Cambridge University Press, 2019).

5. D. M. Kennedy, C. F. Harrington, A. K. Verbos, D. Stewart, J. S. Gladstone, and G. Clarkson, eds., *American Indian Business: Principles and Practices* (Seattle: University of Washington Press, 2017); Miller, *Reservation "Capitalism."*

6. R. K. Akee, K. A. Spilde, and J. B. Taylor, "The Indian Gaming Regulatory Act and Its Effects on American Indian Economic Development," *Journal of Economic Perspectives* 29, no. 3 (2015): 185–208.

7. Miller, Jorgensen, and Stewart, eds., *Creating Private Sector Economies in Native America.*

8. E. Trevan, *Tribal Economies—Planning Strong Tribal Economies—From Profit to GDP* (National Congress of American Indians [NCAI] Annual Conference, Albuquerque, NM, October 2019).

9. M. Emery and C. Flora, "Spiraling-Up: Mapping Community Transformation with

Community Capitals Framework," *Community Development* 37, no. 1 (2006): 19–35; E. S. Trevan, "The Influence of Import Substitution on Community Development as Measured by Economic Wealth and Quality of Life" (PhD diss., Arizona State University, 2016).

10. Emery and Flora, "Spiraling-Up," 19–35; Trevan, "The Influence of Import Substitution on Community Development."

11. R. J. Chaskin, "Building Community Capacity: A Definitional Framework and Case Studies from a Comprehensive Community Initiative," *Urban Affairs Review* 36, no. 3 (2001): 291–323.

12. Trevan, *Tribal Economies.*

13. Miller, *Reservation "Capitalism."*

14. Trevan, "The Influence of Import Substitution on Community Development."

15. T. J. Bartik, "A New Panel Database on Business Incentives for Economic Development Offered by State and Local Governments in the United States," Upjohn Research, prepared for the Pew Charitable Trusts (February 2017); E. Sirolli, *Ripples from the Zambezi: Passion, Entrepreneurship, and the Rebirth of Local Economies* (Gabriola, BC: New Society Publishers, 1999).

16. Miller, Jorgensen, and Stewart, eds., *Creating Private Sector Economies in Native America.*

17. M. Jorgensen, ed., *Rebuilding Native Nations: Strategies for Governance and Development* (Tucson: University of Arizona Press, 2007).

18. McGirt v. Oklahoma, 591 U.S. ___ (2020) 140 S. Ct. 2452 (2020); Nebraska v. Parker, 577 U.S. ___ (2016) 136 S. Ct. 1072; 194 L. Ed. 2d 152; 84 USLW 4154 (2016); Kennedy et al., eds., *American Indian Business.*

19. J. L. Osgood, S. M. Opp, and R. L. Bernotsky, "Yesterday's Gains versus Today's Realities: Lessons from 10 Years of Economic Development Practice," *Economic Development Quarterly* 26, no. 4 (2012): 334–50.

20. Osgood, Opp, and Bernotsky, "Yesterday's Gains versus Today's Realities," 334–50.

21. P. Sabatier, *Theories of the Policy Process* (New York: Routledge, 2019).

22. Osgood, Opp, and Bernotsky, "Yesterday's Gains versus Today's Realities," 334–50.

23. G. Clarkson, K. A. Spilde, and C. M. Claw, "Online Sovereignty: The Law and Economics of Tribal Electronic Commerce," *Vanderbilt Journal of Entertainment & Technology Law* 19, no. 1 (2016).

24. M. E. Porter, "Location, Competition, and Economic Development: Local Clusters in a Global Economy," *Economic Development Quarterly* 14, no. 1 (2000): 15–34.

25. Akee, Spilde, and Taylor, "The Indian Gaming Regulatory Act," 185–208.

26. R. Phillips, E. Trevan, and P. Kraeger, eds., *The Research Handbook on Community Development* (Cheltenham, UK: Edward Elgar Publishing, 2019).

27. Trevan, "The Influence of Import Substitution on Community Development."
28. G. P. Green and A. Haines, *Asset Building and Community Development* (New York: Sage Publications, 2015).
29. First Nations Development Institute, *Reclaiming Native Truth: Changing the Narrative about Native Americans* (2018), https://www.firstnations.org/publications/changing-the-narrative-about-native-americans-a-guide-for-allies/.
30. Trevan, "The Influence of Import Substitution on Community Development."
31. Mohegan Tribe (2020), ilani, https://mohegan.nsn.us/Business/gaming-entertainment/ilani.

GLOSSARY

Agglomerative. The focus on the clustering of certain variables and their impact on society.

Asset-Based Community Development (ABCD). A community development approach that understands the assets in the community and builds on these assets for overall strategy to improve overall quality of life.

Community capital. A framework used to provide value with a variety of community indicators, such as social capital (connections), human capital (knowledge), and economic capital (financial). The community capital framework provides an equitable approach for the application of financial and nonfinancial variables and their impact on all community systems.

Competitive advantage. A strategic approach that identifies a preferred solution to provide optimal benefits. Using different techniques within strategy to provide a preferred solution.

Economic development. Specific actions and strategies implemented to focus on the relationship of trade, not just profits, and measured by Gross Domestic Product (GDP).

Economics. The study of the trade of goods and services using a medium of exchange (i.e., money) under a scarcity of resources for trade.

Economy. Gross Domestic Product (GDP) includes government expenditures (G), overall investment (I), consumption (C), and net exports of exports (X) minus imports (M) (GDP = I + G + C + (X-M).)

Reservation-related economies. Areas of trade (as represented by U.S. county political boundaries) that intersect with Indian lands, reservations, and other trust-related lands specific to Native nations.

Tribal business entity (TBE). These entities are created by tribal law to allow economic activity to take place with the tribe. This includes current-day tribal gaming authorities, other forms of tribal economic activity, and other related economic entities, such as utilizing Section 17 tribal corporations.

Waves of economic development. The waves identify three focus areas of economic development strategy that recruit, retain, and support local entrepreneurial economic innovation.

Human Services for Indigenous Futures

Katie Johnston-Goodstar, Cary B. Waubanascum, and Donald Eubanks

SIGNIFICANT DILEMMAS AND CONTEMPORARY SOCIAL NEEDS MAKE IT NECESSARY for tribes to design and deliver human services in the twenty-first century. This chapter reviews the emergence of human services as a profession and its accepted definitions and values, and reviews the policies and "families of practice" common to tribal administration, including child welfare, financial and emergency assistance, mental health and community service programs. Using Brayboy's Tribal Critical Race Theory framework and Tlostanova and Mignolo's matrix of coloniality to examine the field,[1] we find that human services emerged with a change-oriented and systemic approach to human dilemmas, but has failed to sustain that distinction, becoming complicit in the missionary impulses of colonialism. We urge tribal administrators to reckon with "goals of assimilation" found in contemporary human-services policies and practices, including the normalization of the modern Western family, compliance with neoliberal economies, and a general disregard for Indigenous governance and knowledge. Drawing on those findings, we argue that the time to reimagine human services is overdue. Through the use of tribal case studies, we present possibilities and challenge tribal administrators to embrace human-services designs that reject assimilation and imagine goals and practices in alignment with their original tribal instructions and responsibilities to place and community.

BEST PRACTICES

- Always ask: How is the matrix of coloniality at work here and now? In what ways are the colonial goals of assimilation at work here and now?
- Identify the tribal values, norms, and outcomes you want to promote.
- Remember, tribal human-services designs can produce or discourage Indigenous futures!

WHAT ARE HUMAN SERVICES?

From within the progressive and radical movements of the 1960s, human services emerged as a grassroots field of theory and practice rooted in a holistic approach to the individual, a systemic approach to human dilemmas, and the lived experience of and accountability to the communities being served.[2] As Kincaid detailed, human services is the "multidisciplinary study of processes to facilitate client-determined systemic change at all levels of society," focused less on "what" a human-services professional does, or "where" they do it, but on the processes for change. Human services values an integrated interdisciplinary knowledge base, and the "professional must be seen as a facilitator rather than an expert who dictates or prescribes solutions."[3]

Since its emergence, human services has gained prominence as a profession. Drawing on an interdisciplinary set of theories and practices such as social work, community planning, mental health, and public administration, human services established a commonly held set of professional values and standards.[4] By 1975, the National Organization for Human Services was founded to improve human-services delivery, developing a code of ethics and a set of professional competencies, a newsletter, journals, and an annual conference.[5] The Council for Standards for Human Service Education, created in 1976, provides program accreditation standards and national certification for a host of academic programs developed to educate and train human-services professionals.[6]

Today, multiple families of practice are understood to constitute the field of human services, including corrections, mental health, child care, social services, human resource management, gerontology, developmental disabilities, addictions, recreation, and education. Given the limitations of this chapter, we introduce four of these families for which the tribal administrator is commonly responsible—child welfare, financial and emergency assistance programs, mental health services, and community services—providing a brief overview of the services, program goals, and funding streams. We then explore the implicit goals of these common services, identify pitfalls, and present exemplars that model decolonizing service provision efforts at Menominee Indian Tribe of Wisconsin and Mille Lacs Band of Ojibwe.

Child welfare involves the delivery of child and family services. This may include a range of services that focus on temporary familial crisis, long- or short-term parental well-being, and/or concerns over neglect, abandonment, and abuse of minor children. Child welfare at a tribal level can include active cooperation with non-tribal jurisdictions administering cases under the Indian Child Welfare Act of 1978 (ICWA) in order to "protect the best interests of Indian children and to promote the stability and security of Indian tribes and families" (25 U.S.C. § 1902). Certain state governments mandated by Public Law 280 have "concurrent jurisdiction" in child custody matters, leaving tribes with "service responsibility" to families involved in child welfare proceedings. Tribes with exclusive jurisdiction have the authority to decide child custody matters in their tribal courts.[7] Tribes having "service responsibilities" may include child protection and family assessments, court services, case management and intervention services, kinship and foster care placement, adoptive or nonmedical facility placement.

A second practice, financial and emergency assistance services are often supported by Department of Health and Human Services (HHS)-distributed block grants to design and operate programs such as the delivery of social welfare and financial assistance programs, including seventy tribal TANF programs.[8] Similar to states, tribes are eligible to receive these federal grants. Tribal financial assistance programs often include implementation of Tribal Temporary Assistance for Needy Families (TANF). Tribes may elect to implement their own tribal TANF programs, similar to states. Unlike states, tribal TANF programs do not have the five-year participation limit, and many integrate cultural programming to fit the needs of their communities.[9] Tribal TANF programs adopt federal TANF policy goals to promote work and responsibility, strengthen families, and accomplish one of the four purposes of the TANF program: provide assistance to needy families so that children can be cared for in their own homes; reduce the dependency of needy parents by promoting job preparation, work, and marriage; prevent and reduce the incidence of out-of-wedlock pregnancies; encourage the formation and maintenance of two-parent families.[10] In addition, other grants are available to support the food and energy needs of tribal families. These include the Tribal Low-Income Home Energy Assistance program (LIHEAP)[11] to assist in meeting the costs of home energy, and the U.S. Department of Agriculture (USDA) Food Distribution Program on Indian Reservations (FDPIR) and its alternative, the Supplemental Nutrition Assistance Program (SNAP).[12] FDPIR has recently updated its list of available foods to include traditional foods such as bison, blue cornmeal, wild rice, salmon, and catfish.[13]

Mental health services is a third family of practice. Programs are often guided by the five foundational elements of the Tribal Behavioral Health Agenda created in consultation with the Substance Abuse and Mental Health Services Administration (SAMSHA). These elements are: healing from historical and intergenerational trauma; advancing socio-cultural-ecological approaches to addressing behavioral health in tribal communities; expanding prevention and recovery support; improving behavioral health services and systems; and building national awareness and visibility related to the behavioral health experiences of tribal communities. Various federal funds and collaborations exist to support these efforts, in addition to the Indian Health Service's Division of Behavioral Health, which offers occasional funds for behavioral health, alcohol and substance abuse, and family violence prevention programs.[14] In comparison to many federal policies, funds, and programs, the mental health family of practice is notable in its integration of historic, social, and cultural factors.

Finally, community service programs include a broad array of emergency services and development programs for community members. These can involve public awareness, prevention, legal aid, or case management services for runaway/homeless youth, or transitional living programs, or family violence intervention and shelter services for individuals experiencing urgent safety and housing needs. Programs such as these are often funded through the Family and Youth Services Bureau. Another common community service is found in disability and elder service programs for members of the tribe with longer-term disability or supportive living needs. Federally recognized tribes with at least fifty elders over the age of sixty can receive Title VI program grants under the Older Americans Act of 1978 to provide home-delivered or congregate nutrition services, as well as supportive and caregiver services such as chores, personal care, and transportation services, thereby reducing the need for costly institutional care and medical interventions. Finally, there are services to young people, including prevention, intervention, and treatment approaches to address a range of criminal or antisocial activity and substance abuse disorders and to promote mental health and support youth mentoring and leadership development. These programs are often funded by the Office of Juvenile Justice and Delinquency Prevention, which offers tribal youth grants, or the SAMSHA.

A TIME FOR RECKONING: HUMAN SERVICES AND THE MATRIX OF COLONIALITY

In contrast to earlier "helping professions," human services emerged as a grass-roots, change-oriented, and systemic approach to human dilemmas. The field, however, has failed to sustain that distinction, becoming increasingly entangled in mainstream state and nonprofit services. Human services today are more akin to "resource delivery" than they are to facilitating change-oriented, systemic approaches. Trained "professionals" participate in structures or organizations that individualize and pathologize humans as "service populations," while submersing important social, political, and historical contexts.[15] And specific to Indigenous peoples, human services have not only distanced themselves from the "other," but they have oriented themselves "toward the problematic goal of assimilation."[16]

Human services in the United States operate within and co-construct the four domains of coloniality: economy, authority, normativity, and knowledge.[17] For example, institutions such as the child welfare system, economic assistance divisions, and nonprofit organizations are granted the ultimate authority to interpret policy, train professionals, test for eligibility, decide custody, deliver resources, and ensure compliance with benchmarks of assimilation in state-sponsored policy such as legal marriage, two-parent nuclear households, engagement in paid labor, and the development of normative behavior and households.

According to Abramovitz, these "new" authorities reinforce a colonial family ethic entrenched in Western family structures, patriarchy, and the "proper role of women."[18] They increasingly depend on a punitive, neoliberal logic characterized by notions of individual responsibility, economic competition, free trade, market deregulation, and the privatization of state welfare provision.[19] They reinforce transplanted Victorian notions of the "deserving" and "undeserving" poor. Once fundamental rights like health care, housing, and nutrition become means-tested benefits. Traditional tribal notions of family structure, role, and relationship are deferred;[20] the powerful roles of women are minimized; and cultural understandings of wellness, justice, and ecological interdependence become sidenotes to modern-day policy.

As co-creator and enforcer of these domains of coloniality, human services must reckon with its professional identity. Human services espouse an awareness of the systemic aspects of human dilemmas, but modernization and privatization have worked to "maintain the status quo."[21] As such, human services is operating in "contradiction to its function as a system of care and equal access for those disenfranchised and marginalized."[22] It is losing the "capacit[y] for care and ability to think and teach in ways founded in the living relationship of encounter."[23] The field is gradually being emptied of its commitments to process and client-determined systemic change at all levels of society.[24]

Tribes, like other communities, experience significant dilemmas and pressing social needs, but analyses like these prompt Indigenous providers to ask the critically reflective question "am I a modern-day missionary?"[25] According to the late Seneca scholar John Mohawk, Indigenous peoples have become entangled in our own oppression, perpetuating colonial policies in our "culturally western" forms of governance.[26] Tribal administrators must take extra caution to avoid "taking up colonialist ideas" that could hinder their own sovereignty,[27] and ask critical questions like: In what ways do our human service designs reenact colonial goals of dispossession, displacement, and forced "development"? How do they exploit and assimilate by naturalizing Western values, behaviors, and outcomes? In what ways are they "rooted in imperialism, White supremacy, and a desire for material gain" at the expense of Indigenous peoples and sovereignty? How can tribes reclaim their original teachings and social and economic structures in order to actively counter the erasure of settler colonialism?[28] Finally, how can tribes address these critical questions while continuing to assist their citizens with their pressing everyday needs?

CRAFTING INDIGENOUS FUTURES: CASE STUDIES OF INNOVATIVE TRIBAL SERVICES

Sustainable tribal solutions and human service models, policies, and outcomes are needed. Administrators can play notable roles by designing a holistic and Indigenous-centric platform of human service that does not dehistoricize and individualize human needs or dilemmas, and that has the capacity to imagine a knowable, practical, and anticipated Indigenous futurity.[29] If a funding source has an implicit budgetary bias toward out-of-home placement, if it "does not allow you to provide services with traditional healers in your community or requires your tribal court to make determinations that are counter to your cultural values, this funding source may not be right for your community."[30] If a funding source is not wholly contradictory but remains questionable in terms of outcomes, how can tribal administrators be creative and modify it so that it is in accordance with tribal values, goals, and contexts? While innovations in human services are necessarily tribal-specific, we present two case studies as a jumping-off point.

MENOMINEE TRIBAL TANF PROGRAM

The Menominee Tribe of Indians of Wisconsin provides a unique example of how tribes can struggle with the implicit biases of human-services policies and design programs and services that align better with their own tribal goals and contexts. The Temporary Assistance to Needy Families (TANF) program provides financial assistance to families so that children can be cared for in their own homes. Originally a mother's pension program called Aid to Families with Dependent Children, this program was part of Franklin D. Roosevelt's New Deal in the 1930s. Over the years, it has been debated and modified—the most recent iteration being the Personal Responsibility and Work Opportunity Reconciliation Act of 1996, which explicitly redirected the focus of the program to personal responsibility, family structure, and participation in the workforce. Its primary goals at this time are to reduce the dependency of needy parents by promoting job preparation, work, and marriage; to prevent and reduce the incidence of out-of-wedlock pregnancies; and to encourage the formation and maintenance of two-parent "nuclear" families. Utilizing Brayboy's and

Tlostanova and Mignolo's frameworks to analyze the goals of TANF, we see an implicit bias toward Western norms of gender and family, support for capitalist labor that may or may not align with tribal economic or environmental beliefs, and a generalized ignorance of the historical context of tribal peoples in the United States, including the dispossession of tribal lands and resources, the imposition of historical trauma on Indigenous families, and attacks on tribal language, culture, and social structure.

Within this context, the Menominee Tribe designed and operates their tribal TANF Program to assist community members experiencing economic hardship according to their own self-identified TANF goals:

- To reduce the overall costs of public assistance by promoting work as a means of family support.
- To promote individual employability of TANF recipients through close collaboration and coordination between the TANF Program, PL 102-477 Program, the Education Department, and other programs and services that the tribe operates.
- To reduce generational dependency on public assistance through the development and awareness of work ethics and their value to individual families, their children, and to the community.
- To decrease specific barriers to employment such as drug and alcohol dependence by establishing drug testing as one of the necessary eligibility requirements for TANF benefits.
- To promote self-esteem, independence, and self-sufficiency.

The Menominee tribal TANF program currently serves approximately thirty-one families monthly and provides one-on-one contact with a case worker to create a plan to work towards self-sufficiency that is unique to each family and their circumstances/goals that address the needs of both the client and community. The Menominee TANF program strives to advance cultural revitalization and economic stability by taking advantage of points of intervention that will provide long-term community benefits. The tribe accordingly defined program requirements to address holistic needs in the areas of vocational, economic, and cultural revitalization. Instead of requiring clients to solely submit job applications, clients engage in meaningful activities that build vocational skills, secure employment, economic stability, and cultural engagement. For vocational assistance, clients are matched and placed within tribal departments of their interest, for work experience placements, to gain valuable work ethics and soft skills. A client interested in higher education may be placed within a department at the College of Menominee Nation to gain appropriate skills. Other clients have been placed at the Menominee Culture Museum, Department of Transportation, Food Distribution, Menominee Tribal Clinic, Tribal Utilities, and others. These placements are based on the strengths and desires of the client. The TANF program also supports cultural events such as the Menominee Culture Camp, the annual Sobriety Pow-wow, and Sturgeon Feast and Pow-wow and encourages/provides clients an option to work these events as part of their required TANF work activity hours. The monthly training calendar includes cultural activities to keep our culture alive, such as beading, sewing, and moccasin classes. Clients may also attend cultural healing events as part of their requirements, such as the White Bison, Mending Broken Hearts program that helps people heal from personal and historical trauma, as well as Positive Indian Parenting.[31] The Menominee Tribal TANF program and administration is committed to the holistic well-being of their community members, and this is demonstrated through their social service programs.

MILLE LACS BAND OF OJIBWE ELDER ASSISTED LIVING HOUSING PROGRAM

Another case study can be found in the example of the Mille Lacs Band of Ojibwe Indians and the development of an elder assisted-living housing program. The Mille Lacs Band of Ojibwe, located in east-central Minnesota, has a government based on a division of powers to help ensure proper checks and balances. The legislative branch, composed of a secretary-treasurer and three district representatives (Band Assembly), enacts laws that regulate the band's affairs and appropriates money for band programs and services. The executive branch implements band laws and administers the band's programs and services and is led by the chief executive, who is responsible for conducting external relations. The judicial branch, or Tribal Court, upholds the band's laws and ensures justice is served equally to all band members.[32] The tribe is guided by a set of values that form the foundation of their lives and are predicated on their language:

Gwayakwaadiziwin (Honesty): To achieve honesty within yourself is to recognize who and what you are. Do this and you can be honest with all others.

Dabaadendiziwin (Humility): Humble yourself and recognize that no matter how much you think you know, you know very little.

Debwewin (Truth): To learn Truth, to live Truth, to walk Truth, and to speak Truth.

Nibwaakaawin (Wisdom): To have Wisdom is to know the difference between good and bad and to know the result of your actions.

Zaagi'idiwin (Love/Compassion): Unconditional love and compassion is to know that when people are weak, they need your love and compassion the most.

Manaadendamowin (Respect): The Mille Lacs Band of Ojibwe has community values: Respect others, their beliefs. Respect yourself. When you practice respect, respect will be given back to you.

Aakwade'ewin (Bravery/Courage): Have bravery and courage in doing things right even though it may hurt you physically and mentally.

In 1997, the Band Assembly and Chief Executive Marge Anderson passed a resolution to build and manage assisted living units for band elders. Rapidly aging elders of the baby boomer generation faced various levels of infirmity, and maintaining health while living at home had become an issue for many. The only services provided near the reservation were nursing homes in surrounding counties. Isolation and reports of biased treatment in these facilities was common. Western norms and notions around family and the age of "elderhood" informed the design and delivery of their services. These factors were vital considerations in the creation of the resolution.

Utilizing Brayboy's and Tlostanova & Mignolo's frameworks, we can see that the band's decisions were driven by their beliefs and values, and rooted in their history, culture, and future. The commissioner of Health and Human Services led the effort of designing and building the tribe's new assisted living units. Through consultation with elders, elected officials, band members, and health care providers, each facility included support services such as nutritional support (breakfast and lunch for all elders), nursing stations, and other supportive services. Each unit included a kitchenette, one bedroom, and a living area. Mille Lacs Band's reservation consists of three districts composed of several distinct communities. District 1 is the largest district and received a twenty-unit facility. Districts 11 and 111 each received ten-unit facilities.

The band decided that these units would be designed in consultation with and located within the community, thus promoting access to family support and continuation of the community's values. They additionally decided to provide this housing free of charge to all enrolled band members fifty-five years or older, which is *not* "compliant" with Western expectations of age and neoliberal economy but *is* responsive to the current context of tribal health, life expectancy, and needs for community care and the tribe's values. The Band Assembly ultimately decided to fund this project independently, without assistance from federal, state, or county funding, in order to allow the tribe to design, deliver, and retain full control over the housing and referral to the assisted living program.

PRACTITIONER PERSPECTIVE

Tribal human services are tasked with addressing everyday, real-life dilemmas of their citizens. These human services are housed within larger tribal governance structures where many are actively carrying out strategic plans for revitalizing their own Indigenous futures and addressing the vestiges of colonialism. This often results in a collision between worldview, structure, and goals. Navigating and reconciling these contradictions is the work of the decolonizing tribal administrator. Through this chapter, we have provided a review of human services, frameworks for analysis, and examples of innovative tribal human services from our own professional experiences. We hope that these examples are helpful in promoting critical reflection of service provisions and your future designs. We encourage you to apply these concepts to your own administration and reckon with "goals of assimilation" found in mainstream human services; to consider how coloniality is present; to explore how tribal values, norms, and outcomes can be privileged, and how Indigenous futures can be central to your work.

NOTES

1. Bryan McKinley Jones Brayboy, "Toward a Tribal Critical Race Theory in Education," *Urban Review* 37, no. 5 (2005): 425–46; Madina Vladimirovna Tiostanova and Walter Mignolo, *Learning to Unlearn: Decolonial Reflections from Eurasia and the Americas* (Columbus: Ohio State University Press, 2012).

2. Hans Skott-Myhre, Brad McDonald, and Kathleen S. G. Skott-Myhre. "Appropriating Care and Hijacking Desire: Thought and Praxis in Human Services under 21st Century Capitalism," *Journal of Progressive Human Services* 28, no. 3 (2017): 164–78.

3. Susan O. Kincaid, "Defining Human Services: a Discourse Analysis," *Human Service Education* 29, no. 1 (2009): 18–19.

4. Fran Burnford and Joann Chenault, *The Current State of Human Services Professional Education*, no. 7. Project Share, 1978.

5. "Ethical Standards for Human Services Professionals," National Organization for Human Services, 2015, https://www.nationalhumanservices.org/ethical-standards-for-hs-professionals.

6. Council for Standards in Human Service Education (2020), https://cshse.org.

7. Native American Rights Fund (n.d.). Indian Child Welfare Guide Online: Jurisdiction, https://narf.org/nill/documents/icwa/faq/jurisdiction.html#Q12.

8. "About TANF," U.S. Department of Health and Human Services, 2017, https://www.acf.hhs.gov/ofa/programs/tanf/about.

9. Heather Hahn, "A Descriptive Study of Tribal Temporary Assistance for Needy Families (TANF) Programs," Urban Institute, 2014, https://www.urban.org/research/publication/descriptive-study-tribal-temporary-assistance-needy-families-tanf-programs.

10. U.S. Department of Health and Human Services, "About TANF."

11. "Tribal LIHEAP Program Characteristics," U.S. Department of Health and Human Services, 2020, https://liheapch.acf.hhs.gov/tribal.

12. "Supplemental Nutrition Assistance Program (SNAP)," U.S. Department of Agriculture, 2020, https://www.fns.usda.gov/snap/supplemental-nutrition-assistance-program.

13. "Food Distribution Program on Indian Reservations (FDPIR)," U.S. Department of Agriculture, 2020, https://www.fns.usda.gov/fdpir/food-distribution-program-indian-reservations.

14. "The National Tribal Behavioral Health Agenda," Substance Abuse and Mental Health Services Administration, 2020, https://store.samhsa.gov/product/The-National-Tribal-Behavioral-Health-Agenda/PEP16-NTBH-AGENDA.

15. National Organization for Human Services (n.d.). "Ethical Standards for Human Services Professionals," https://www.nationalhumanservices.org/what-is-human-services#whatarethey; Eve Tuck, "Suspending Damage: a Letter to Communities," *Harvard Educational Review* 79, no. 3 (2009): 409–28.

16. Brayboy, "Toward a Tribal Critical Race Theory in Education," 425–46, 436.

17. Tiostanova and Mignolo. *Learning to Unlearn.*

18. Abramovitz, Mimi. *Regulating the lives of women: Social welfare policy from colonial times*

to the present. South End Press, 1996.

19. V. Navarro, "Neoliberalism As a Class Ideology; or, the Political Causes of the Growth of Inequalities." *International Journal of Health Services: Planning, Administration, Evaluation* 37, no. 1 (2007): 47–62; Jessica Toft, "Words of Common Cause: Social Work's Historical Democratic Discourse," *Social Service Review* 94, no. 1 (2020): 75–128.

20. Leo Kevin Killsback, "A Nation of Families: Traditional Indigenous Kinship, the Foundation for Cheyenne Sovereignty," *Alternative: an International Journal of Indigenous Peoples*, 15, no. 1 (2019): 34–43; Katie Johnston-Goodstar, "Decolonizing Youth Development: Reimagining Youthwork for Indigenous Youth Futures." *AlterNative: An International Journal of Indigenous Peoples* 16, no. 4 (2020): 378–86.

21. Paul Kivel, "Social Service or Social Change," in *Incite, The Revolution Will Not Be Funded*, by INCITE! Women of Color Against Violence (Durham: Duke University Press, 2007), 129–49, 3.

22. Skott-Myhre, McDonald, and Skott-Myhre. "Appropriating Care and Hijacking Desire," 164–78, 167.

23. Skott-Myhre, McDonald, and Skott-Myhre. "Appropriating Care and Hijacking Desire," 164–78, 169.

24. M. Reisch and J. Andrews. *The Road Not Taken: a History of Radical Social Work in the United States* (New York: Routledge, 2014); Katie Johnston-Goodstar and Ross VeLure Roholt, "Unintended Consequences of Professionalizing Youth Work: Lessons from Teaching and Social Work," *Child & Youth Services* 34, no. 2 (2013): 139–55.

25. M. Hart, "Am I a Modern Day Missionary? Reflections of a Cree Social Worker," *Native Social Work Journal* 5 (2003): 299–313.

26. John Mohawk, "Racism," in *Thinking in Indian: A John Mohawk Reader*, ed. J. Barreiro(Golden, CO: Fulcrum Publishing, 2020), 224–31.

27. Brayboy, "Toward a Tribal Critical Race Theory in Education," 425–46, 431.

28. J. K. Kauanui, "'a Structure, Not an Event': Settler Colonialism and Enduring Indigeneity," *Lateral* 5, no. 1; P. Wolfe, "Settler Colonialism and the Elimination of the Native," *Journal of Genocide Research* 8, no. 4 (2016): 387–409.

29. E. Tuck and R. A. Gaztamide-Fernández, "Curriculum, Replacement, and Settler Futurity," *Journal of Curriculum Theorizing* 29, no. 1 (2013).

30. "Tribal Leadership Series: Funding Child Welfare Services," National Indian Child Welfare Association, 2018, https://www.nicwa.org/wp-content/uploads/2018/11/Funding.pdf.

31. "Mending Broken Hearts," White Bison, https://whitebison.org/mending-broken-hearts/; National Indian Child Welfare Association (2020); NICWA Training Institutes: Positive Indian Parenting, https://www.nicwa.org/training-institutes/.

32. "Government," Mille Lacs Band of Ojibwe, 2020, www.millelacsband.com.

GLOSSARY

Coloniality. The quality of or set of beliefs associated with colonialism, and the practices of European nations to extract from and occupy the lands of other cultures by force and coercion.

Domains of coloniality. Otherwise known as the colonial matrix of power, it has been defined by scholar Anibal Quijano as a matrix of power where colonizing nations/cultures seek control over four interrelated domains of the society they are colonizing: control of economy; authority; gender, sexuality, and family; and knowledge.

Historical trauma. Multigeneration trauma experienced by a group—often a racial, ethnic, or religious minority group that has been persecuted by another (for example, the experience of traumatic events such as forced removal of children to boarding schools, or massacre). This trauma can manifest itself across generations in patterns of poor physical and mental health.

Neoliberalism. A political and economic ideology that sees competition as the defining characteristic of human behavior/relations. It emphasizes minimal state intervention in favor of the free market, which is believed to produce the most efficient allocation of resources.

Tribal critical race theory. Developed by Lumbee scholar Brian Brayboy, it is a framework that seeks to explain the unique racial and political experiences of education and educational policies in the United States.

Tribal TANF. The Tribal Temporary Assistance for Needy Families is a financial assistance program for federally recognized Indian tribes that allows tribes the flexibility to design their own welfare programs that promote work and responsibility and strengthen families.

Community Wellness

Linda Bane Frizzell and Candice Skenandore

AMERICAN INDIANS AND ALASKA NATIVES (AI/AN) COLLECTIVELY CONTINUE TO experience striking disparities when compared to the rest of the U.S. population. High rates of poverty and unemployment, barriers to accessing higher education, poor housing, lack of transportation, and geographic isolation all contribute to poor health and wellness outcomes for AI/AN communities. However, the fact that AI/AN peoples exist today is testament to their inherent strengths and numerous paths of resiliency. These characteristics speak to fortitude in the face of ongoing genocide, historical trauma, destructive federal policies, forced removal/relocation, boarding schools, land dispossession, and continuing threats to culture, language, and access to traditional foods.

Historic and persistent underfunding of AI/AN health services has resulted in problems of access, and has limited the ability of AI/AN provider systems to deliver a full range of medical, behavioral, environmental health, wellness, and public health services that could help prevent or reduce the complications of chronic diseases, co-occurring disorders, and premature death. AI/AN communities must and will continue to advocate for their needs while pursuing their own effective traditions and innovations.

BEST PRACTICES

The holistic approach to individual and collective life shared among many AI/AN communities fully anticipates and aligns with the best contemporary public health models. Best and promising practices that Native communities can deploy in the interest of wellness include:

- cultivation and support for culturally grounded services
- encouragement and facilitation of traditional food systems
- consideration of holistic community-environment well-being
- equitable law, justice, and economic development
- knowledgeable and competent engagement with federal contracting and compacting
- strategic use of general public-health service capacity and health care and services billing
- collaborative transportation, financial, housing, and family services
- innovative community health aide, dental health aide, and telehealth programs

IHS

Established in 1955, the U.S. Indian Health Service (IHS) is a federal agency within the Department of Health and Human Services (HHS) that provides a health service delivery system specifically for AI/ANs. Members and qualifying descendants of federally recognized AI/AN tribes are eligible for services provided by the IHS. It is important to understand that the IHS does not administer a type of "health insurance." Rather, it is a system of health service delivery. It is also important to recognize that the IHS has never been funded at the appropriate level for fulfilling U.S. health service obligations to tribal nations. Historically, the funding range fluctuates between 40 percent and 60 percent of need. An issue is that the IHS is not requesting the amounts it needs to adequately fund the agency. For example, in the Fiscal Year (FY) 2021 IHS Budget Justification, the IHS requested $6.23 billion in discretionary funds, yet the Tribal Budget Formulation Workgroup identified a need of over $9.1 billion in total discretionary appropriations. This failure is primary among the causes for the continued decline in relative health status of AI/AN peoples.

The contemporary AI/AN–oriented health system consists of IHS (federal), tribal, and urban Indian health services programs. This constellation of service pathways is often referred to collectively as ITUs. Tribes may choose to receive health services directly from the IHS and/or administer their own health services, programs, functions, or activities, or a portion thereof, through contracting or compacting agreements under the amended Indian Self-Determination and Education Assistance Act (ISDEAA). The ITU system delivers health services in over six hundred IHS and tribal health service facilities scattered across thirty-six states, mostly in rural and isolated areas. As of 2020 the IHS directly operates twenty-four hospitals (service units), fifty health centers (clinics), eleven school health centers (clinics), twenty-four health stations (satellite clinics), and seven regional youth treatment centers. Tribes and tribal organizations, through ISDEAA contracting and compacting, operate over 80 percent of the IHS health system. Tribes operate 22 hospitals, 285 health centers, 5 school health centers, 54 health stations, 127 Alaska Native village clinics, and 5 youth regional treatment centers. Additionally, the IHS provides limited funding for urban Indian health centers in thirty-four urban areas throughout the country.[1] The urban clinics receive approximately 1 percent of the IHS budget to operate their health care programs. Therefore, urban clinics rely heavily on other funding sources, including grants, which rarely cover costs such as maintenance and repairs to aging facilities.

A FAILURE OF FINANCIAL AND HUMAN RESOURCES

In December 2018 the U.S. Commission on Civil Rights released a report titled *Broken Promises: Continuing Federal Funding Shortfall for Native Americans*. This report provided an update to the 2004 report *Broken Promises: Evaluating the Native American Health Care System*. Both of these documents validate the unforgivable inequity of federal funding for health services and rights guaranteed to AI/AN communities under the trust obligation. Over the fifteen years between reports, conditions had only slightly improved. Moreover the updated report found that federal programs serving Indian Country not only continue to be underfunded, but in many cases have endured resource regressions.

As discussed elsewhere in this handbook, AI/AN communities are comprised of sovereign entities (federally recognized tribes n=574) that have entered into government-to-government relationships with the United States. These relationships entail a treaty-based trust responsibility by which the federal government has pledged to provide for the ongoing health of AI/AN peoples. To be American Indian or Alaska Native is to be part of a political classification. AI/AN community members are dual citizens of the United States and of their respective Native nations. The trust responsibility and this political status of AI/AN peoples provides the fundamental rationale for federal policy regarding AI/AN health. Specifically, an individual may be considered eligible for IHS services "if he is regarded as an Indian by the community in which he lives as evidenced by such factors as tribal membership, enrollment, residence on tax-exempt land, ownership of restricted property, active participation in tribal affairs, or other relevant factors in keeping with general Bureau of Indian Affairs practices in the jurisdiction."[2]

The Indian Health Care Improvement Act (IHCIA) was originally enacted on September 30, 1976. This statute was instrumental in setting national policy to improve the health of Indian people, and it was the initial authorization for the IHS, tribal providers, and urban Indian health programs to bill Medicare, Medicaid, and the Children's Health Insurance Plan. Yet this billing authorization is starkly inadequate to address the depth and breadth of health needs. In testimony from the National Indian Health Board, FY 2019, IHS appropriations were at only about $5.8 billion. Per capita medical expenditures within IHS were $4,078 in FY 2017, compared with $9,726 in national per capita spending for Medicare that same year. Although the IHS budget has nominally increased by 2–3 percent each year, these increases are barely sufficient to keep up with rising medical and nonmedical inflation, population growth, facility maintenance costs, and other expenses.[3]

As independent, sovereign nations, tribal governments do not operate within state regulatory structures, and often must compete with their own state governments for resources. Tribes are regularly left out of statewide public health plans and federal funding decisions for public health programs. Without a local tax base and little (if any) outside funding, tribal communities are often the most in need of public health dollars. Tribes continue to be ignored during the budget formulation of the U.S. public health system; knowledgeable communities, professionals, and individuals who understand tribal governments and their authority are vital for redressing this wrong. Moreover, Medicaid reimbursement is only available through a state Medicaid authority. To date there have been many government-to-government challenges for tribes to collaborate with state governments to ensure their populations have access to health services. This inequality is exacerbated by the frequently limited knowledge among state employees regarding federal responsibility for AI/AN health services.

The IHS budget comes out of the Interior-Environment appropriations bill and not out of the Labor, Health and Human Services, and Education appropriation bill, which funds the HHS. This posed a problem for tribes and tribal organizations during the COVID-19 pandemic when Congress provided funds to tribes via HHS departments like the Centers for Disease Control and Prevention; Substance Abuse and Mental Health Services Administration; Health Resources and Services Administration. Unlike the IHS, these entities do not have existing funding mechanisms in place to get funds out to tribes quickly. This resulted in delays of receiving funds needed to combat the virus early on. Tribes asked these departments to work with the IHS to enter into interagency agreements to allow COVID-19 funds to run through existing ISDEAA agreements, but because these departments are funded out of the HHS budget and the IHS is funded out of the Interior budget, tribes were told this was impossible.

Some federal health care programs such as Medicare and Medicaid are not subject to annual appropriations. The Veterans Health Administration (VHA) and the IHS are subject to appropriations and must deliver services within their service areas. There may be times when the number of patients within a service area has increased without seeing an increase in funding. The VHA is funded by the Veterans Administration, which is afforded the authority of advance appropriations—an appropriation of new budget authority that becomes available one or more fiscal years after the fiscal year for which the appropriation providing it is enacted.[4] The IHS does not have this authority; therefore tribes may see a lapse in funding due to continuing resolutions or government shutdowns.

Unsurprisingly, chronic and pervasive health staffing shortages—for everything from physicians to nurses to behavioral health practitioners—stubbornly persist across Indian Country, with over fifteen hundred consistent healthcare professional vacancies documented as of 2016. For example, a Government Accountability Office (GAO) report from August 2018 found an average 25 percent provider vacancy rate for physicians, nurse practitioners, dentists, and pharmacists across two-thirds of IHS Areas (GAO 18-580). In addition, many tribes do not have housing for health care professionals. In these communities, even if the providers were hired they would not have a place to live.[5] The health needs of AI/AN communities require uniquely qualified providers. Colonization, genocide, war, forced relocation, boarding schools, discrimination, broken treaties, unfulfilled promises, economic conditions, and political injustice all create practice environments that often overwhelm health service professionals, leading to early burnout and limited years of service.

Healthcare access issues both arise from and exacerbate underfunding and understaffing. From the reservation and rural AI/AN perspective, there are multiple barriers to access routine health services and tremendous issues for culturally considerate and specialized services. In reality, access to primary care often comes down to a "choice of one" (or, in some cases, none) and requires an ability to travel (not only by land but in some cases by air and by sea) and to have technological resources for accessing basic professional health services.

There has been a major population shift of AI/ANs from rural to metropolitan areas in recent decades. Throughout the 1990s to 2014, generally the population was fifty-fifty, half on the reservations and the other half in urban areas. The 2010 Census reveals that 78 percent of the AI/AN live outside of tribal statistical service areas. Twenty-two percent of AI/ANs live on reservations or other trust lands. In 2017, the ten states with the largest American Indian/Alaska Native populations were California, Oklahoma, Arizona, Texas, New Mexico, Washington, New York, North Carolina, Florida, and Alaska.[6] Unique issues have arisen due to this major shift of AI/ANs from rural to metropolitan areas. This scenario puts more stress on basic health services in rural America, as AI/ANs often travel back and forth between urban residences and their usually rural cultural and extended family communities. Complex implications for ensuring access to culturally sensitive services thus arise. As economic conditions continue to offer limited employment in rural areas, this "migration" is expected to continue. To further compound access issues, rural hospitals and clinics are increasingly closing. Over the course of the last ten years, more than 120 rural hospitals have ceased operations, further limiting access to care for populations that are older, less healthy, and less affluent than urban counterparts.[7]

An example of how this plays out can be seen in the simple fact that geographic location and availability of cancer screening services are related.

Individuals in areas with higher AI/AN population concentrations have large gaps in the availability, utilization, and distance to providers when compared to other areas. Despite recommendations for cancer screening for breast and colorectal cancer among the Medicare population, preventive screening rates are often lower among vulnerable populations, such as the small but rapidly growing older American Indian and Alaska Native population.[8]

HEALTH DISPARITIES

The devastating lack of funding, human resources, and health care access discussed above has contributed to conditions in AI/AN communities, where the people

- have life expectancies 5.5 years shorter than the national average
- experience infant mortality rates 1.6 times higher than non-Hispanic whites and 1.3 times the national average
- experience suicide rates 1.6 times the national average, and for Native male youth 2.5 times higher than the national average
- require treatment for alcohol and drug abuse at nearly twice the national average (18.0 percent versus 9.6 percent)
- have a drug-related death rate that is 1.8 times the national average (22.7 deaths per 100,000 versus 12.6 deaths per 100,000)
- have a diabetes diagnosis rate over twice the national average (15.1 percent versus 7.2 percent)[9]

Age-adjusted mortality rates, listed in the table below as cases per 100,000, likewise reflect the striking disparities experienced by AI/AN communities. Table 1 is drawn from the most recent comprehensive sources.[10]

There are also clearly gendered and racialized contours of the above mortality rates. AI/AN populations collectively suffer from one of the nation's highest rates of crime and victimization, and Native women are ten times more likely to be murdered and four times more likely to be sexually assaulted than the national average. AI/AN individuals are being killed in police encounters at a higher rate than any other racial group, and these deaths likely remain undercounted by federal agencies.[11]

Table 1. Comparative Mortality Rates

	AI/AN RATE	U.S. ALL GROUPS	RATIO: AI/AN TO ALL GROUPS
ALL CAUSES*	999.1	747.0	1.3
heart disease	194.1	179.1	1.1
cancer	178.4	172.8	1.0
accidents/unintentional injuries	93.7	38.0	2.5
diabetes	66.0	20.8	3.2
alcohol-induced	50.5	7.6	6.6
chronic lower respiratory diseases	46.6	42.2	1.1
stroke	43.6	39.1	1.1
chronic liver disease	42.9	9.4	4.6
influenza and pneumonia	26.6	15.1	1.8
drug-induced	23.4	12.9	1.8
kidney disease	22.4	15.3	1.5
suicide	20.4	12.1	1.7
Alzheimer's disease	18.3	25.1	0.7
septicemia	17.3	10.6	1.6
homicide	11.4	5.4	2.1
essential hypertension diseases	9.0	8.0	1.1

*Unintentional injuries include motor vehicle crashes.

Source: Indian Health Service, "Disparities," https://www.ihs.gov/newsroom/factsheets/disparities/

SOLUTIONS AND INNOVATIONS

Time and again it is revealed as critical that federally recognized tribes are dealt with as sovereign entities as affirmed in the U.S. Constitution. The ongoing COVID-19 pandemic is yet another staggering moment in which such nation-to-nation relations are paramount. If tribes had been properly engaged, the HEROES Act would have been fashioned and implemented far more effectively. The following passage excerpted from 2020 testimony provided by the National Indian Health Board to the U.S. Commission on Civil Rights underscores both the challenges at hand and the need for tribes to be innovative as sovereign nations:

> Centuries of genocide, oppression, and simultaneously ignoring our appeals while persecuting Our People's ways of life persist—now manifest in the vast health and socioeconomic inequities we face during COVID-19. The historical

and intergenerational trauma our families endure, all rooted in colonization, are the underpinnings of our vulnerability to COVID-19. Indeed, we tell our stories of treaties, Trust responsibility and sovereignty here—over and over—and it often appears the listeners are numb to our historic and current truths. But the truth does not change: that is the ground we stand on.

Across the country, we hear heart wrenching accounts of Our People experiencing racism at the hands of our neighbors while battling a pandemic that continues to lay bare how under resourced our Indian health system is and how vulnerable are our economies. We hear baseless stories about how "dirty Indians" are causing the outbreaks, or how private hospitals are refusing to accept referrals to treat Our People. These same sentiments echoed across all previous disease outbreaks that plagued Our People, from Small Pox to HIV to H1N1. This begs the painful question: what has changed?[12]

From a tribal administration perspective, this question can be reoriented as "What must change?" There is a critical need for tribes to insist on and collaborate to improve the medical and health professional workforce at IHS, in tribal facilities, and within urban Indian service providers. This necessitates increasing the pipeline of AI/AN community members going into medicine and allied health services, providing better incentives for all health professional staff to work in Indian Country, and expanding associated scholarship and loan repayment programs. Tribal governments manage a wide range of services, including primary clinics, behavioral health services, Supplemental Nutrition Assistance Program (SNAP), Special Supplemental Nutrition Program for Women, Infants and Children (WIC), senior centers, elder nutrition sites, preventative rabies veterinary care, injury prevention programs, and many other efforts and initiatives. When compared to IHS direct services, tribal programs tend to be more grounded in the cultural practices and norms of the community members they serve.

IHS should be an entitlement with mandatory funding, or at the very least have advance appropriation authority so that tribes do not have a lapse in funding during times of continuing resolutions and government shutdowns. The IHS needs to request full funding to perform its required duties and uphold its trust responsibilities. The IHS should work in collaboration with tribes to determine its level of need funding and make those needs known to Congress.

The ISDEAA has been the most successful federal Indian policy in history and nearly all Indian nations utilize contracts and/or compacts. For more than three decades, Self-Determination and Self-Governance has proved to be an effective and efficient approach to implementing the government-to-government relationship that exists between the U.S. and tribal governments. Tribes should have the ability to incorporate concepts of the ISDEAA such as reprogramming, redesigning, reallocating, and lower administrative burden when providing HHS programs, services, functions, and activities. The one-size-fits-all approach does not work in Indian Country as each tribe has its own unique challenges and cultures. Incorporating these concepts will provide tribes the flexibility needed to address their communities' needs in a more efficient and effective manner. One way to better improve and maintain the health, safety, and welfare of tribal communities is by expanding the ISDEAA into the HHS. The growth and success of ISDEAA into the IHS is best documented by the over 360 tribes currently participating in contracts and compacts, as compared to the fourteen tribes that first entered into agreements in 1993/1994. In 2003, the HHS concluded that a Self-Governance demonstration project was feasible and a Tribal Federal Workgroup provided guidance in 2014. Expanding ISDEAA into HHS will fix the delay in funding, allow tribes to build capacity, tailor programs to fit their needs, allow for better planning, and allow more time helping the community as opposed to spending time on administrative work.

Culturally grounded approaches to food systems hold great promise to positively impact the high rates of food insecurity, diabetes, obesity, and related ailments within AI/AN communities. While the counties with a majority of AI/ANs represent less than 1 percent of the counties nationwide, as many as 60 percent of them are classified as food insecure.[13]

The Patient Protection and Affordable Care Act (ACA) included the permanent reauthorization of the IHCIA. The ACA offers important opportunities to increase health services and insurance coverage for AI/ANs to reduce long-standing disparities. According to the Kaiser Family Foundation policy report "Health Coverage and Care for American Indians and Alaska Natives," nine in ten uninsured American Indians and Alaska Natives have incomes in the range to qualify for these coverage expansions.[14] The ACA offers particularly significant opportunities to begin ameliorating the impact of behavioral health issues upon the lives of AI/AN communities. Mental illness and substance use disorders have been profoundly underestimated and culturally undefined in AI/AN populations. Most troubling is the fact that much of the personal and societal burden of behavioral health conditions and issues could be prevented or alleviated if people at risk for experiencing these conditions had access to and received culturally appropriate prevention and treatment care and services.[15]

Among AI/AN people there are a wide range of beliefs about illness, healing, and health. The concept of mental illness and beliefs about why and how it develops have many different meanings and interpretations among diverse AI/AN communities. Substance use disorders are likewise often understood in deep conjunction to related factors. Every tribe has its own cultural traditions at the foundation of how holistic well-being is understood, sought, achieved, and maintained. Successful behavioral health services make clear that regard for and use of those traditions to ground healing practices are most effective. Physical complaints and psychological concerns are often not distinguished for AI/AN patients, who may express emotional distress in ways not readily accounted for by standard diagnostic categories.[16]

Practitioner Perspective

Many times patients will forgo their appointments with specialists because the out-of-pocket costs are prohibitive, including loss of work time, child/elder care, home heating maintenance (freeze-up for those who only have wood as a heating source), livestock care, and home security issues. Currently, there is little literature available that assesses these expenses. These out-of-pocket costs create an extra hardship for AI/ANs, who may choose to feed their families and suffer the consequences of postponing their medical appointments until they require extensive and more costly procedures to save their lives. Certainly telemedicine will have a role in reducing some of these disparities, but the policies need to be further developed from a rural cost perspective. The Centers for Medicare and Medicaid, during the COVID-19 emergency, has shown how changing the criteria for paid telehealth encounters has greatly improved access to services for all populations. Previous to this change, reservations and rural areas had extremely limited access to any professional health services. Now, it is imperative that these reimbursable telemedicine encounters continue. Honestly speaking, telemedicine will save our health services on the reservations, as well as in all rural populations.

American Indians and Alaska Native people have long experienced lower health status when compared with other Americans. Lower life expectancy and disproportionate disease burden exist perhaps because of limited educational opportunities, disproportionate poverty, discrimination in the delivery of health services, and cultural differences. It is fundamentally necessary to understand that the AI/AN health and wellness system is unlike any other. It serves the poorest, sickest, and most remote populations in the United States. Each tribe's culture undergirds and guides their elected leadership to meet their respective unique needs in this complex environment. The Constitution, treaties, executive orders, and laws establish the federal government's responsibility to provide certain rights, protections, and health services to AI/ANs as a government-to-government relationship requirement.

Current knowledge about AI/ANs is severely lacking among the general public (including many state public-health staff), resulting in egregious actions because of failure to comprehend AI/AN health and wellness needs. There is little if any understanding that there are 574 federally recognized tribes, each totally unique. Often, the public has little to no knowledge of the accurate history of our country. Without this acknowledgment of knowing the history and status of tribes, the public-sector staff literally have no awareness of tribal governments, and this is resulting in a health status of AI/ANs that continues to decline to this day. Following is an example from a former student about the seriousness of public ignorance: The student's daughter, grade 3, was in a class that was celebrating "Heritage Week." When asked by the teacher, "What is your heritage?" the child responded, "I am an Indian." The teacher's response was: "Oh no, that is not correct, there are no Indians left."

NOTES

1. Indian Health Service, "IHS Profile," www.ihs.gov/newsroom/factsheets/ihsprofile/.
2. 42 CFR 36.12.
3. Testimony of National Indian Health Board—Stacy A. Bohlen. Hearing on Reviewing the Broken Promises Report: Examining the Chronic Federal Funding Shortfalls in Indian Country. House Committee on Natural Resources, Subcommittee on Indigenous Peoples of the United States, November 19, 2019, 10:00 a.m.
4. "Indian Health Service: Spending Levels and Characteristics of HIS and Three Other Federal Health Care Programs," December 10, 2018, https://www.gao.gov/assets/

gao-19-74r.pdf/, p. 12.

5. Testimony of National Indian Health Board—Stacy A. Bohlen.

6. U.S. Department of Health and Human Services. Office of Minority Health. "Profile: American Indian/Alaska Native," March 28, 2018, https://minorityhealth.hhs.gov/omh/browse.aspx?lvl=3&lvlid=62.

7. "As Rural Hospital Closure Crisis Deepens, New Research from The Chartis Center for Rural Health Reveals Scope of Hospitals Vulnerable to Closure," February 11, 2020, https://www.businesswire.com/news/home/20200211005662/en/Rural-Hospital-Closure-Crisis-Deepens-New-Research.

8. S. D. Towne Jr., L. M. Smith, and M. G. Ory. "Geographic Variations in Access and Utilization of Cancer Screening Services: Examining Disparities among American Indian and Alaska Native Elders." *International Journal of Health Geographics* 13 (2014).

9. U.S. Commission on Civil Rights. "Broken Promises: Continued Federal Funding Shortfall for Native Americans," https://www.usccr.gov/pubs/2018/12-20-Broken-Promises.pdf, p. 208.

10. Indian Health Service, "About HIS," https://www.ihs.gov/aboutihs.

11. U.S. Commission on Civil Rights, "Broken Promises," 207.

12. National Indian Health Board Written Testimony Submitted to the United States Commission on Civil Rights, July 17, 2020. Briefing "COVID-19 in Indian Country," July 17, 2020, https://www.nihb.org/covid-19/wp-content/uploads/2020/07/FINAL-NIHB-TESTIMONY-USCCR-COVID19-July-16-2020.pdf.

13. Feeding America, 2017. "Map the Meal Gap: Highlights for Overall and Child Food Insecurity," https://www.feedingamerica.org/sites/default/files/research/map-the-meal-gap/2015/2015-mapthemealgap-exec-summary.pdf.

14. Samantha Artiga, Rachel Arguello, and Philethea Duckett, Henry J. Kaiser Family Foundation. "Health Coverage and Care for American Indians and Alaska Natives," October 7, 2013, http://kff.org/disparities-policy/issue-brief/health-coverage-and-care-for-american-indians-and-alaska-natives/.

15. National Indian Health Board. "Indian Health 101," July 2014, http://www.nihb.org/tribal_resources/indian_health_101.php.

16. American Psychiatric Association, APA Fact Sheet, "Mental Health Disparities: American Indian and Alaska Natives," 2017, https://www.psychiatry.org/File%20Library/Psychiatrists/Cultural-Competency/Mental-Health-Disparities/Mental-Health-Facts-for-American-Indian-Alaska-Natives.pdf.

GLOSSARY

Cultural humility. A lifelong quest toward achieving positive outcomes in work with all populations and communities. It is essential that health care and health service providers learn about the respective cultures of the populations they serve. In order to practice true cultural humility, a person must also be aware of their own cultural traditions and mindful of historic realities such as legacies of violence and oppression against certain groups of people.

Health disparity. Generally preventable differences in the burden of disease, injury, violence, or opportunities to achieve optimal health and wellness that are experienced by minority populations.

Health equality. Giving everyone the same thing, no matter what the size, location, or economic status is of the population.

Health equity. Increasing opportunities for everyone to live the healthiest life possible, no matter what race, ethnicity, where people live, economic status, or population size. Health equity includes addressing assets (including strengths, resilience) and acknowledging disparities.

Health funding. The Indian Health Service (IHS) is required to work within yearly budgets approved by Congress and does not receive enough funds to meet all the health needs of American Indians and Alaska Natives. That is why IHS does not offer certain services and why some services aren't available at certain times of year. In fact, the IHS budget only meets about half of the need.

Health Service Law. A basis for guidance of the specific health and social justice rights for American Indians and Alaska Natives, including P.L. 93-638 and P.L. 94-437.

Health status. A state of complete physical, mental, and social well-being, and not merely the absence of disease or wellness. Health status can be considered in terms of a person's body structure and function and the presence or absence of disease or signs and symptoms, and the extent to which the environment, social disparities, and disabilities affect a person's normal life.

Historical American Indian and Alaska Native Health Services. A brief history of American Indians pre- and post-colonization as it relates to the health and wellness of present-day American Indians and Alaska Natives.

Indian Health Service. The federal agency that provides health services to American Indians and Alaska Natives. Located in the Department of Health and Human Services since 1955.

Tribal Natural Resources

Kekek Jason Stark

FOR MANY TRIBES, THE NATURAL RESOURCES OCCUPYING THE LAND AND WATERS encompassing their traditional territories contain deeply rooted principles grounded in culture, tradition, and law.[1] Tribes continue to utilize the natural resources of their territories for religious, ceremonial, medicinal, subsistence, and economic needs.[2] This article will discuss various aspects pertaining to tribal natural resources, including Indian title, Indian rights, the implementation of rights associated with traditional territories as well as on-reservation rights, and cultural resource sustainability.

BEST PRACTICES

- Remain mindful that the natural resources occupying the land and waters encompassing tribal traditional territories contain deeply rooted principles grounded in culture, tradition, and law.
- Realize that tribes continue to utilize the natural resources of their territories for religious, ceremonial, medicinal, subsistence, and economic needs.

- Remember that tribes possess exclusive rights to the natural resources that encompass reservation lands.
- Recognize that tribes have maintained the power of self-government within their territories, which includes the ability to regulate on- and off-reservation hunting, fishing, and gathering.

Case Study

This article will examine as a case study the Lake Superior and Mississippi Bands of Ojibwe. These bands, pursuant to the Treaties of 1837, 1842, and 1854, reserved their inherent right to hunt, fish, and gather in their traditional treaty territories (ceded territories) as well as on-reservation.

Original Indian (Aboriginal) Title

Under the theory of original Indian title, tribes have legal rights in the territories that they occupied.[3] Original Indian title, also known as aboriginal title, means the interests that tribes possess in their land based solely upon the rights acquired by them as the original inhabitants by virtue of possession and inherent tribal sovereignty.[4]

Proof of actual original Indian title depends on a showing of actual exclusive and continuous use and occupancy of a region for a long time.[5] The actual possession in the strict sense is not essential, and Indian title may be established through the tribe's intermittent contacts in the areas they controlled. Joint and amicable possession of property by two or more tribes or groups will not defeat Indian title.[6] A tribe's contention that it used and occupied an area since time immemorial is sufficient proof of Indian title or the right of occupancy because an accepted principle of federal Indian law is that tribes held "aboriginal title" to the territories they inhabited from time immemorial.[7]

Indian (Aboriginal) Rights

Deriving from a tribe's original Indian title are the inherent Indian (aboriginal) rights associated with that title. Indian rights include the rights to traditional lands and waters, all rights to practice traditional customs and religion, all rights to retain and develop Indian languages and cultures, and the rights to self-government.[8] Indian rights derive from ancestral use, that is, the use of a specifically allocated area for traditional purposes and cultural expression, which entails the use of the land and water for hunting, trapping, fishing, traditional cultivation, irrigation, transportation, and domestic uses.[9] Indian rights are: aboriginal rights, customary rights, usufructuary rights, usual privileges of occupancy, or permissive occupancy. Broadly defined to include all "beneficial incidents" of occupancy, Indian title includes the Indian rights to hunt, fish, and gather.[10] Treaties solidified Indian rights because the treaty was not a grant of rights to the Indians, but a grant of rights from them, a reservation of those not granted.[11] It is important to note that Indian rights can be severed from the tribe's original Indian title and continue to exist after a tribe's original Indian title is extinguished.[12]

Traditional Territories (Off-Reservation Treaty Reserved Territories)

Once a tribe establishes that it possessed original Indian title to its traditional territory, and that part and parcel of possessing Indian title are the Indian rights associated with that title, we then must examine whether those Indian rights continue to exist. It is a general principle that the Indian rights to use, harvest, and manage natural resources in a tribe's traditional territory was extinguished when the tribe's reservation was established unless these Indian rights were expressly reserved, typically in a treaty.[13] In the case of the Ojibwe, the tribes pursuant to the Treaties of 1837, 1842, and 1854 reserved the rights to hunt, fish, and gather in their traditional territory as defined in their treaty territories (ceded territories).

TREATY RESERVED RIGHTS ARE COMMUNAL RIGHTS

Once a tribe establishes that its Indian rights were expressly reserved and continue to exist, we then need to understand who possesses those rights. Treaty reserved rights are held communally by all treaty signatory tribes, and not individual tribal members.[14] Each tribal member has the right to exercise treaty rights, subject to their own tribe's authorization and regulation, because when and how an individual tribal member may use treaty rights is an "internal affair" of the tribe.[15]

Ojibwe treaty (off-reservation) reserved rights are intertribally shared. That means all of the treaty signatory tribes reserved these rights collectively.[16] This stems from the Ojibwe clan system principle that wherever you go as an individual, there is always a place for you among your fellow clan relatives in other communities. This concept of collective identity was recognized in Article V of the 1842 Treaty with the Chippewa, which established "whereas the whole country between Lake Superior and the Mississippi, has always been understood, as belonging in common to the Chippewas, party to this treaty." The implications of these rights being intertribally shared are that the tribes must undertake effective management programs and adopt and enforce regulations consistent with reasonable and necessary conservation, public health, and public safety standards; stay within the tribal allocation of the resources; and engage in intertribal co-management to effectively manage and regulate the treaty resources.

INTERTRIBAL COORDINATION OF TREATY RESERVED RIGHTS

Tribes that communally possess treaty reserved rights must intertribally coordinate the exercise of those rights in their treaty territories (ceded territories). The effect of an uncoordinated harvest system is that the state could have the ability to regulate treaty-related harvest activity by claiming state regulation is a necessity to limit the harvest of a particular resource. As a matter of law, tribes typically have a collective allocation consisting of a maximum of 50 percent of the total allowable harvest equation. By not effectively self-coordinating tribal harvest, the state could impose allocations as a means of limiting the tribal harvest by ensuring that the tribes will not overharvest and thereby protect the resource. The state could also compel state regulation of treaty harvest activities if the tribes have not enacted sufficient tribal regulations. Tribal regulations must adequately address legitimate state concerns in the areas of conservation of the resources and public health and safety. By not having tribal codes in place that address these concerns, the state can argue for the application of state regulations to tribal treaty harvest activities.

TREATY RESERVED RIGHTS CAN BE EXERCISED THROUGHOUT THE TREATY TERRITORIES

Once a tribe establishes that its Indian rights were expressly reserved and continue to exist, and that those rights are communal and need to be shared intertribally, we then need to understand where those rights can be exercised. In the Great Lakes region, the only limit on the exercise of Ojibwe reserved rights is to the areas within the treaty territory.[17] The Treaties of 1837, 1842, and 1854 do not contain any language restricting the tribes' treaty reserved rights to only certain areas.[18] The Court recognized that with respect to allocation of the resources, the tribes were required to take their 50 percent share throughout the treaty territory, and that they could not concentrate their harvest in a particular area (e.g., the establishment of tribal management zones and the prohibition on establishing zones of exclusivity regarding the harvest of walleye).[19] The Court recognized that the Ojibwe were divided into separate bands, and that each band occupied a fairly distinct territory:

> The Chippewa were divided into independent bands. Each band had its own chief and each occupied a fairly distinct territory. The territories were based on use by a family or a group of families or by the natural resources of the territory. The roving habits of the Chippewa as a whole and the Chippewa's territoriality tended to disperse the Indian population in the ceded territory while avoiding the exhaustion of the natural resources. This dispersal diminished, however, as the Chippewa became increasingly involved in trade … As among Chippewa members, the Chippewa economy was a system of reciprocity. An important element of this system was sharing. The scarcer a resource became, the more willing the Chippewa were to share it.[20]

COMMERCIAL ACTIVITY AND TREATY RESERVED RIGHTS

Once a tribe establishes that its Indian rights were expressly reserved and continue to exist and that those rights are communal, that the rights need to be shared intertribally, and that the rights can be exercised throughout the treaty territory, we then need to understand whether those rights can be utilized for commercial purposes. Historically, the Ojibwe were clearly engaged in commerce throughout the treaty era and that commercial activity was a major factor in Ojibwe subsistence.[21] The court decided that the "fruits" of the exercise of treaty reserved rights may be traded and sold today to non-Indians, employing modern methods of distribution and allocation, and are not limited to any particular technique, methods, devices, or gear.[22]

RESOURCE ALLOCATION STANDARD AND TREATY RESERVED RIGHTS

Off-reservation treaty reserved rights are generally not exclusive rights, but, rather, shared with non-members.[23] Deriving from the notion of sharing the natural resources associated with Indian rights is the resource allocation standard. The resource allocation standard is grounded on the premise that both tribal and non-tribal users are entitled to a "fair share" of the harvest in the treaty territory, or the area subject to nonexclusive treaty harvest activities.[24] Tribes are entitled to take nonexclusive resources sufficient to ensure a moderate living, up to a maximum of 50 percent of the harvestable resources.[25] The 50 percent cap applies even if tribal harvest of all the resources would not be sufficient to provide the Indians with a moderate living.[26] The Court has further determined that in unusual circumstances, such as a drastic decline in tribal population or tribal abandonment of the resources, the tribal allocation could be modified downward.[27]

Instead of a pro rata allocation of the resources, the bands in the *Mille Lacs* litigation created management plans to allow for the gradual development of treaty harvests. In light of these plans, the bands asserted that there was no need to allocate the resources between Indian and non-Indian harvesters. The bands took the position that the 1837 Treaty provides them a nonexclusive right to the harvestable resources in the Minnesota portion of the treaty territory, not an unlimited right. Therefore, the bands acknowledged that non-Indian harvesters have a right to a fair share of the resources. The Court held that given the fact that the bands' Management Plan and Code restricts the bands' harvest well below the equal share of the available harvest, the state could not show the bands' harvest would impinge on the non-Indians' right to a fair share requiring the allocation of a fixed share of the resource.[28] The Court went on to discuss that the allocation of the resources is only appropriate when the circumstances involved in the case are fully developed.[29] The Court pointed out that the bands should be allowed to fully develop their capacity to exercise their treaty rights before any allocation of the resources is required.[30] In *LCO VII*, the court only agreed to make an allocation for deer because the heavy demand between the Indian and non-Indian harvesters exceeded the available supply.[31] The Court discussed:

> The non-Indian demand for antlerless deer exceeds the available supply. In this sense, deer hunting is unlike non-Indian angling which is essentially self-regulating ... The showing of heavy competition establishes the predicate for addressing the issue of allocation. The full development of the record makes it possible to do so.[32]

THE TRIBAL OFF-RESERVATION SELF-REGULATION STANDARD

Once a tribe establishes its share or allocation of treaty reserved resources, we then need to understand who gets to regulate those harvest activities. The tribes possess the authority to regulate their members in the exercise of treaty rights off-reservation in the treaty territory. Effective tribal self-regulation of a particular resource or activity precludes state regulation.[33] Where the tribes responsibly ensure that conservation and public health and safety goals are met, the legitimate interests of the state are not contravened. If a tribe can show that it is adequately regulating its members to ensure perpetuation of the resource, state regulation is unnecessary. The state may regulate only in the absence of effective Indian tribal self-regulation.[34]

The tribes may regulate their members exclusive of state regulation so long as the tribal self-regulation is effective. For purposes of preclusion of state regulation, the following must occur: tribal regulations must adequately address legitimate state concerns in the areas of conservation of resources and public health and safety; there must be effective enforcement mechanisms, including competent and adequately trained enforcement personnel; there must be a form of official tribal identification for tribal members exercising treaty reserved rights in the treaty territory; and there must be a full exchange of information between the tribes and the state, including scientific and management information, and harvest data of any given resource in any geographic area.[35]

THE STATE OFF-RESERVATION REGULATION STANDARD

Tribes and states possess concurrent authority to regulate the off-reservation tribal exercise of treaty rights in the interests of conservation or the public welfare; however, effective tribal regulation precludes concurrent state regulation.[36] A state may only regulate treaty-rights-related activities if the regulations are reasonable and necessary, the regulation does not discriminate against the Indians, and it is the least restrictive alternative available to accomplish its purpose.[37]

A regulation is determined to be *reasonable* when it is appropriate to its purpose. A regulation is deemed to be appropriate when the essential nature of the regulation depends upon showing that there is a need for the regulation; the particular regulation is reasonable to effectuate the necessary measure; the regulation's application to the tribes is necessary; and the particular regulation for the Indians cannot be achieved solely through the regulation of non-treaty users of the resource.

A regulation is *necessary* if proven essential. The nondiscrimination prong requires that the regulation, in language and effect, shall not discriminatorily harm the Indian harvest; and the regulation, in language and effect, shall not discriminatorily favor non-treaty harvesters.[38] Once these stipulations are met, the state may still only regulate treaty rights so long as the regulations imposed are the least restrictive alternative available to accomplish their purpose.

THE ELEMENTS OF AN EFFECTIVE OFF-RESERVATION TRIBAL SELF-REGULATION SYSTEM

Tribes may block state regulation if tribes effectively regulate themselves and protect legitimate state conservation, health, and safety interests.[39] Tribal laws are deemed to be "effective" if they are capable of achieving conservation and health safety goals, i.e., perpetuation of the resource with a reasonable margin of safety against extinction, and of preventing a substantial risk to public health and safety. Conservation (or health and safety) goals are distinct from management goals. State management goals may include distribution among user groups, development of "trophy" specimens, and promoting tourism. Tribal management goals may include the enhancement of nutrition, economic development, perpetuation of traditions, and promoting tourism. Conservation goals may be expressed in terms of population numbers, distribution, harvestable numbers, escapement numbers, and the number of breeding pairs.

The effectiveness of a tribal self-regulation system is judged by evaluating each tribe or group of tribes according to the following criteria:

- The tribe must have an organized tribal government.
- The tribe must possess codified laws that protect the natural resources, public safety, and public health.
- The tribe must have adequate personnel to enforce the laws.
- The tribe must have an organized judicial system.
- There must be experts in natural resources and natural-resource management.
- The achievement of resource management and conservation goals should be met through intergovernmental cooperation.

TRIBAL LANDS (ON-RESERVATION)

Once a tribe establishes that it possessed original Indian title to its traditional territory, and that part and parcel of possessing Indian title are the Indian rights associated with that title, when a tribe's reservation is established, it is a basic premise of federal Indian law that tribes possess exclusive rights to the natural resources that reservation lands encompass. These exclusive rights are implied, and do not need to be mentioned in the action that established the reservation (whether by treaty, executive order, statute, or agreement).[40] This general rule applies unless the right to use the natural resources has been expressly abrogated by treaty or statute.[41] With regard to trust and restricted lands, the United States as trustee also owes an obligation to the tribe (or allottee) to oversee the management of these natural resources pursuant to its trust responsibility. As the beneficial owner of its natural resources, Indigenous nations are able to directly develop its natural resources.[42] In the absence of direct development, many Indigenous nations lease their lands for use by others for mining, timber harvesting, grazing, agriculture, and general surface uses.

When an extraction project is proposed affecting tribal resources, it is important that tribes develop the expertise and capacity to understand the proposed project as well as the potential impacts to the natural resources. This includes a specific fact and location analysis. It is important that tribes require a permit or lease applicant to anticipate and solve problems with their extraction plans before they occur, as the history of extraction projects has shown that often problems cannot be adequately fixed once they begin. Tribes must ensure that the process provides enough flexibility to address changes to the project or unexpected information.

REGULATION OF ON-RESERVATION RIGHTS

Tribes have maintained the power of self-government within their reservations, which includes the ability to regulate hunting, fishing, and gathering.[43] Unlike off-reservation lands, where a state has the ability to regulate tribal treaty rights upon a showing of conservation or public, health, and safety purposes, on-reservation lands may only be regulated by a state in "exceptional circumstances."[44] Absent exceptional circumstances, a state is precluded from regulating the usage of on-reservation natural resources.[45]

FEDERAL REGULATION

Federal agencies may regulate tribal natural resources, on- and off-reservation, if the regulation is supported by congressionally delegated powers, is warranted by the tribe's treaty, and is consistent with the agency's trust responsibilities. The Tenth Circuit upheld interim game regulations established by the Department of the Interior when the two cooperatively governing tribes, the Shoshone and Northern Arapaho, were unable to reach agreement on a uniform code.[46] The application of federal laws to tribes does not affect tribal powers or treaty rights unless Congress specifically intends them to, or a tribe specifically agrees to their application. Federal laws modifying or affecting tribal natural-resource rights must specifically show, either in the body of a law or in the legislative history, Congress's intent to interfere with those rights. An additional tool for tribes is the Lacey Act, which makes it a federal crime for any person to traffic in fish, wildlife, or plants taken in violation of federal, tribal, or state law.[47]

CULTURAL RESOURCE SUSTAINABILITY

The Ojibwe have a mutual duty and respect for the resources of their territories. From this relationship, the Ojibwe have been able to develop harvest and management protocols as key components of Ojibwe cultural preservation matching the needs of the Ojibwe with the capability of the earth to produce and sustain the natural resources. The wide range of resources harvested by the Ojibwe means that a wide range of healthy ecosystems are necessary to support those resources. A disruption to the ecosystems that sustain Ojibwe harvest practices equates to a disruption to Ojibwe culture. As a result, the interests of the Ojibwe in the sustainability of their natural resources can be qualitatively different than those of other citizens. The Ojibwe must reconcile historic Ojibwe adaptability and resiliency with how much ecological disruption is too much for Ojibwe culture to endure. As a result, the Ojibwe have increasingly become involved in environmental issues that affect numerous ecosystems within their territories. When the state is considering actions affecting tribal natural resources (on-reservation as well as in treaty territories) consultation is required. The Ojibwe often look to federal agencies as the treaty signatory to help ensure the protections of treaty resources.

PRACTITIONER PERSPECTIVE

My takeaways for tribal natural-resource managers is to encourage managers to engage natural-resource regulatory systems to ensure that these systems, encompassing the tribal code, management plans, and regulatory protocols, adequately reflect tribal custom, values, and traditions. As a manager it is your responsibility to uphold your obligations to the tribe, the tribal membership, as well as to the resources themselves. In this regard, I encourage managers to talk about their natural-resource management systems with the harvesters, elders, knowledge keepers, and the membership at large. In doing this, you will ensure that your natural-resource regulatory systems retain their unique tribal characteristics.

NOTES

1. Sarah Laslett, *The Ancestor's Breath in the Voice of the Water: Connecting Land and Language in the Ojibwe Revitalization Movement*, 2:1 Oshkaabewis Native Journal 15 (1995).

2. Ann McCammon-Soltis and Kekek Jason Stark, "Fulfilling Ojibwe Treaty Promises— An Overview and Compendium of Relevant Cases, Statutes and Agreements," in *Minwaajimo: Telling a Good Story—Preserving Ojibwe Treaty Rights for the Past 25 Years* (Odanah, WI: Great Lakes Indian Fish and Wildlife Commission Press, 2011).

3. Michael J. Kaplin, *Proof and Extinguishment of Aboriginal Title to Indian Lands.* 41 A.L.R. Fed. 425.

4. *Id.*

5. Wilcomb E. Washburn, *Original Indian Title (Revisited)*, in *Readings in American Indian Law: Recalling the Rhythm of Survival*, edited by Jo Carrillo, citing *U.S. v. Seminole Indians of the State of Florida*, 180 Ct. Cl. 375, 1967.

6. *Confederated Tribes of Warm Springs Reservation v. United States.* 177 Ct. Cl. 184 (1966); *United States v. Pueblo of San Ildefonzo.* 513 F2d 1383 (1975).

7. *Narragansett Tribe of Indians v. Southern Rhode Island Land Development Corp.* 418 F. Supp. 798 (DC RI 1976). See Felix Cohen, *Original Indian Title*, 32 Minn. L. Rev. 28 (1947).

8. Michael Asch, *Home and Native Land: Aboriginal Rights and the Canadian Constitution* 27 (Methuen Publications 1984).

9. Richard Bartlett, *Aboriginal Water Rights in Canada: A Study of Aboriginal Title to Water and Indian Water Rights* 56 (Canadian Institute of Resources Law 1986).

10. *Shoshone v. United States*, 299 U.S. 476, 496 (1937); *United States v. Minnesota*, 466 F. Supp. 1382, 1385 (D. Minn. 1977).

11. *U.S. v. Winans*, 198 U.S. 371, 381 (1905).

12. *Lac Courte Oreilles Band of Lake Superior Chippewa v. Wisconsin (LCO I)*, 700 F.2d 341, 352 (7th Cir. 1983).

13. *United States v. Santa Fe P.R. Co.*, 314 U.S. 339, 347 (1941).

14. *United States v. Washington*, 520 F.2d 676, 688 (9th Cir. 1975); *United States v. Michigan*, 471 F. Supp 192, 271 (W.D. Mich. 1979), *aff'd as modified*, 653 F. 2d 277 (6th Cir. 1981); *Lac Courte Oreilles v. Wisconsin (LCO III)*, 653 F. Supp. 1420 (W.D. Wis. 1987); *Mille Lacs Band v. State of Minnesota*, Case No. 3-94-1226 (D. Minn. 1996) (unpublished decision).

15. *Winans*, 198 U.S. at 381 (1905); *Settler v. Lameer*, 506 F. 2d. 231, 237–238 (9th Cir. 1974); *United States v. Washington*, 384 F. Supp. 312, 340–342 (W.D. Wash. 1974), *aff'd*, 520 f.2d 676, 686 (9th Cir. 1974); *Washington v. Wash. State Commercial Passenger Fishing Vessel Ass'n*, 443 U.S. 658, 684 (1979); *Michigan*, 471 F. Supp. at 273; *United States v. Felter*, 546 F. Supp. 1002, 1022–1023 (D. Utah 1982), *aff'd*, 752 F.2d 1505 (10th Cir. 1985); *Lac Courte Oreilles v. Wisconsin (LCO IV)*, 668 F. Supp 1233, 1241 (W.D. Wis. 1987); *United States v. Oregon*, 787 F. Supp. 1557, 1566 (D. Or. 1992) *aff'd*, 29 F.3d 481 (1994).

16. See *Lac Courte Oreilles*, 653 F. Supp. at 1420.

17. *Mille Lacs Band*, Case No. 3-94-1226, at 40.

18. *Id.*

19. *Id.* citing *Lac Courte Oreilles v. Wisconsin (LCO VII)*, 740 F. Supp. 1400, 1418 (W.D. Wis. 1990); See also *Lac Courte Oreilles v. Wisconsin (LCO VI)*, 707 F. Supp. 1034, 1418 (W.D. Wis. 1989).

20. *Mille Lacs Band*, Case No. 3-94-1226, at 40 citing *Lac Courte Oreilles*, 653 F. Supp. at 1424–1425.

21. *Lac Courte Oreilles*, 653 F. Supp. at 1430.

22. *Id.* See also *Mille Lacs Band v. State of Minnesota*, 861 F. Supp 784 (D. Minn. 1994).

23. *Puyallup Tribe v. Department of Fish and Game (Puyallup I)*, 391 U.S. 392, 398 (1968); *Lac Courte Oreilles*, 740 F. Supp. at 1416.

24. *Washington*, 443 U.S. 658, 684 (1979).

25. *Id.* at 686; *Lac Courte Oreilles*, 740 F. Supp. at 1418.

26. *Lac Courte Oreilles v. Wisconsin (LCO V)*, 686 F. Supp 226, 227 (W.D. Wis. 1988). An exception to this general rule is that the tribes have had the occasional opportunity to harvest more than 50 percent of the harvestable surplus on a particular water body, while not creating "zones of exclusivity."

27. *Washington*, 443 U.S. at 686–687; *Lac Courte Oreilles*, 740 F. Supp. at 1418.

28. *Mille Lacs Band v. State of Minnesota*, 952 F. Supp. 1362, 1388–1389 (D. Minn. 1997); See also *Idaho ex. rel. Evans*, 462 U.S. 1017, 1027 (1982).

29. *Id.*

30. *Id.*

31. *Lac Courte Oreilles*, 740 F. Supp. at 1414.

32. *Id.*

33. See *Washington*, 520 F.2d at 686 n. 4; *Michigan*, 471 F. Supp at 274; *Lac Courte Oreilles*, 668 F. Supp at 1241–1242; *Lac Courte Oreilles*, 707 F. Supp at 1055; *Mille Lacs Band*, 952 F. Supp. at 1369–1375.

34. *Lac Courte Oreilles*, 668 F. Supp at 1241–1242.

35. *Id.*; *Mille Lacs Band*, 952 F. Supp. at 1374.

36. *Washington*, 520 F.2d at 686 n. 4; *Michigan*, 471 F. Supp. at 274; *Lac Courte Oreilles*, 668 F. Supp. at 1241–1242; *Mille Lacs Band*, 861 F. Supp. at 836; *Mille Lacs Band*, 952 F. Supp. at 1374.

37. See *Puyallup*, 391 U.S. at 398. See, e.g., *United States v. Michigan*, 653 F.2d 277, 279 (6th Cir. 1981); *Lac Courte Oreilles*, 740 F. Supp. at 1421–1422; *Mille Lacs Band*, 861 F. Supp. at 836–838.

38. See *Puyallup*, 391 U.S. at 398; *Michigan*, 653 F.2d at 279; *Lac Courte Oreilles*, 668 F. Supp at 1236.

39. *Lac Courte Oreilles*, 668 F. Supp. at 1237–1239; See *Washington*, 384 F. Supp. at 340–341.

40. *Menominee Tribe v. United States*, 391 U.S. 404, 406 (1968); *United States v. Aanerud*, 893 F. 2d 956, 958 (8th Cir. 1990).

41. *United States v. Shoshone Tribe*, 304 U.S. 111 (1938).

42. See, e.g., Thomas H. Shipps, *Tribal Energy Resource Agreements: A Step toward Self-Determination*, 22 Nat. Res. & Env't 55, 56 (Summer 2007).

43. *New Mexico v. Mescalero Apache Tribe*, 462 U.S. 324, 330 (1983).

44. *Id.* at 331–332.

45. *Id.* at 332 n.15.

46. *Northern Arapaho Tribe v. Hodel*, 808 F. 2d 741 (10th Cir. 1981).

47. Lacey Act, 16 U.S.C. § 3372(a).

GLOSSARY

Indian rights. The term Indian rights, also known as aboriginal rights, means the rights derived from ancestral use, that is, the use of a specifically allocated area for traditional purposes and cultural expression, which entails the use of the land and water for hunting, trapping, fishing, traditional cultivation, irrigation, transportation, and domestic uses.

Indian title. The term Indian title, also known as aboriginal title, means the interests that tribes possess in their land based solely upon the rights acquired by them as the original inhabitants by virtue of possession and inherent tribal sovereignty.

Intertribal. The term intertribal refers to the tribes or bands that collectively possess Indian rights in common.

LCO litigation. The term LCO litigation refers to the *Lac Courte Oreilles Band v. Wisconsin* line of cases involving the existence, nature, and scope of the Indian rights reserved pursuant to the 1837 and 1842 Treaties with the Chippewa.

Mille Lacs litigation. The term Mille Lacs litigation refers to the *Minnesota v. Mille Lacs Band* line of cases involving the existence, nature, and scope of the Indian rights reserved pursuant to the 1837 Treaty with the Chippewa.

Regulation. The term regulation refers to codified laws that protect the natural resource, public safety, and public health.

Traditional territories. The term traditional territories refers to the geographical area that a tribe or band historically used and occupied.

PART 3

Sovereign Tribes Engaging Settler Governments

HISTORICALLY, TRIBES FORMED INTERGOVERNMENTAL AGREEMENTS WITH EACH other and established trade networks that spanned throughout North and South America. Diplomacy was a critical component to survival and cooperation. When the Europeans arrived with their sights set on conquest and manifest destiny, tensions quickly arose between the original inhabitants and the new immigrants. Colonization, assimilation, and removal efforts over generations left Indigenous people not only minorities in their own homelands, but often subject to the laws of settler governments. This is our reality today. We are now charged with navigating complex jurisdictional rules involving tribal members and tribal lands, understanding federal lawmaking processes that impact tribal governments, negotiating mutually beneficial agreements with settler governments, and considering wielding our collective power to influence settler elections.

Jurisdiction and Law in Indian Country

Krystal L. John

THIS CHAPTER DISCUSSES CONGRESS' PLENARY POWER OVER FEDERAL INDIAN law and the resultant criminal and civil jurisdiction in Indian Country through analysis of Public Law 280 and case law. It also discusses treaty making, law-making, tribal constitutions and citizenship, and enrollment in Indian Country. Laced throughout such discussions will be underlying tribal/federal relations, including the federal government's trust responsibility and tribal/state relations.

BEST PRACTICES

- Review case law and applicable laws to understand basic criminal and civil jurisdiction.
- Consider the current legal and political environment, including the U.S. Supreme Court, federal appellate courts, and federal district courts, when making decisions that may challenge tribal jurisdiction/ sovereignty.
- Understand and monitor pending threats to tribal jurisdiction/ sovereignty.
- Consider the impacts an adverse legal decision would have within your own community and throughout Indian Country.

- Discuss with other tribal nations (hereinafter "nations") who may have encountered similar scenarios.
- Advocate for and participate in federal legislation that works to keep tribal sovereignty and jurisdictional problems at the forefront.
- Seek feedback/counsel from your nation's legal representative before acting.

INTRODUCTION

Our nations have occupied the lands now considered the United States for centuries, and our governments predate all forms of American democracy.

The term "sovereignty" is used across Indian Country, but is exercised uniquely in each community and often with much confusion. Nations were never expected to exist in 2020, and yet here we are, still arguing in our own communities, with other local governments and tribal governments, with the federal government, and sometimes even internationally about our ability to self-govern based on our sovereignty.

Williams v. Lee defined "sovereignty" as the right to make laws and be governed by them.[1] Tribal sovereignty does not fit neatly into many standard definitions of sovereign nations, and are often mutual sovereigns whose boundaries, and therefore jurisdictions, overlap with other sovereigns. Sovereignty is always messy—tribal sovereignty is especially messy. To understand it, one must understand inherent versus delegated sovereignty.

Inherent sovereignty most closely embodies the textbook definition of "sovereignty" and represents power our nations hold as governments exerting their own authority. However, the United States has claimed that our nations' sovereign immunity has been limited through treaties, federal laws, and/or court decisions. Delegated sovereignty is power that Congress gives to tribes. An example of delegated sovereignty is the granting of criminal jurisdiction to tribes over non-tribal members in certain statutes, like the Violence Against Women Act (VAWA), which in actuality restored inherent authority that had been previously taken by the courts.

It is through this inherent and delegated sovereignty that nations exercise jurisdiction (the ability to carry out and enforce governance) and sovereign immunity. Just as sovereignty can look different for each tribal nation, jurisdiction and the applicability of sovereign immunity often vary from one nation to another.

PLENARY POWER OF CONGRESS

Congress has claimed plenary power to pass laws impacting Indian tribes,[2] which has proven to be dangerous for our nations through several dark eras of federal Indian law and policy such as treaties, allotments, and assimilation and termination. Congress's federal Indian law and policy has transitioned through the following eras:

- Treaties: The first federal policy was to enter treaties with nations, which recognized their sovereignty and self-governance.
- Allotments and Assimilation: Then federal Indian policy pushed assimilative goals to break up tribal landholdings and to assimilate Indian people into mainstream society. The Dawes Act of 1887 and other allotment acts during this time authorized the President to subdivide tribal land holdings into allotments for individual tribal members and families' heads of household. The allotments given to tribal members and families remained in trust status for twenty-five years, then were transferred to the individual in fee status with citizenship. This terminated the federal government's trust responsibility over the land, which, in turn, resulted in taxation, possible tax foreclosure, and the ability to fully alienate the land. Pursuant to allotment, Indian land decreased from 138 million acres to only 48 million acres, of which nearly 20 million acres were desert lands.[3]
- Reorganization: After allotment and assimilation goals failed to assimilate Indians into mainstream society, federal policy swung to reorganization. Among other things, the Indian Reorganization Act of 1934 stopped the allotment process and provided a mechanism for tribes to rebuild their land bases.[4]
- Termination Era: After reorganization, federal policy again focused on minimizing the trust responsibility owed tribes by terminating

federal recognition and with it the trust responsibility owed to various nations.

- Self-Determination Era: We are in the self-determination era, where the goal of federal policy is to exercise the trust responsibility, recognizing that individual nations are in the best position to identify what is and is not in their nation's best interests. In this era, we see the Indian Civil Rights Act (addressing tribes' punitive capabilities by increasing the amount of fines that can be imposed and duration of incarceration); the Native American Grave Protection and Repatriation Act (secures Native burial sites and sacred remains and requires their keepers to return them to tribes even if held by a museum); the Violence Against Women Act (giving tribes limited jurisdiction over non-tribal members for violent crimes committed against women on reservations); and the Helping Expedite and Advance Responsible Tribal Home Ownership (HEARTH) Act (transferring the responsibility for approving leases on tribal trust land from the Department of Interior–Bureau of Indian Affairs to nations meeting HEARTH Act requirements).

Treaties and Their Relationship to Federal Indian Legislation

The original recognition of tribal sovereignty by the federal government was the practice of dealing with tribes on a government-to-government basis by entering treaties with nations. The majority of the treaties were related to nations ceding land to the federal government in exchange for limited rights of continued use and occupancy protected by the federal government. All tribal treaties were required to be signed by both parties and required approval from Congress.[5] The treaty-making era lasted from 1774 to 1871.[6] After the practice of entering treaties ended, tribal sovereignty was subject to interpretation by the U.S. Supreme Court, and the only method for Congress to transact with nations became legislation.

In deciphering the meaning of treaties, courts construe them in favor of tribes, settle ambiguities in favor of tribes, and interpret them in the manner the tribes would have originally understood them.[7]

These guidelines of interpretations were developed in large part due to the language barriers that existed, the uneven bargaining power between tribes and the federal government, and the federally appointed negotiators who were not always recognized tribal leaders. As a result, the judiciary has the goal of making lasting law by restoring trust.

Treaties entered between nations and the federal government continue to impact the applicability of federal laws. For example, federal statutes of general applicability, like the Endangered Species Act, apply to tribal members even on reservations, unless specifically excluded from the law by Congress. However, the guidelines of interpretation for treaties, in some circumstances, have been expanded to federal statutes, largely those regarding tribes' reserved rights. In these circumstances, some courts will construe statutes in favor of tribes, even when they are not mentioned in the statute, by limiting the general applicability rule to require express intent by Congress to cancel treaty rights.[8]

When considering whether a treaty or statute applies, the general rule is that whichever became effective later in time is the provision that stands. That means that when Congress was both entering treaties and legislating, Congress could have promised land-use rights to nations in a treaty and then passed a statute a year later taking those property rights away. Where a property right is taken away by statute, the tribal nation must be compensated pursuant to the Takings Clause of the Constitution, but Congress is not required to pay for taking governance rights.[9]

TRIBAL SOVEREIGNTY AS INITIALLY FRAMED BY THE U.S. SUPREME COURT

The Marshall Trilogy is a set of three landmark cases, all authored by Justice John Marshall, that framed the legal depth of tribal sovereignty and jurisdiction, which, subject to further elaboration/modification, continues to provide the legal framework for tribal sovereignty and jurisdiction today. The first case was *Johnson v. McIntosh*. It birthed the "discovery doctrine," stating the "discovering" party (which was Britain and transferred to the United States) has all title rights, subject only to the Indian right of occupancy. The second case was *Cherokee Nation v. Georgia*. It coined the term "domestic dependent nations" in reference to tribes and recognized the relationship between the federal government and tribes as that of a guardian and ward. The final case was *Worcester v. Georgia.* It held that tribes retain the right of self-governance, the federal government has sole authority over tribes, states' laws have no force within Indian Country, and states may not act where Congress has chosen not to.

JURISDICTION IN INDIAN COUNTRY

Jurisdiction and property in Indian Country is very messy because old statutes, policies, and treaties were never overturned or terminated; rather they were layered on top of one another. The determination of jurisdiction can depend on a combination of the following factors:

- Which state you are in
- Which nation you are dealing with within the state
- Which treaties/statutes apply
- What was the conduct
- What is the title status of the land where the activity occurred
- If criminal, was the person who committed the crime Indian or non-Indian
- If criminal, was the victim Indian or non-Indian

Criminal Jurisdiction

Table 1 summarizes criminal jurisdiction for crimes committed within Indian Country in states where Public Law 280 does not apply (Public Law 280 is explained more thoroughly later in this chapter).

Civil Jurisdiction

Civil jurisdiction in Indian Country starts with the assumption from *Worcester v. Georgia* that tribes retain the right to self-government and that the laws of the state have no force within Indian Country. If nations were treated as states when exercising civil jurisdiction, they would have the authority to regulate all

Table 1. Criminal Jurisdiction in Indian Country

DEFENDANT	VICTIM	FEDERAL JURISDICTION	TRIBAL JURISDICTION	STATE JURISDICTION
Indian	Indian	Major Crimes* General Fed. Crimes[†]	All Crimes—*perhaps only non-major crimes*[‡]	None
Indian	Non-Indian	Major Crimes Enclave Crimes[§] Assimilated Crimes[ǁ] General Fed. Crimes	All Crimes—*perhaps only non-major crimes*	None
Indian	None	Assimilated Crimes General Fed. Crimes	All Crimes	None
Non-Indian	Indian	Enclave Crimes[#] Assimilated Crimes General Fed. Crimes	None**	None††
Non-Indian	Non-Indian	General Fed. Crimes	None	All Crimes‡‡
Non-Indian	None	Enclave Crimes[§§] Assimilated Crimes General Fed. Crimes	None	Apparentlyǁǁ

*. Major Crimes Act (MCA), 18 U.S.C. §§ 1153, 3242. Federal jurisdiction may exist over lesser included offenses if the defendant requests a lesser included offense jury instruction. See *Keeble v. United States*, 412 U.S. 205, 211-12 (1973). Indian against Indian crimes otherwise covered by the ICCA are expressly exempted, which also makes the ACA inapplicable.

†. Several courts have held that generally applicable federal criminal laws that are not limited by the location of the act apply regardless of assignment of criminal jurisdiction in Indian Country. *See, e.g., United States v. White*, 237 F.3d 170, 172-74 (2d Cir. 2001) (federal tax reporting law); *United States v. Wadena*, 152 F.3d 831, 840-42 (8th Cir. 1998) (federal election conspiracy law), *cert. denied*, 526 U.S. 1050 (1999); *United States v. Yannott*, 42 F.3d 999, 1003-04 (6th Cir. 1994) (federal firearms laws), *cert. denied*, 513 U.S. 1182 (1995).

‡. It is an open question if federal jurisdiction under the MCA is the only applicable jurisdiction to major crimes. Compare *Solem v. Bartlett*, 465 U.S. 463, 465 n. 2 (1984) ("Tribes exercise concurrent jurisdiction over certain minor crimes by Indians") with *United States v. Antelope*, 430 U.S. 641, 643 n.2 (1977) ("Except for the offenses enumerated in the Major Crimes Act, all crimes committed by enrolled Indians against other Indians within Indian Country are subject to the jurisdiction of tribal courts."), with *Wetsit v. Stafne*, 44 F.3d 823, 825 (9th Cir. 1995) ("A tribal court . . . in compliance with the Indian Civil Rights Act is competent to try a tribal member for a crime also prosecutable under the Major Crimes Act.").

§. Indian Country Crimes Act (ICCA), 18 US.C. § 1152, creates federal jurisdiction for certain offenses committed by Indians against non-Indians and for all offenses committed by non-Indians against Indians. *But see United States v. Langford*, 641 F.3d 1195, 1196 (10th Cir. 2011) (an ACA case held "federal courts do not have authority over victimless crimes committed by non-Indians in Indian Country"). Federal jurisdiction exists unless the tribe adjudicates the Indian defendant. 18 U.S.C. § 1152.

ǁ. Assimilative Crimes Act (ACA), 18 U.S.C. § 13.

#. Crimes by non-Indians otherwise prosecutable under the Major Crimes Act are not federally prosecutable because the defendant must be an Indian.

**. *Oliphant v. Suquamish Indian Tribe*, 435 U.S. 191, 205 (1978).

††. *Williams v. United States*, 327 U.S. 711, 714 (1946).

‡‡. *United States v. McBratney*, 104 U.S. (14 Otto) 621, 624 (1882) (holding states have exclusive jurisdiction over crimes committed by non-Indians against non-Indians in Indian Country); *accord Antelope*, 420 U.S. at 643 n. 2.

§§. Note the position of the U.S. Department of Justice: "The *McBratney* rationale seems clearly to apply to victimless crimes so as, in the majority of cases, to oust Federal jurisdiction. Where, however, a particular offense poses a direct and immediate threat to Indian persons, property, or specific tribal interests, Federal jurisdiction continues to exist, just as is the case with regard to offenses traditionally regarded as having as their victim an Indian person or property . . . [E]ven where Federal jurisdiction is thus implicated, the States may nevertheless be regarded as retaining the power as independent sovereigns to punish non-Indian offenders charged with 'victimless' offenses of this sort." 3 Op. Off. Legal Counsel 111, 112-12 (1979).

ǁǁ. *Solem v. Bartlett*, 465 U.S. 463, 465 n.2 (dictum); *United States v. Langford*, 641 F.3d 1195, 1197 (10th Cir. 2011); *State v. Harrison*, 238 P.3d 869, 874-75 (N.M. 2010); *People v. Ramirez*, 148 Cal. App. 4th 1464, 1474 n. 9 (2007); *State v. Sebastian*, 701 A.2d 13, 22 n. 21 (Conn. 1997), *cert. denied*, 522 U.S. 1077 (1998); *State v. Vandermay*, 478 N.W.2d 289, 290-91 (S.D. 1991); *State v. Snyder*, 807 P.2d 55, 56-58 (Idaho 1991); *State v. Burrola*, 669 P.2d 614, 615 (Ariz. Ct. App. 1983).

conduct within their boundaries by any party, regardless of title status of the land or citizenship of the actor, but that is not the case. Nations are generally able to exercise civil jurisdiction over

- All tribal members (regardless of whether they reside on the reservation)
- All non-tribal members entering consensual/contractual relationships with them that include provisions consenting to tribal civil jurisdiction
- All land owned by the tribe within the reservation boundaries
- All land owned by tribal members within the reservation boundaries

Civil jurisdiction is important to understand and will likely be where nations spend the majority of their efforts exercising sovereignty. For me, in Oneida, the bulk of my day-to-day work is assisting management to assert sovereignty from state/local civil regulations and exercise civil jurisdiction through our ordinances, including zoning, eviction and foreclosure, land uses and leasing, environmental requirements, etc. Due to Oneida's checkerboard reservation, enforcement can be tricky, so land status and tribal member status are the first questions I ask when advising who has jurisdiction. Once I've gathered the facts, I compare our situation to the landmark case in tribal civil jurisdiction, *Montana v. United States*, and ensuing cases that further limited tribal civil jurisdiction.

In *Montana*, the Court looked at tribal civil regulatory jurisdiction and provided that when it comes to regulation of non-member conduct within the reservation on non-Indian fee land, presume that tribes lack authority to regulate except

- The activity of non-Indians may be regulated (i.e., taxed, licensed, etc.) if they enter consensual relationships with the tribe or tribal members through community dealings, contracts, leases, etc.; OR
- The activity of non-Indians may be regulated by nations when such conduct threatens or has some direct effect on the political integrity, economic security, or health and security of the tribe—the title status of the land is just one factor in this analysis.[10]

The *Montana* Court said that this is self-governance (which is true), but emphasized tribes as limited sovereigns by recognizing that nations have jurisdiction over their citizens, but finding their territorial jurisdiction to be conditional.

After *Montana*, the Supreme Court handed down more decisions limiting tribal civil jurisdiction. For example, the Court held that there is a duty to exhaust remedies in tribal court before filing in federal court, including issues tribes bring to the Supreme Court under diversity jurisdiction.[11] This lengthened the path to the Supreme Court for tribal matters.

Then, in *Strate* the Court tightened the analysis under *Montana*'s first exception by looking at who was injured instead of the nature of the actions and their relation to the contract. It also said that while the second exception read broadly, its application is narrow.[12] After *Strate*, the *Hicks* Court looked at non-Indian conduct on tribal land and unanimously denied tribal jurisdiction and required self-governance be implicated to exercise tribal regulatory jurisdiction over non-members. In addition, the *Hicks* Court was the first to require that the consent to jurisdiction arise from a commercial relationship, which represents another tightening of *Montana*. Lastly, the *Hicks* Court explains that tribal courts are not courts of general jurisdiction presumed and required to hear federal claims, but rather that there is a presumption that tribal courts lack authority to hear federal claims unless such authority is specifically delegated by statute.[13]

Taxation in Indian Country

As far as nations' authority to tax, nations can impose taxes on non-Indians that are conducting business on the reservation as an inherent power pursuant to tribal sovereignty, and no approval from the secretary of the Interior is required.[14] However, nations cannot tax on non-Indian fee land within reservation boundaries because it does not satisfy the second *Montana* exemption.[15]

When it comes to states' authority to tax nations and their citizens, states cannot tax Indian reservation land or Indian income from activities happening on Indian land, but they can tax Indians going beyond reservation boundaries pursuant to nondiscriminatory state laws otherwise applicable to all citizens of the state.[16] In addition:

- Trust property cannot be taxed by states without express authority from Congress; this includes allotments still held in trust too.
- Generally, income earned on the reservation by a tribal member living on the reservation is not subject to state taxation, but state law may affect the qualifications. For example, under Wisconsin case law, the tribal member must be living on their own reservation in order for their earned income to be excluded from state taxation.[17] State sales tax is inapplicable to Indians on reservations; and
- Federal taxes apply to Indians on reservations with the exception of trust-based income.

Public Law 280

Public Law 280 (P.L. 280) is a federal statute that transfers jurisdiction (mostly criminal, but in some cases also civil) that is otherwise vested in the federal government and transfers it to states. When jurisdiction is assumed pursuant to P.L. 280, the state's jurisdiction extends within tribal borders, taking the place of the federal government's, and applies state laws with the same force and effect within the reservation as they apply outside of the reservation.[18] There are two types of P.L. 280 states, mandatory and optional.[19] In mandatory states, neither the state nor the tribe has an option as to the assumption of otherwise federal jurisdiction by the state. In optional states, the "option" originally referred only to the option of the states and did not require tribes' consent to assume jurisdiction, which allowed states to decide which tribes they would exercise jurisdiction over, including how much and which type. This meant states could assume only limited jurisdiction and could pick and choose which tribes within the state to apply it to. Tribal consent was not required for a state to assume P.L. 280 jurisdiction in optional states until 1968 through the Indian Civil Rights Act, which focused on goals of self-determination. Ten states assumed jurisdiction before consent of tribes was required, and since then no tribe has consented to a state's assumption of jurisdiction.

Mandatory states receive both general criminal jurisdiction and some civil jurisdiction. In optional states, the state receives only adjudicative civil jurisdiction and not regulatory or tax authority,[20] and the state must give tribal ordinances/customs full force and credit within state court unless they are preempted by federal or state law.

Tribes, both mandatory and optional, and/or states may request retrocession of any or all P.L. 280 jurisdiction through the Department of the Interior, with the decision being made by the secretary.[21] Retrocession can be costly for tribes because it will require them to divert already precious resources to providing services and infrastructure that were previously provided by the state (e.g., jails, additional police officers, development of criminal/civil legislation).

Concurrent Civil Jurisdiction

Where there is concurrent civil jurisdiction between a tribal nation and a state, states will often have mechanisms for transferring the matter to tribal court. For example, in the State of Wisconsin, a civil matter with concurrent jurisdiction in both state and tribal court can be transferred to the sole jurisdiction of the tribal court through one of two ways. The first is based in case law established in *Teague v. Bad River Band of Indians* and requires the court to consider a range of factors to determine if the tribal court's jurisdiction is most appropriate for the matter. The second is called a discretionary transfer pursuant to Wis. Stat. §801.54. It allows the circuit court, on its own motion or by motion of either party, to transfer the action to tribal court following notice and hearing on the transfer where the court must make a threshold determination that there is concurrent jurisdiction. Some of the factors considered in both instances include:

- whether the action requires analysis of tribal laws, constitution, resolutions, or case law;
- whether the action involves traditional or cultural matters of the tribe;
- whether the tribe is party to the action, and tribal sovereignty, jurisdiction, or territory is at issue;
- the tribal membership status of the parties;
- where the claim arises;
- any contract that applies selection of forum for disputes or governing law;

- which court can most expeditiously handle the matter; and
- the relative burdens on the parties, including cost, access to and admissibility of evidence, and process.[22]

TRIBAL CONSTITUTIONS, COURTS, LAWMAKING, AND CITIZENSHIP

About 250 of the 333 tribal constitutions in the United States were modeled on the Indian Reorganization Act.[23] Tribal constitutions determine how tribes govern themselves, including the authority and requirements to adopt laws and determine their citizenship. However, many IRA modeled constitutions do not include separation of powers or any independent judicial branch of government.[24] As tribes' governments evolve and take back ownership in crafting their own self-governance, outside of the IRA model, many tribes are revisiting their constitutions to include stronger checks and balances and incorporate their judiciary branches. By 2013 over sixty tribes were considering amendments to their constitutions, including the Oneida Nation.[25] We successfully amended our constitution in 2014 to incorporate our judicial branch and modify our election practices.

As tribes work towards constitutional amendments, it is important to note that inclusion in tribal constitutions is not required in order for tribes to establish their courts, determine their citizenship, or write laws (unless citizenship is included in a current constitution and would contradict the tribe's revisions). This is because the authority to establish courts, write laws, and determine citizenship is not derived from delegated federal authority, but rather from their retained inherent authority. The U.S. Constitution does not apply when tribes exercise their inherent authority because that authority existed prior to the existence of the Constitution. However, tribal actions are subject to limitation by Congress's plenary powers, including the Indian Civil Rights Act, which specifically places limitations on tribal self-governance that are similar to provisions in the U.S. Constitution.[26]

PRACTITIONER PERSPECTIVE

We cannot protect and advance our sovereignty without first understanding it and our histories completely. At home in Oneida, we just celebrated a massive legal victory affirming our sovereignty when the Seventh Circuit Court of Appeals overturned the district court's decision in *Oneida Nation v. Village of Hobart*. The Village of Hobart asserted that the Oneida Nation had to apply for and receive permits from the village in order to hold our Big Apple Fest within our reservation boundaries on tribal trust and fee land.[27] If upheld, the decision would have limited Oneida's ability to self-govern strictly to trust lands. By understanding our history and applicable case law, we were able to protect our inherent right to self-govern within our entire reservation, not just on our trust lands. The win doesn't just protect Big Apple Fest, it also protects our commercial enterprises, supports our positions with other local governments that our laws apply within our boundaries, and supports our positions in fee-to-trust applications/appeals, to name just a few focal points.

We must digest the intricacies of our scenarios and the implications on sovereignty and jurisdiction, because a loss for one nation can quickly become a loss for all of Indian Country. For example, a bad decision in Wisconsin district court may potentially impact all eleven nations in Wisconsin. Then, if that bad decision had been upheld on appeal, the appellate court's decision may potentially affect all tribes in the Seventh Circuit. Finally, had we lost our appeal, we would have likely appealed to the Supreme Court, where a loss could potentially have impacted all tribes throughout Indian Country.

Sovereignty and jurisdiction in Indian Country are complicated and unlike any other area of law. It is difficult for non-tribal attorneys to understand, as I often find myself explaining components of federal Indian law to my counterparts when representing my clients, and even more difficult for tribal staff without legal backgrounds to understand. I encourage tribal attorneys to work to explain their positions to management and break down some of the silos between the legal world and the management world. We should be discussing our nations' sovereignty regularly—how to protect it and how to expand it—and should be working towards a conversational understanding and an openness that allows tribal management to feel comfortable letting their legal team know when they have questions or need more explanation. I try to live this with all of my internal clients in Oneida, and am most proud of the progress we have made with our Comprehensive Housing Division, where we have recently

- Adopted a HEARTH Act leasing law that allows Oneida to approve our own trust leases based on our own standards;
- Retailored our HUD-funded rental and rent-to-own programs to maximize the self-governance afforded pursuant to NAHASDA[28] to make our policies truly our own;
- Created a program in partnership with our Bay Bank that promotes both reacquisition of reservation lands and homeownership by creating a dual closing, with the homeowner buying the improvements subject to a residential lease and the nation buying the land; and
- Adopted a landlord-tenant law and a mortgage and foreclosure law to solidify our policies and provide transparency, accountability, and consistent enforcement.

These examples show how beneficial it can be for nations to assess their programs to see how to use tribal sovereignty to make their programs work best for the nation's specific needs.

Our sovereignty existed before there was ever a United States, and through our ancestors' perseverance, it has remained intact despite genocide, racism, slavery, poverty, and countless other devastations. Our sovereignty is a muscle that must be exercised enthusiastically and consistently so we are prepared when we must flex the muscle again to fight for continued existence.

NOTES

1. Black's Law Dictionary.
2. *U.S. v. Kagama*, 118 US 375 (1886).
3. David H. Getches et al., Cases and Materials on Federal Indian Law, 140–87 (6th ed. 2011).
4. *Id.* at 187–200.
5. American Indian Treaties, National Archives (October 4, 2016), https://www.archives.gov/research/native-americans/treaties.
6. *Id.*
7. See *United States v. Washington*, 384 F.Supp. 312 (W.D. Wash 1974), *aff'd*, 520 F.2d 676 (9th Cir. 1975); *State v. Tinno*, 497 P.2d 1386 (Idaho 1972); *United States v. Winans*, 198

U.S. 371 (1905).

8. See *Id.*

9. See *United States v. Dion*, 476 U.S. 734 (1986).

10. *Montana v. United States*, 450 U.S. 544 (1981).

11. *National Farmers Union Insurance Co. v. Crow Tribe of Indians*, 471 U.S. 845 (1985).

12. *Strate v. A-1 Contractors*, 520 U.S. 438 (1997).

13. *Nevada v. Hicks*, 533 U.S. 353 (2001).

14. *Merrion v. Jicarilla Apache Tribe*, 455 U.S. 130 (1982). *Kerr-McGee Corp. v. Navajo Tribe*, 471 U.S. 195 (1985).

15. *Atkinson Trading Company, Inc. v. Shirley*, 532 U.S. 645 (2001).

16. *Washington v. Confederated Tribes of the Colville Indian Reservation* (holding that while tribes do have an interest in raising revenue for essential governmental programs, that interest is strongest when the revenues are derived from value generated on the reservation by activities involving the tribes and when the taxpayer is the recipient of the tribal services.

17. *Joan La Rock v. Wisconsin Department of Revenue*, 232 Wis. 2d 474 (2001).

18. 28 U.S.C. §1162.

19. The following are the six mandatory states: Alaska, California, Minnesota, Nebraska, Oregon, and Wisconsin (excluding the Menominee Tribe). 18 U.S.C. §1162(a).

20. *Bryan v. Itasca County*, 426 U.S. 373 (1976).

21. 25 U.S.C. §1323.

22. See Wis. Stat. §801.54(2)(a)-(k); *Teague v. Bad River Band of Indians*, 236 Wis.2d 384 (2000).

23. Jean Hopfensperger, *Tribes across the country are re-examining the constitutions*, Star Tribune (July 6, 2013).

24. *Id.*

25. *Id.*

26. 25 U.S.C. §1302.

27. *Oneida Nation v. Village of Hobart*, No. 19–1981 (7th Cir. 2020).

28. Native American Housing Assistance and Self-Determination Act of 1996.

GLOSSARY

Adjudicative. The entry of a decree by a court in respect to the parties in a case, it implies a hearing by a court, after notice, of legal evidence on the factual issue(s) involved.

Assimilation. The process of becoming similar to another through absorption and integration of people, ideas, or culture.

Concurrent jurisdiction. Two or more courts from different systems simultaneously have jurisdiction over a case.

Inherent. Existing in something as a permanent, essential, or characteristic attribute.

Jurisdiction. The official power to make legal decisions and judgments.

Sovereign immunity. A legal doctrine whereby a sovereign cannot be sued without granting its own consent.

Sovereignty. The authority of a state to govern itself or another state.

Trust responsibility. The highest moral and legal obligation that the United States must meet to ensure the protection of tribal and individual Indian lands, assets, resources, and treaty and similarly recognized rights.

Federal Lawmaking and Policy

Kirsten Matoy Carlson, Wendy Helgemo, Tadd M. Johnson, and Laura Paynter

POLICYMAKERS REGULARLY MAKE DECISIONS ABOUT FEDERAL POLICY THAT impact the daily lives of tribal people. Indian nations have a long history of influencing federal policymaking. Tribal leaders and administrators have to understand how the federal legislative process works to improve the federal policies and programs affecting their communities. The U.S. Congress, the legislative branch of the federal government, has the power to make laws. There are two types of federal laws: (1) authorizing laws that create federal programs, and (2) appropriations laws that fund federal programs. This chapter explains how the federal government makes these laws, explains how to read them, and provides insights into how Indian tribes can participate in the legislative process.

BEST PRACTICES

- Know how Congress makes law and policy through authorizing legislation.
- Build relationships with the members of the committee of jurisdiction when advocating for a bill.

- Concisely state your issue and proposed solution when seeking a policy change, asking for money, or testifying before Congress.
- Know how to read a bill.
- Participate in hearings on bills that affect your community.

INTRODUCTION

The federal government has a government-to-government relationship with Indian nations. A central aspect of this relationship is the trust relationship between the United States and Indian nations. The Supreme Court first recognized the trust relationship in *Cherokee Nation v. Georgia* in 1831. The Court acknowledged that the trust relationship comes from the preexisting sovereignty of Indian nations and international law, which states that stronger sovereigns take on an obligation of protection when assuming authority over a weaker one.[1] The United States promised protection to tribes and their citizens as part of land transactions and thus took on a trust responsibility towards Indian nations.[2]

The modern trust responsibility is based on treaties, statutes, court decisions, and the course of dealings between the United States and tribes. In treaties and later statutes, the U.S. government promised to provide tribes with protection, education, health care, and other benefits in exchange for tribal lands. The trust relationship obligates the federal government to support tribal self-government and economic prosperity and to protect tribal lands, assets, and resources. These responsibilities are legally enforceable obligations on the part of the United States. The Supreme Court has held that the trust responsibility includes legal duties, moral obligations, and the fulfillment of understandings and expectations that have arisen over the entire course of the relationship between the federal government and the tribes.[3]

The U.S. Constitution gives Congress exclusive legislative power over Indian affairs.[4] Congress has a constitutional obligation to fulfill the trust responsibility by creating and funding programs for tribes. Federal laws passed by Congress fulfill the federal trust responsibility to tribes; establish or enlarge existing trust responsibilities; and clarify rights from religious freedom to civil rights, to the sacramental use of peyote, to civil and criminal jurisdiction. Congress can also overturn Supreme Court decisions, restore tribes that were terminated, or reverse policies from decades past. On the dark side, Congress can unilaterally abrogate treaties, remove tribes from their homelands, take away tribal land rights, and even terminate the legal recognition of tribes by the U.S. government. Tribes must learn about and actively participate in the legislative process in order to survive and endure.

No one knows the needs of Indian people better than tribal leaders and administrators. Members of Congress rely on input from tribal leaders and administrators to fulfill the trust responsibility. Indian nations are more likely to receive programs and money to serve their communities when they participate in the legislative process.

Indian nations more effectively participate in the legislative process when they understand the two kinds of laws Congress enacts. Authorizing laws create programs, policies, and agencies. Appropriations laws fund the federal programs, services, and activities set out in an authorizing law. Indian nations can influence both authorizing laws and appropriations. You can more successfully influence federal law if you understand how those laws are made.

AUTHORIZING LAWS

Congress makes law through bills, which are proposed statutes or laws. By passing bills, Congress can create, expand, and change federal agencies, programs, and activities.[5] A bill goes through several stages and may or may not be passed by Congress. These stages include drafting the bill, introduction of the bill, referral to a committee, committee consideration of the bill, a floor vote, passage, referral to the other body of Congress, consideration by the other body of Congress, and presentment to the President.[6] Figure 1 shows how a bill proceeds through each of these stages.

Starting the Legislative Process

Tribes often need federal legislation to fix problems they are having with the federal government or federal programs, or protect their sovereignty, their

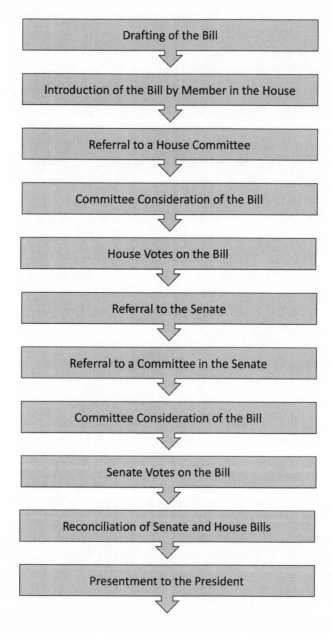

Figure 1. How a Bill Becomes a Law

SOURCE: KIRSTEN MATOY CARLSON.

land, their jurisdiction, and their natural resources. Indian nations have used legislative advocacy to advance tribal sovereignty by initiating new policies, reversing court decisions, and encouraging the oversight and implementation of existing policies.[7]

Tribes that develop strong relationships with their congressional delegation and other members of Congress may more readily navigate and influence the legislative process. Tribes may also use their relationships with their congressional delegation to influence other branches of government. For example, your member of Congress may call the BIA or another agency on your behalf if your tribe runs into problems getting something done.

Tribes seek one of three kinds of bills: pan-tribal bills, which have an overriding purpose of developing federal Indian policy by addressing an issue faced by all Indians (e.g., the Helping Expedite and Advance Responsible Tribal Home Ownership (HEARTH) Act or the Indian Gaming Regulatory Act); tribe specific bills, which do not seek to establish general federal Indian law or policy but address a specific issue for one or a few but not all tribes (e.g., the Gun Lake Trust Reaffirmation Act or the Nevada Native Nations Land Act); and general bills, which have a substantive focus other than Indians (e.g., health, education, employment, etc.) but specifically mention Indians (e.g., Violence Against Women Act).[8]

The advocacy strategy used depends on the kind of bill. For example, for tribe specific bills, tribes may work closely with their member of Congress to introduce and manage the bill as those bills are rarely passed without the support of the congressional delegation. Several Nevada tribes used this strategy in securing the enactment of the historic Nevada Native Nations Land Act.[9] In contrast, for pan-tribal bills, tribes may work with other tribes in a coalition across Indian Country and have a national legislative strategy involving many congressional delegations. The advocacy for the HEARTH Act is an illustration of this strategy. The New Mexico Pueblos united and built a coalition with other tribes through the National American Indian Housing Council to propose a bill to change federal law so they would have tribal leasing authority and would not have to get approval of the secretary of the Interior when they wanted to lease their own lands.[10] Tribes often engage in even broader coalitions when working on general legislation. For example, NCAI and tribal leaders joined forces with immigrant and LGBTQ activists to ensure passage of the Violence Against Women Act.[11]

Anyone can come up with an idea for a bill. If tribal leaders or administrators have an idea for a bill, they can share the idea with their congressional delegation, lawyers, or lobbyists. If others support the idea, congressional staffers or the tribe's lawyers or lobbyists may draft language for a bill. The tribe may work closely with their congressional delegation on the language of the bill. If the bill affects the local or state government or other stakeholders, they may also be involved in the drafting of the bill.

Introducing a Bill

Once the bill language is ready, a member of Congress has to introduce it and it is assigned a number, such as H.R. 24 in the House or S. 7 in the Senate, for tracking it through the legislative process. Developing strong relationships with your local congressional delegation or other members of Congress makes it easier to get a bill introduced. Ideally, members of the tribe's congressional delegation introduce the same bill in both the House and the Senate around the same time to increase its chances of enactment, but this doesn't always happen. It is not always possible to get the support of both a senator and a representative to introduce a bill.

Committee Work

Once a bill is introduced, it is referred to at least one committee. Advocating for a bill at the committee level is important because the majority of bills never make it out of committee. If you are in favor of the bill, you want the bill to go to only one committee, preferably the committee most favorable to your interests. In the Senate, the preferred committee for bills relating to Indians is usually the Senate Committee on Indian Affairs, which has broad authority over issues related to American Indians, Native Hawaiians, and Alaska Natives.[12]

The House does not have a similar committee with general authority over Indian affairs. The Subcommittee on Indigenous Peoples of the House Committee on Natural Resources exercises jurisdiction over some American Indian, Alaska Native, and Native Hawaiian issues.[13] Indian-related bills, however, are

Table 1. House Committees with Jurisdiction over American Indians, Alaska Natives, and Native Hawaiian Issues

HOUSE COMMITTEE	AREAS OF JURISDICTION RELATED TO INDIANS
House Committee on Natural Resources	Bureau of Indian Affairs
House Committee on Education and Labor	Education; 477 programs
House Judiciary Committee	Tribal Courts; Justice
House Committee on Energy and Commerce	Indian Health Service; Administration for Native Americans
House Committee on Financial Services	Housing and Urban Development

frequently referred to other committees. Table 1 shows some of the House committees that hear bills related to Indians.[14]

Once a bill is referred to a committee, the chairman of the committee decides whether or not to move the bill forward. The committee can ignore the bill, rewrite or mark up the bill, schedule a hearing, or refer the bill to a subcommittee (usually in the House). Building a relationship with the chairman and committee staff may help to build support for your bill and keep it moving through the legislative process.

The purpose of a hearing is to gather information on the bill. The chair decides who to invite to testify on the bill, which may include advocates for and against the bill. Hearings provide an opportunity to engage in targeted advocacy on proposed laws. Many legislative advocates testify at hearings because they deem it an important activity and wisely use it to access and influence lawmakers.[15] Hearings provide access to lawmakers, allow for the presentation of carefully reasoned arguments and technical information about the bill, and shape the legislative record.[16] Even if you are not a witness, anyone can submit testimony, which will become a part of the hearing record.

After holding a hearing, the chairman can hold a markup, which is an opportunity to make changes or amend the bill. During markup, members of the committee may debate the bill and propose amendments to the language, which may come from testimony. The ideal purpose of the markup is to strengthen the bill, but it is sometimes used to weaken it. Many members of Congress prefer that a bill have a hearing and a markup in the committee to develop a legislative record showing the need for the legislation.

At the end of a markup session, the committee votes on whether to report the bill to the full body for further consideration. If the committee reports out the bill, a written report accompanies the bill and it goes to the full body for consideration. The committee report includes an explanation of the bill and its purpose; its procedural history (e.g., earlier introductions, progress in committee, etc.); all committee votes; a section-by-section analysis of the bill; the committee views on the bill; minority and supplementary views (if submitted); cost estimates; and information on the bill's regulatory impact. The committee report usually contains a separate analysis from the Congressional Budget Office, a nonpartisan office of Congress, about how much it will cost to implement the bill over the next five or ten years. This is a key part of the report because members of Congress may be reluctant to support a bill if it costs too much. Committee reports serve to educate legislators, judges, and the public about the bill and how it developed over time.

Floor Vote

Once a committee reports out a bill, it has to be placed on the chamber's calendar for floor consideration. Bills that make it to the floor may be debated. Debates rarely change votes, but members use them to publish their positions and include remarks for the legislative history. Bills may also be amended on the floor in accordance with Senate and House rules. Members of Congress may use amendments strategically to defeat a bill or to add unrelated provisions to it. For example, the provision ending treaty-making was added to an unrelated bill. Many bills, however, are passed without floor amendments. Once a bill passes the House or the Senate, it is sent to the other body for consideration. It proceeds through the committee and to the floor for enactment.

Reconciling House and Senate Bills

If the House and Senate enact different versions of the same bill, then they have to agree on one version before the bill can be enacted. Sometimes one body simply decides to accept the version passed by the other body. Other times the House and Senate exchange bills several times until they are able to agree on the provisions in the two bills and come up with a bill they both accept. Still other times, the two bodies cannot reach an agreement on a bill and one body will call for a conference. Conferees are appointed from each body and they meet to negotiate a bill that both the House and Senate will accept. A formal conference is very rare except for very large pieces of legislation such as the Farm Bill.

Presidential Approval

Once the House and the Senate pass the same version of a bill, it is presented to the President, who has ten days (not including Sundays) to sign or veto it. If the President vetoes a bill, it is returned to Congress. Congress may override the veto if two-thirds of those voting in each body vote to enact the bill. If a veto is overridden, the bill becomes law without the President's signature. If the President takes no action on a bill within the ten-day period, then the bill usually becomes law without the President's signature. A bill does not become law, however, if Congress adjourns before the end of the ten-day period and the President has not signed it. The President has to accept or reject the entire bill and cannot reject only the provisions of a bill that s/he does not like. Sometimes if the bill is important to the President, Congress, or the advocate, s/he will have a signing ceremony. Examples of signing ceremonies for Indian bills have been water rights and land settlements and the Violence Against Women Act.

APPROPRIATIONS LAWS

Congress has to pass an appropriations law to fund the federal programs, policies, and activities set out in an authorizing law. Tribal leaders need to make sure that they are involved in the appropriations process to get money for their people. Many programs and agencies serving Indian Country are chronically underfunded, and the needs of many Indian nations and their people go unmet. You can more successfully influence the appropriations process to make sure the needs of your community are met if you know how the process works. The appropriations process is similar to the process for authorizing legislation, but differs in that it is part of the federal budgeting process.

How to Read a Bill

Tribal leaders and administrators who know how to read a bill may more readily navigate and influence the legislative process. All bills follow a similar pattern, consisting of three main parts: a title, an enacting clause, and a body. These main parts of the Gun Lake Trust Land Reaffirmation Act are shown in figure 2.

Each bill starts with a title. The title informs legislators and the public of the subject matter of the bill and may be used to refer the bill to the appropriate legislative committee. For example, the title for the bill below is "To reaffirm that certain land has been taken into trust for the benefit of the Match-E-Be-Nash-She-Wish Band of Pottawatomi Indians, and for other purposes."

Immediately following the title is the enacting clause, which simply explains that the bill is being enacted by either the House or the Senate. For example, the enacting clause of the Gun Lake Trust Reaffirmation Act reads, "Be it enacted by the Senate and House of Representatives of the United States of America in Congress assembled."

The body or main part of the bill comes next and contains what the bill is going to do and how it is going to do it. Section 2 of the Gun Lake Trust Reaffirmation Act is the body of that bill. It reaffirms the trust status of lands taken into trust by the secretary of the Interior for the Match-E-Be-Nash-She-Wish Band of Pottawatomi Indians.

Two other important parts of the body of a bill are the definitions and the severability clause. Knowing how words are defined in a bill makes it easier to understand the bill. Congress can give a word any meaning it wants. A bill can give specific meaning to words that would otherwise be read more broadly or narrowly from common usage. Not all bills include definitions (the Gun Lake Trust Reaffirmation Act does not). Nor do all bills use the same definition for the same word. For example, federal laws currently contain different definitions for the word "Indian."

In reading a bill, tribal leaders and administrators should also check to see if the bill has a severability clause. Severability clauses tell courts that the legislative intent is to preserve as much of the bill as possible in case part of it is invalidated.

Public Law 113–179
113th Congress

An Act

To reaffirm that certain land has been taken into trust for the benefit of the Match-E-Be-Nash-She-Wish Band of Pottawatami Indians, and for other purposes.

Sept. 26, 2014
[S. 1603]

Be it enacted by the Senate and House of Representatives of the United States of America in Congress assembled,

SECTION 1. SHORT TITLE.

This Act may be cited as the "Gun Lake Trust Land Reaffirmation Act".

Gun Lake Trust Land Reaffirmation Act.

SEC. 2. REAFFIRMATION OF INDIAN TRUST LAND.

(a) IN GENERAL.—The land taken into trust by the United States for the benefit of the Match-E-Be-Nash-She-Wish Band of Pottawatomi Indians and described in the final Notice of Determination of the Department of the Interior (70 Fed. Reg. 25596 (May 13, 2005)) is reaffirmed as trust land, and the actions of the Secretary of the Interior in taking that land into trust are ratified and confirmed.

(b) NO CLAIMS.—Notwithstanding any other provision of law, an action (including an action pending in a Federal court as of the date of enactment of this Act) relating to the land described in subsection (a) shall not be filed or maintained in a Federal court and shall be promptly dismissed.

(c) RETENTION OF FUTURE RIGHTS.—Nothing in this Act alters or diminishes the right of the Match-E-Be-Nash-She-Wish Band

Figure 2. Gun Lake Trust Land Reaffirmation Act

PRACTITIONER PERSPECTIVE

Wendy Helgemo is a member of the Ho-Chunk Nation and senior legislative attorney at Big Fire Law & Policy. In her work in Washington, DC, in a tribal nonprofit and public service, three experiences highlight how Indian nations, coalitions, and tribal organizations can steer and influence the legislative process.[17]

VAWA 2013

During my time serving as advisor on Indian Affairs for U.S. Senator Harry Reid (D-NV), the Violence Against Women Act (VAWA) expired and had to be reauthorized by Congress. Originally passed in 1994, tribes were included in the law in 2005 in a new Title IX—Safety for Indian Women. In 2011, U.S. Senator

Daniel Akaka (D-HI), then chairman of the Indian Affairs Committee and the only Native Hawaiian to have served in the Senate, introduced the "Stand Against Violence and Empower (SAVE) Native Women Act" to reauthorize VAWA Title IX. Staff on the Senate Indian Affairs Committee worked closely with staff of the Judiciary Committee and Senator Patrick Leahy (D-VT), then chairman of the Judiciary Committee, to include Senator Akaka's bill in the larger VAWA bill. Indian nations and organizations built a coalition with LGBTQ and immigration advocates and together fought hard for the bill, which included specific protections for their communities. Overcoming Republican opposition, the coalition was successful in getting everything included in the Violence Against Women Reauthorization Act of 2013 (P.L.113-4). One of the most critical provisions of the law reversed a portion of a U.S. Supreme Court decision (*Oliphant v. Suquamish Indian Tribe*, 435 U.S. 191 (1978)) and restored tribal jurisdiction over all persons who commit domestic violence crimes on tribal lands. President Barack Obama held a special signing ceremony at the U.S. Department of the Interior for the VAWA bill, which women advocates, tribal leaders, members of Congress, and administrative officials attended. To date, dozens of tribes are exercising restored criminal authority under this law.

The HEARTH Act

When I worked at the National American Indian Housing Council, the New Mexico Pueblo housing authorities wanted to change federal law so they had tribal leasing authority and would not have to get approval of the secretary of the Interior when they wanted to lease their own lands. They formed a coalition and proposed legislation to extend the Navajo Nation's authority to lease their own lands for agricultural, residential, and other surface uses, under the Indian Long-Term Leasing Act of 1955 to all tribes. The tribal coalition worked closely with former U.S. Rep. Martin Heinrich (D-NM) (now U.S. Senator Heinrich (D-NM)) to introduce the Helping Expedite and Advance Responsible Tribal Home Ownership (HEARTH) Act of 2011 (H.R.205). Senator John Barrasso (R-WY), then vice-chairman of the Indian Affairs Committee, introduced a companion bill in the Senate (S.703). Due to effective advocacy by Indian housing authorities, tribes, tribal organizations, and financial institutions for this bipartisan, non-controversial, low cost bill, and broad support in the House Financial Services

Committee, Senate Indian Affairs Committee, and the Obama administration, Congress speedily passed it (P.L.112-151). President Barack Obama held a special signing ceremony in the Oval Office for the HEARTH Act, which tribal leaders, members of Congress, and administrative officials attended. To date, fifty-six tribes are exercising their new authority under this law.

Nevada Native Nations Land Act

When I was advisor on Indian Affairs for Senator Harry Reid (D-NV), six Nevada tribes requested his assistance to return much-needed lands to them. Senator Reid introduced the Nevada Native Nations Land Act (S.1436), which would convey federal Bureau of Land Management and U.S. Forest Service land to tribes. Senator Reid's staff worked closely with the tribal coalition, the U.S. Department of the Interior, and the U.S. Department of Agriculture to develop maps to depict the requested acreage and address any public land uses to clear the way for the conveyance. These issues included grazing permits, mining, cattle watering holes, bighorn sheep hunting, roads, gates and an airport. U.S. Rep. Mark Amodei (R-NV) introduced a companion bill in the House of Representatives (H.R.2733). The tribal coalition and congressional delegation worked tirelessly to clear the many local small hurdles for the bill to pass (P.L.114-232). This bipartisan, low-cost bill set a new precedent that tribal and county lands requests do not need to be tied together in the same legislation, as had been the practice in the West. The Nevada Native Nations Land Act returned about 80,000 acres of land to Nevada tribes.

CONCLUSION

Federal laws affect almost every aspect of the daily lives of American Indians. Indian nations must engage in the legislative process to fix problems they are having with the federal government or federal programs and to protect their sovereignty, their land, their jurisdiction, and their natural resources. Effective participation in the federal legislative process requires an understanding of the two kinds of laws Congress enacts, the processes for enacting each, and an ability to read and understand federal laws.

NOTES

Thanks to Benjamin Yawakie and An Garagiola-Bernier.

1. Cherokee Nation v. Georgia, 31 U.S. 1 (1831).

2. Treaty of Hopewell, 1785.

3. U.S. v. Mitchell, 463 U.S. 206 (1983); Seminole Nation v. United States, 316 U.S. 286 (1942).

4. U.S. Const. art. I, § 8, cl. 3.

5. This discussion follows a traditional or textbook explanation of the federal legislative process. The purpose is to familiarize readers with the process rather than to explain all the possible routes that bills may take to enactment. Bills can start in the House or the Senate. This explanation has bills originating in the House because all appropriations bills have to start in the House.

6. ESKRIDGE ET AL. 2014. CASES AND MATERIALS ON LEGISLATION AND REGULATION (5th ed.), at 23–34. *See also* ABNER J. MIKVA ET AL., LEGISLATIVE PROCESS (4th ed. 2015).

7. Kirsten Matoy Carlson, Lobbying as a Strategy for Tribal Resilience, 2018 BYU Law Review 1159.

8. Kirsten Matoy Carlson, Congress and Indians, 86 University of Colorado Law Review 77, 124 (2015); CHARLES F. WILKINSON, AMERICAN INDIANS, TIME, AND THE LAW (1987). Approximately 10 percent of all Indian-related bills are pan-tribal, 36 percent are tribe specific, and 40 percent are general. Kirsten Matoy Carlson, Congress and Indians, 86 University of Colorado Law Review 77, 124 (2015).

9. S. Rep. No. 114-216 (Feb. 29, 2016); H. Rep. No. 114-487 (April 16, 2016).

10. H. Rep. No. 112-427 (April 16, 2012).

11. Kirsten Matoy Carlson, Lobbying as a Strategy for Tribal Resilience, 2018 BYU Law Review 1159; RESTORATION OF NATIVE SOVEREIGNTY & SAFETY FOR NATIVE WOMEN, Vol. 10(1) (March 2013); *Advocating and Protecting Native Women; NCAI Violence Against Women Task Force Leads VAWA Meetings on Capitol Hill*, NATIONAL CONGRESS OF AMERICAN INDIANS (July 5, 2012), http://www.ncai.org/news/articles/2012/07/05/advocating-and-protecting-native-women-ncai-violence-against-women-task-force-leads-vawa-meetings-on-capitol-hill; Laura Garbes, *SAVE Native Women Act: Addressing Domestic Violence on Reservations*, CULTURAL SURVIVAL (July 12, 2012), https://www.culturalsurvival.org/news/save-native-women-act-addressing-domestic-violence-reservations; Ashley Parker, *House Renews Violence Against Women Measure*, N.Y. TIMES (Feb. 28, 2013), https://www.nytimes.com/2013/03/01/us/politics/congress-passes-reauthorization-of-violence-against-women-act.html (noting that "more than 1,300 women's and human rights groups signed a letter supporting the Senate legislation").

12. Senate Committee on Indian Affairs, About the Committee, https://www.indian.senate.

gov/about-us.

13. The subcommittee exercises jurisdiction over natural resources and land management, ownership, and leasing to Indian health care, tribal criminal justice, development of reservation economies, enhancement of social welfare, and improvement of energy efficiency and renewable energy development initiatives on tribal lands. For more information on the subcommittee, see https://naturalresources.house.gov/subcommittees/subcommittee-for-indigenous-peoples-of-the-united-states.

14. David E. Wilkins & Heidi K. Stark, American Indian Politics and the American Political System (3d ed. 2011).

15. Kay Lehman Schlozman and John T. Tierney, Organized Interests and American Democracy 295 (1986).

16. *Id.* at 296.

17. Wendy Helgemo, Big Fire Law and Policy Group.

GLOSSARY

Appropriations. Laws passed by Congress to fund the federal programs, policies, and activities set out in an authorizing law.

Authorizing legislation. Laws passed by Congress to create federal programs, policies, and agencies.

Trust responsibility. Obligation of the U.S. government to fulfill the promises it made to provide protection, education, health care, and other benefits to tribes in treaties and statutes.

Navigating the Federal Budget Process to Empower Tribal Budgeting and Decision-Making

Lawrence S. Roberts

Quinault Indian Nation and ncai president Fawn Sharp said, "When tribal nations agreed to cede millions of acres of land, the federal government promised to safeguard their right to govern themselves, and to provide them adequate resources to deliver essential services effectively. These obligations are the foundation of the government-to-government relationship that exists between tribal nations and the United States." It is these obligations that form the core of the United States' responsibilities in the federal budgeting process.

This chapter provides an overview of the federal budgeting process and the role effective federal budgets can serve in meeting treaty and trust responsibilities to tribal nations. During the Obama administration, I was appointed by the President to serve in a number of capacities in the Assistant Secretary's Office for Indian Affairs, including acting assistant secretary, and led Indian Affairs for the last year of the administration. In this role, I was involved in every aspect of preparing and implementing the Indian Affairs budget, including working directly with tribal leaders; managing the Bureau of Indian Affairs, the Bureau of Indian Education, and coordinating with Interior staff to develop and implement multiple budgets; testifying before Congress; working with the Office of Management and Budget (omb); and assisting the White House Council on Native American Affairs with coordinating federal investment and resources. Much of what follows is based on my direct experience in working in these multiple capacities.

Effective federal budgets increase the likelihood that tribal revenues are available to serve tribal governance priorities. This chapter will discuss

- the overall federal budget process;
- the role of the OMB in formulating federal budgets and the relevance of OMB circulars to appropriations impacting tribal nations;
- how departments, such as the Department of the Interior, and agencies, such as the Bureau of Indian Affairs, the Bureau of Indian Education, and Interior's Office of Policy, Management and Budget, work to impact federal appropriations;
- additional opportunities to increase federal funding for trust and treaty obligations outside the typical agency appropriations process; and
- effective tools for tribal nations to meaningfully impact federal budgets.

This chapter will use examples of successes by tribal nations to increase federal budgets by providing a roadmap of short-term planning (one to three year) and long-term planning (five to ten year) strategies. We will also cover recent examples and strategies to overcome administration proposals to reduce federal funding necessary to implement federal trust and treaty obligations.

BEST PRACTICES

- Discuss the importance of data with key tribal leadership.
- Identify tribal/federal agency offices that maintain data relating to particular program needs, shortfalls, and current or potential outcomes.
- Identify data gaps and develop short- and long-term strategies to address those gaps.
- Collect data and real-life examples that key tribal leadership can share with federal counterparts.
- Develop proposed solutions with proposed metrics to demonstrate results.

- Research federal administration and congressional priorities for alignment with tribal priorities.
- Utilize intertribal organizations to keep up on regional and national trends regarding federal budget.
- Educate federal staff and officials locally and in Washington, DC, regarding the importance of a federal budget increase and projected results from that increase.
- Provide written and oral testimony during federal appropriations hearings.
- Communicate your progress and results to tribal leadership and federal counterparts.

INTRODUCTION

How does Congress decide to increase or flatline funding for tribal social services or law enforcement? Why does Congress cut funding for needed programs like tribal housing improvement? Who do tribes meet with to advance funding to meet tribal needs for the twenty-first century? What approaches for increased funding have a higher likelihood of success? Should federal funds be provided through one federal agency or spread across multiple departments? Why is it that attorneys call what they do "practice?"

With the exception of the last question, the answer to which is self-evident, this chapter sets forth the budgeting process as it should be and how it often actually occurs. This discussion is followed by an overview of the offices to work within the federal government to support tribal funding priorities. Finally, this chapter closes with tribal strategies, based on real life examples, that resulted in budget increases.

THE FEDERAL BUDGETING PROCESS

The federal budgeting process is an annual process that formally begins with submittal of the President's budget proposal to Congress. Appropriations committees and subcommittees in the House and Senate then typically hold multiple hearings on the proposed budget—hearings where tribal leaders are typically invited to testify. After those hearings, the appropriations committees will draft and pass out of committee appropriations bills for particular departments. Those bills then move to the full body for action. Some appropriations bills will move forward on their own, while others may be combined into a larger appropriations bill referred to as an omnibus bill. It is not uncommon for Congress to enact an omnibus bill that funds all or most of the government programs.

Throughout the process, congressional and executive branch staff are key players in formulating the federal budget. From preparing the draft budget to deciding who testifies at a particular hearing, to preparing the report to move the bill out of committee, congressional and executive branch staff are the behind-the-scenes advocates for increasing or cutting funding of particular programs.

Appropriations Cycles

Generally speaking, federal programs administered by agencies and tribes are budgeted on one-year and sometimes two-year cycles. The annual federal budget runs from October 1 to September 30 of the following year. In recent years, Congress has failed to enact appropriations legislation prior to the expiration of the current fiscal year. When this occurs, Congress either enacts a continuing resolution, which provides funding for programs at current levels for a discrete period of time, or the government shuts down due to a lack of appropriations.

Congress's inability to pass a budget on time has a direct impact on tribal governments. Under a continuing resolution, tribes must devote time and resources to develop a plan should Congress fail to enact a budget. If Congress fails to enact a budget and the federal government shuts down, tribes are forced to shoulder the budget burden temporarily or to close programs until Congress enacts a budget. Many in Congress recognize the impacts of federal budget dysfunction on tribes. Some agencies, such as the Bureau of Indian Education, have programs that are forward-funded by Congress. Forward funding is funding for the year in advance of the budget year so that if there is a lapse in appropriations those programs continue to receive funding. There is a push by many tribes and members of Congress to have all federal tribal programs move to forward funding or mandatory appropriations.

The timing of the federal budget process requires long-term planning by tribes in order to have a meaningful impact. For example, let's examine a fictional scenario in which tribal elections seat a tribal council in November 2019. In December 2019, the tribal council decides that it wants to advocate for budget increases for public safety. Based on the normal federal budget timetable, shown in Table 1, the earliest a tribal council could expect to see their efforts have a positive effect on the regular law enforcement budget would be generally in the 2022 budget, which would begin in October 2021.

Practice Tip

Appropriated program funding generally must be obligated by the agency before the end of the fiscal year, September 30th. Funding not obligated is returned to the Treasury. If the funding returned is significant, it is difficult for the agency to advocate for additional funding for that particular program. Federal agencies will begin work in early summer to identify programs that are not on track to obligate their current year funding. Typically, federal leadership will work with staff to ensure funding is obligated. This situation sometimes presents opportunities for tribes to receive limited funding for projects that can utilize the funding immediately. For example, an agency may have $30,000 of unobligated natural-resource funding in July that must be used before the end of the fiscal year. A tribe could request such funding be used for a long-needed study on impacts to fishery habitat. See Table 1 for the General Budget Timeline.

The Executive Branch—The President's Budget

The President's budget is typically delivered to Congress in February of each year. Every president identifies specific, broad administration priorities for increased funding. For example, President Obama's fiscal year 2017 budget proposed prioritized funding to address climate change. That proposal included increased funding to tribal nations to prepare for and respond to the impacts of climate change. While the President's budget is delivered in February, the administration's budget development process is virtually year-round. At any given time, the executive branch is working on three fiscal-year budgets—implementing the current budget, defending the proposed budget, and developing the budget for the year following the proposed budget.

Table 1. General Budget Timeline

	EXECUTIVE BRANCH	HOUSE	SENATE
DECEMBER 2019	Federal agencies in the final stages of working with the Office of Management and Budget to draft the President's proposed budget for October 2021.		
JANUARY 2020	President previews priorities and budget proposal in State of the Union Address.		
FEBRUARY 2020	President proposes budget for October 2021.		
MARCH 2020		Committee hearings on budget	Committee hearings on budget
APRIL 2020	Federal agencies begin work on drafting October 2022 proposed budget.	Congress passes budget resolution to guide decisions by congressional appropriations committees.	
MAY 2020	Federal agencies work to obligate, use, or lose 2020 funds. Federal agencies also continue to work on 2022 proposed budget.	Committee hearings on budget	Committee hearings on budget
JUNE 2020			
JULY 2020		Votes on budget bills	Votes on budget bills
AUGUST 2020			
SEPTEMBER 2020		Votes on budget bills	Votes on budget bills
OCTOBER 2020	2021 Budget begins on October 1		

Shortly after the proposed budget is delivered to Congress, each department and agency works with OMB to explain and defend the budget in congressional briefings and hearings held that spring. Typically, OMB will issue planning guidance to the agencies in the spring regarding preparation of the next budget proposal.

In the spring and summer, agencies work internally with their political leadership, the department's budget team, and with OMB to examine the efficacy of current programs, to identify priorities, and to identify areas of concern. Agencies further work to develop a budget proposal to be submitted to OMB.

In September, each department will submit a budget request to OMB. OMB reviews the submittals, and works to align those submittals with the President's priorities and likely budget constraints. OMB then makes recommendations to the President for each agency and department. After this process is concluded, OMB provides a "passback" to each department with a proposed budget. This typically occurs in late November or early December. There is generally a short window for department leadership to appeal passback decisions to OMB leadership or the President in December or early January.

The Role of OMB and OMB Circulars

The Office of Management and Budget performs a number of functions for the President. In addition to developing and overseeing implementation of the President's budget, OMB oversees each department's performance, reviews proposed, and final administrative rules; reviews and approves agency testimony submitted to Congress; and is involved in the preparation of presidential memoranda and executive orders.

OMB is comprised of almost entirely career staff—about 90 percent of the positions in any particular administration. Organized by subject matter and department, many of the same individuals that have a role in overseeing an agency's budget also have a role in reviewing agency regulations and testimony. For example, Interior and other executive-branch written testimony cannot be submitted to Congress before it is approved by OMB. It is critical for tribes to meet with OMB as part of any strategy to increase funding for a particular program. Career staff in each of the resource management offices work directly with the budget offices in each department as well as with senior leadership in each of the federal agencies. If OMB has a concern with the effectiveness of a particular program, or the President has a particular program focus, OMB will meet with senior program staff to develop benchmarks for that program.

In addition to working with departments, agencies, and tribes to develop and oversee implementation of the budget, OMB issues regulations, circulars, and other guidance to assist funding recipients with implementation. Circulars are instructions or information issued by OMB to federal agencies for the administration of funding and policies and are expected to have a continuing effect of two years or more. The primary regulations relating to tribes are found at 2 C.F.R. Part 200.[1] These regulations set forth uniform administrative requirements, cost principles, and audit requirements for non-federal recipients of federal funding. In 2011, OMB created the Council on Financial Assistance Reform (COFAR), which is comprised of executive branch officials to provide "recommendations to OMB on policies and actions necessary to effectively deliver, oversee, and report on grants and cooperative agreements, as well as sharing with executive departments and agencies best practices and innovative ideas for transforming the delivery of this assistance."[2] OMB disbanded the COFAR in 2017 and replaced it with the Chief Financial Officers Council (CFO).[3] The CFO website provides resources, such as a FAQ document, that provides guidance to recipients relating to implementation of Part 200.[4]

Federal Departments and Agencies

Each department works with OMB to develop the President's budget and to implement the budget passed by Congress. Within each department, there is an office dedicated to overseeing preparation of the department's overall proposed budget, including each of the agencies within that department. Further, each agency may have its own budget office that works with agency program staff, the department's budget office, and OMB. In the case of the Department of the Interior and Indian Affairs, the secretary of the Interior will identify certain priorities for implementation across the department. For example, Interior Secretary Sally Jewell prioritized addressing climate change, greater engagement of youth in the outdoors, and the development of Conservation Corps. Interior's Office of Policy, Management and Budget (PMB) works with each of the assistant secretaries and their budget offices to develop a proposed budget for the department that would incorporate those priorities. In turn, the assistant secretaries work with their senior leadership teams to identify needs and opportunities to advance those priorities. In this example, the assistant secretary/Indian Affairs worked with BIA and BIE, the regional directors for both of those agencies, tribes, and the principal deputy assistant secretary and the deputy assistant secretary/Management to develop programs to assist tribes with climate change and implementation of Youth Conservation Corps.

Some agencies, such as BIA, BIE, and IHS, have tribal-agency budget committees to assist in preparation of the proposed budget. For BIA and BIE, such budget committees meet quarterly and are co-chaired by the assistant secretary and two tribal leaders. Each region is represented on the committee by the regional director and two tribal leaders. The committee identifies proposed budget increases, data gaps, and policies to improve the efficacy of federal funding and programs. It is common for OMB and the department's Policy, Management and Budget Office to attend committee meetings.

Just as it is important to think about how a tribe's budget priorities fit within the President's priorities, it is important to track each department leader's and assistant secretary's priorities to identify opportunities to advance tribal priorities. Depending on the tribe's budget priorities, it may make sense to reach out to some or all of the offices identified within the department to ensure that they have accurate information regarding the role the tribe's goals play in the preparation of the department's proposed budget.

Practice Tip

Do not wait until the late November–January time period to reach out to federal agencies and OMB regarding the President's budget to be issued in February; it is too late for staff at those entities to make major modifications to the budget proposal.

The Legislative Branch—The House and Senate

Once the President's budget is delivered to Congress, the House and Senate hold hearings and prepare the budget legislation. The various appropriations committees take the lead on these tasks; however the committees with jurisdiction over the substantive topics also hold hearings and work with appropriations staff. Full committees often invite tribal leaders from national intertribal organizations to testify on the President's budget. Subcommittees with jurisdiction over appropriations concerning tribes often receive testimony from tribal leaders across the country, typically in March.

Appropriations Committees

Both the Senate and House appropriations committees are organized with sub-committees focused on particular departments across the federal government. The House Committee on Appropriations has fifty-three members and twelve subcommittees.[5] The full committee receives draft legislation from each of the subcommittees and then meets during a "markup" to offer amendments to the draft legislation and to vote each bill out of committee. Once voted out of committee, the bill moves to consideration by the full House of Representatives.

The Senate Committee on Appropriations is structured similar to the House Committee, with thirty-one senators and twelve subcommittees.[6] Each of the subcommittees prepares legislation to be considered first in subcommittee hearings and then moved forward for consideration by the full committee. The full committee holds a "business meeting" to consider proposed amendments to the subcommittee's forwarded legislation. After the legislation is moved out of the full committee it will be considered by the full Senate.

Appropriations Subcommittees

As discussed above, the subcommittees take the lead in developing budget legislation. The House subcommittee responsible for BIA, BIE, and IHS budgets is the Subcommittee on Interior, Environment, and Related Agencies.[7] The Senate subcommittee responsible for BIA, BIE, and HIS budgets is the Senate Subcommittee on Interior, Environment, and Related Agencies.[8] Subcommittee hearings on the President's budget are typically held in March of each year.

It is critical that tribes engage with both the House and Senate subcommittee and committee staff regarding budget priorities. Committee staff often have years of expertise on federal tribal programs and budget issues. Like OMB, Senate and House staff will typically want budget proposals to include data regarding the issue, a description of how the increase in funding will be implemented by the particular program, and proposed metrics to track results. Metrics are the parameters by which you will measure the data—for example, the period of time it takes for the Bureau of Indian Affairs to issue a decision to accept a particular parcel of land into trust. Data and metrics can then be used to support future investments. In formulating appropriations legislation, members and staff on the committee will engage with their colleagues in the House and Senate, tribes, OMB, and the various levels of leadership within the executive branch responsible for oversight or implementation of the programs.

Subject Matter Committees

In addition to the appropriations committees, it is critical to educate members and staff of the committees with subject matter jurisdiction over the particular program for which the tribe is seeking increased funding. For tribes, the leading committee in the Senate is the Senate Committee on Indian Affairs.[9] The leading committee in the House is the Committee on Natural Resources.[10]

Senators and representatives focused on Indian Country matters may serve on both the appropriations committee and the subject matter committee. For example, during the 116th Congress, Senator Murkowski chaired the Senate Subcommittee on Interior, Environment, and Related Agencies while also serving on the Senate Committee on Indian Affairs. Likewise, Senator Udall served as vice-chair of the Senate Committee on Indian Affairs and ranking member of the Senate Subcommittee on Interior, Environment, and Related Agencies. The subject matter committees have jurisdiction over authorizing legislation for new programs and amendments to existing laws. If a new proposed program does not fit within an existing authorized program, the tribe will need to work with the subject matter committees to enact legislation to authorize the program.

Members

Finally, tribes will want to educate the various senators and representatives that are advocates for the particular services and programs, including the particular tribe's elected members of Congress. Staff in each member's personal office are able to help tribes frame the substantive proposal, navigate the various committees, and engage with executive branch agencies, including OMB. Staff can also help to build support among other individual members of Congress to advance a particular budget initiative.

OPPORTUNITIES FOR ADDITIONAL FUNDING OF TRUST AND TREATY OBLIGATIONS

Rahm Emanuel said, "You never want a serious crisis to go to waste. What I mean by that is it is an opportunity to do things you think you could not do before." In addition to the annual appropriations process, at times Congress will enact legislation to address a particular national crisis. Prominent examples are the American Recovery and Reinvestment Act of 2009 (Recovery Act) and the Coronavirus Aid, Relief, and Economic Security Act of 2020 (CARES Act). Both acts, enacted on an expedited basis, included substantial revenues to tribes outside the typical appropriations process.

Emergency Appropriations Legislation

The $787 billion Recovery Act funding focused on investments in infrastructure, education, and health to generate jobs and stimulate the economy. The Recovery Act provided approximately $2.5 billion specifically for tribes. The funds resulted in an number of substantial investments in Indian Country, including funds for the construction or repair of schools, repair and replacement of roads, and construction of new housing. The CARES Act provided $8 billion to tribes to use for expenditures incurred due to the Coronavirus public health emergency.

Typically, the aim of such legislation is to provide a direct infusion of resources into the economy. As such, the legislation is often targeted to projects and programs that can be implemented immediately. For example, the Recovery Act focused on "shovel-ready" projects for which planning had been completed and all that was needed was resources to actually build or repair the particular infrastructure.

Given the emergency nature of the appropriation, it is nearly impossible to plan in detail for a particular bill. However, those tribes that maintain strong data and planning programs will be better positioned to ensure they are able to maximize their inclusion in a particular emergency bill.

Use or Lose Funding

In addition to emergency legislation, virtually every federal agency's annual funding must be obligated before the end of the fiscal year. Obligated does not mean that it has to actually be spent in that fiscal year, but that it must be transferred to the tribe through a contract or a contract entered into by the federal agency committing the agency to the expenditure of the funds. As discussed above, BIA is an agency for which funds that are not spent within the fiscal year will be returned to the Treasury. Most administrations direct agencies to obligate as much of the appropriated funds as possible before the end of the fiscal year.

Authorization of Pilot Projects

Another opportunity for additional funding is to participate in pilot projects launched by agencies. Agencies will often receive an increase in funding to develop and implement a pilot project that will produce data to support further budget increases in a new area or program. For example, in years past, Congress has appropriated budget increases to implement pilot projects focused on law enforcement and social services.

Effective Strategies for Tribes to Impact Federal Budgets

Not surprisingly, the best ideas and solutions for delivering services and programs within Indian Country come from tribes. Setting aside budget shortfalls for a moment, too often tribally driven solutions are not implemented broadly because federal decision-makers are unaware of the scope of the challenge and the tribally driven solution. That is why it is critical for tribes to tell their story. Over and over again. Persuasive, interesting stories begin with a hook—the tribe's connection to the issue. It then moves to the challenge and consequences if things remain unchanged. Importantly, it closes with a solution and why that solution will improve the lives of Native people and the broader community.

Even if a potential solution seems obvious, it remains difficult to achieve substantial budget increases despite a significant, unquestionable, unmet need. Why is that? An obvious reason is that it often feels impossible to increase the budget to meet the unmet need because programs have been underfunded for generations. However, a primary reason for the lack of significant new investment is the lack of reliable data. Without data to show how the funding will be used effectively, the agency, OMB, and other executive branch decision-makers are less likely to push a significant investment. If it's not in the President's budget, the House and Senate are less likely to increase funding without data to support that decision. At a macro-level, significant funding increases are driven by the President's budget. If the House or Senate disagrees with the budget proposal but lacks data for any significant increase, a likely outcome is status quo from the previous year or a slight. Therefore, it is preferable to be included in the President's budget, and data supporting the investment in the solution is an often necessary ingredient.

Finally, the tribally driven solution must include metrics to measure the efficacy of the increased funding. These metrics can spur budget increases in future years and will themselves provide data to support those increases. Metrics will also help to demonstrate success of the tribally driven solution. Sharing the success with those that work on federal budgets is critical. Too often, the conversation turns to the next challenge of the moment and there's a lack of focus on what's working well and why. That part of the story—the investment is working well and here's why—helps to solidify funding in future budgets. Finally, a successful solution can have a snowball effect that supports other budget initiatives.

Telling Your Story

Telling your story is critical to the budget process. Billy Frank Jr., one of the most effective advocates, reminded us to tell our story over and over again. He shared this story to educate others of the importance of improving the environment:

> The directors of the federal government, the directors of the state of Washington, they've retired. And I've watched them. I went to their retirement ceremonies. They've all left. They've left us with poison.
>
> Us tribes, we can't leave. The Lummis are there. Makah there. Quinault. Duwamish. Nisqually. We can't move where the sunshine is or nothing. This is our home here, so we got to stay here with the poison. That's not a good documentary for the people who run this country, but that's what happened.
>
> But we're on a course; we've been on a course; we're trying to make change. And we will make that change because we have to survive. For our children, our grandchildren, and all of us together.
>
> You know, you have to give a lifetime to what I'm talking about. You can't just be here today and gone tomorrow. You have to tell this story of change continually for the rest of your life.... This is a big giant picture that we're talking about. And it isn't no easy one, and it's not gonna be done overnight. There have to be increments of change. We'll be way out—100 years of planting trees, getting our watersheds back, getting our oceans clean . . . but we're gonna do it. We've got to do it.

Sharing how a particular program has real-life impacts on tribal communities is the essential human element often missing in the budgetary process. Those real-life impacts, combined with a proposed solution, stick with federal decision-makers as the budget is being formulated. Even if the tribe's challenge and proposed solution does not fit perfectly within the broader administration priorities, it is possible that the tribe's story will spur adjustments to address that story.

Perhaps this concept is best illustrated by a story. During the Obama administration there were a number of heart-wrenching tragedies involving Native youth on a particular reservation. The administration was working with the tribe and within the federal government more broadly to identify solutions to address the crisis. During one meeting with the tribal community, a young single mother shared that she needed help with classes on how to be a parent, she needed help with developing job search skills, she needed assistance with basic necessities, but that all of the programs designed to help families in her situation were siloed, uncoordinated, and that even if she knew all of the different programs to access that there were gaps between the programs. Building on the young parent's story, a tribal official described how they were reacting to crisis and didn't have the resources to plan a proactive approach to serving their community.

Out of this story, the administration launched the Tiwahe ("family" in Lakota) pilot project. The five-year program focused on providing resources to a number of tribes to develop a structure for the delivery of services to families in their communities. Recognizing that social services, job training, and education are interconnected in the health and welfare of the family, funding was provided to each tribe to develop a framework for coordination of services with metrics to measure effectiveness. Metrics and data from these pilot locations would then serve to frame expansion of the program or adjustments to the program.

Data, Data, Data

The importance of data cannot be overstated. The primary question OMB and budget staff in the House and Senate ask agencies for is data to support the need, and data to show that increased investment will be effective. In a normal budget process, data drives decisions.

Unfortunately, data can be elusive for tribes for many reasons. Rightly, tribes are reluctant to share some data for both historical and modern reasons. In other situations, data may not exist—either because the federal agency or tribe does not have the infrastructure to collect the data, or the data that has been collected is not reliable. Any planning for federal budgets must include not only a plan to collect data but also a plan on what types of data will be shared with federal officials.

A concrete example of the importance of data is the BIA Office of Justice Services (OJS) High Priority Performance Goal Initiative (HPPG) launched in 2009. Tribes, OJS, and the administration advocated that funding for staffing of tribal law enforcement at levels commensurate with local and state jurisdictions would result in a decrease of crime on reservations. The lack of data showing that increased staffing would lead to a decrease in crime resulted in pushback from OMB and other budget staff. The concept of HPPG was simple. Fund staffing at a number of reservations commensurate with state and local levels and collect data over a two-year time period to determine whether an increase in staffing actually lowered crime. Metrics were developed to measure the results.

The initiative showed that across four reservations, the crime rate on every reservation initially went up. It went up because residents saw that there was an active law-enforcement presence that had the resources to respond to and investigate crimes. The initiative also showed that over the course of the period that violent crime rates dropped 35 percent over two years. On one reservation the violent crime rate dropped by 68 percent. The results showed that budget increases in this area resulted in an overall lower crime rate. The data and metrics were critical to further budget increases for tribal law enforcement.

PRACTITIONER PERSPECTIVE

Too often, tribal advocates will only tell part of the story—the background and the challenge. Effective tribal advocates will also propose solutions in consumable increments. Let's return to the Tiwahe example. There, the tribe and its community identified a long-term goal—healthy families and communities—and proposed solutions that would lead to that goal. The initial proposed solution was to establish some funding for planning purposes—what does coordinated family services look like for their community? The planning would then lead to implementation steps. Short-term steps could be establishing family coordinators that could advise and direct access to different programs, or relocating the social services programs closer to law enforcement so that people would feel safer when accessing social services. Long-term steps could include modernizing how the tribe organizes its particular services and programs, and physical infrastructure to support that approach. The tribe's inclusion of proposed solutions that were achievable within the constraints of time and overall budget helped federal decision-makers advocate internally for increased budgets.

Showing Investment Is Smart

A component of proposing solutions as part of the federal budget process is explaining why the solution makes sense from a budgeting perspective. In addition to trust and treaty responsibilities, increased budget proposals often show how upfront investment will reduce costs in the long term. The law-enforcement HPPG initiative demonstrated that not only did increased law-enforcement personnel result in a lower violent crime rate, but that it led to a better long-term outcome because of intervention at an earlier point with resources to help both the victim's family and in some cases the offender, rather than a system of long-term incarceration.

Communicating Results

Finally, it is critical to communicate results to all of the components that play a role in developing, proposing, authorizing, and implementing federal budgets. Communicating results addresses either a vacuum of information or actual misinformation and continues building support for the initiative. Communicating negative results is often just as important as communicating positive results. For example, in the initial stages of the HPPG initiative the results were negative—tribes were reporting dramatic increases in crime. If communication stopped then, a federal budget official's takeaway might have been that the pilot program was a bust, or that there needed to be significant changes to the program.

Through communication it became apparent that this wasn't unique to one particular tribe, but was happening at all pilot locations. The communication led to the conclusion that the increase wasn't because of a sudden uptick in crimes, but the fact that the local communities felt confident that reports would actually be acted upon. Continued communication over a longer time period shared that violent crime actually decreased significantly at each location. Tribes and OJS shared this outcome broadly and repeatedly to support increases in law enforcement budgets. In doing so, other federal commissions and entities pointed to these results as data, not only to support increased budgets but to advocate for improvements to federal policy.[11]

NOTES

1. https://www.govinfo.gov/content/pkg/CFR-2014-title2-vol1/pdf/CFR-2014-title2-vol1-part200.pdf.

2. OMB Memorandum M-12-01, https://obamawhitehouse.archives.gov/sites/default/files/omb/memoranda/2012/m-12-01.pdf.

3. OMB Memorandum M-17-26, https://www.whitehouse.gov/sites/whitehouse.gov/files/omb/memoranda/2017/M-17-26.pdf.

4. *CFO Home Page.* CFO.gov. (n.d.). Retrieved October 12, 2021, from https://cfo.gov/grants/grants-resources/.

5. *House Committee on appropriations.* House Committee on Appropriations. (n.d.). Retrieved October 12, 2021, from https://appropriations.house.gov/.

6. *United States Senate Committee on appropriations.* Home | United States Senate Committee on Appropriations. (n.d.). Retrieved October 12, 2021, from https://www.appropriations.senate.gov/.

7. *Interior, environment, and Related Agencies (116th congress).* House Committee on Appropriations. (n.d.). Retrieved October 12, 2021, from https://appropriations.house.gov/subcommittees/interior-environment-and-related-agencies-116th-congress.

8. *Interior, environment, and related agencies: United States Senate Committee on appropriations.* Subcommittee | Subcommittee List | Subcommittees | United States Senate Committee on Appropriations. (n.d.). Retrieved October 12, 2021, from https://www.appropriations.senate.gov/subcommittees/interior-environment-and-related-agencies.

9. *Home: The United States Senate Committee on Indian affairs.* Home | The United States Senate Committee on Indian Affairs. (n.d.). Retrieved October 12, 2021, from https://www.indian.senate.gov/.

10. *The House Committee on Natural Resources.* Natural Resources Committee. (n.d.). Retrieved October 12, 2021, from https://naturalresources.house.gov/.

11. "A Roadmap for Making Native America Safer," Report to the President and Congress of the United States, Indian Law and Order Commission (May 2015), https://www.aisc.ucla.edu/iloc/report/.

GLOSSARY

Appropriations bill. Legislation under the jurisdiction of the House and Senate Committees on Appropriations that provides budget authority for federal programs or agencies.

Continuing resolution. Legislation in the form of a joint resolution enacted by Congress, when the new fiscal year is about to begin or has begun, to provide budget authority for federal agencies and programs to continue in operation until the regular appropriations acts are enacted.

Executive order. A declaration by the President that has the force of law, usually based on existing statutory powers. It does not require any action by the Congress to take effect.

Forward funding. Funding that becomes available beginning late in the budget year and is carried into at least one following fiscal year.

Mandatory appropriation or spending. Spending budget authority and outlays controlled by laws other than annual appropriations acts.

Office of Management and Budget (OMB). The White House agency that assists the President in overseeing the preparation of the federal budget and supervises its administration in executive branch agencies. In helping to formulate the President's spending plans, OMB evaluates the effectiveness of agency programs, policies, and procedures; assesses competing funding demands among agencies; and sets funding priorities.

OMB circular. Instructions or information issued by OMB to federal agencies. These are expected to have a continuing effect of two years or more.

Omnibus bill. A bill that combines many individual appropriations bills together and is passed as one combined package.

Passback. The Office of Management and Budget's formal response to the federal departments and agencies on their budget submissions. The Office of Management and Budget will increase, decrease, and/or maintain budget totals. Usually, by Thanksgiving, initial decisions by OMB are made and "passed back" to federal departments and agencies.

Presidential memoranda. Very similar to executive orders, except they are not required by law to be printed in the Federal Register; they are not required to cite the President's legal authority (see 1 C.F.R. § 19.1); and the Office of Management and Budget is not required to issue a "Budgetary Impact Statement" on executive memoranda.

President's Budget. The document sent to Congress by the President in January or February of each year, as required by law (31 U.S.C. § 1105), requesting new budget authority for federal programs and estimating federal revenues and outlays for the upcoming fiscal year and four subsequent outyears.

Use or lose funding. Funding that must be obligated by the agency prior to the end of a fiscal year, typically September 30th.

Tribal-Local Intergovernmental Agreements

Nicholas C. Zaferatos

NATIVE AMERICAN TRIBES DEFINE THEIR FUTURE VISION THROUGH POLICIES that reflect their community's particular values and priorities. It is not uncommon for the policies of tribal communities to diverge from those of surrounding non-Indian communities as policies reflect differences in community needs and circumstances. Intergovernmental agreements (IGAs) provide a tool with which tribes and regional governments may overcome discrepancies in policy that may adversely affect tribal rights both on reservations as well as in off-reservation areas where treaty rights extend.[1] Efforts that promote mutual understanding between tribes and local governments help lead to conflict avoidance and to beneficial forms of cooperation that foster cultural diversity, equity, and inclusion among the communities that occupy a shared region. This chapter reflects the experiences of the Swinomish Indian Tribal Community in Washington State, which has employed intergovernmental cooperation as a key strategy in its efforts to strengthen its governance control over its reservation affairs and to advance its treaty rights in ceded territories.

BEST PRACTICES

Several important lessons have emerged as best practices in improved intergovernmental relations and are evidenced in experiences between tribes, states, and local governments:

- Regional cooperation between tribes and regional governments becomes possible when based on a government-to-government approach and the recognition of the historic circumstances that created conflicts.
- The parties' willingness to cooperate invariably boils down to individual leaders' willingness to form and maintain long-term relationships.
- Long-standing barriers to institutional communication must be broken.
- Commitment to intergovernmental cooperation requires personal and professional commitments by elected officials and staff tasked with resolving complex and often contentious issues. Time and resources must be dedicated to education and the development of skills among policymakers and staff involved in the intergovernmental relationship.
- Unforeseen events that arise require constant monitoring in order to protect the relationship. The process requires the capacity to address conflicting issues through consultation, including a forum for dispute resolution.

REGIONAL DIVERSITY, EQUITY, AND INCLUSION

Native Americans are increasingly asserting their aboriginal, treaty, and reserved inherent self-governance rights to the management of land, natural and cultural resources, and reservation affairs. Although their approach to affirming their rights may vary depending on particular circumstances, they often rely on the judicial system. The legal process has in some cases resulted in shifting the balance of power in the political landscape when tribal interests are affirmed. The emerging recognition of Indian rights by federal, state, and in some cases local governments has begun to alter what had predominantly been an exclusive state governing system with new forms of regional cooperation inclusive of tribal interests. The presumption of state regulatory authority in the management of natural resources, environmental quality, and land use within reservations in particular is shaken whenever a court affirms the validity of a tribal claim of injury to property rights or to a tribe's assertion of its political authority. In some cases, the courts have mandated new forms of resource management that require comanagement by both the tribes and the states, as in the case of the treaty fisheries decision in *United States v. Washington.*[2]

Building intergovernmental relationships provides an effective way for tribes to have their voices heard and to influence decisions both within and beyond their reservation boundaries. The rise of cooperative tribal–state planning structures that accommodate tribal interests is a response to the recognition of tribal rights under the federal self-determination policy and by the courts. The result has been an expansion of governance approaches that include comanagement with states, increased consultation with tribal stakeholders by regional governments, and the recognition of Native traditional knowledge in environmental management. Coordinated planning processes have emerged at the state and local level based on the federal government-to-government relationship model reflected in the federal Indian self-determination policy. Cooperative governance helps to avoid conflict while simultaneously advancing tribal objectives. However, the attainment of mutual governance necessitates the often difficult negotiations among former adversarial governments in the transition from a state-centered system of governance to a pluralistic regional system of governance that integrates tribal interests in regional decision-making.

Benefits of Cooperative Management

Cooperation between tribes and local governments can produce quantitative benefits that include greater efficiencies in the provision of local government services as well as qualitative benefits by reducing jurisdictional conflicts and tensions that many tribes face in their regions. Many states encourage local governments to create joint agreements with other local governments to promote economic growth, emergency services, environmental protection, land-use and transportation planning, and other aspects of regional planning.[3] Although cooperation among local governments is commonplace, less progress has been experienced in the coordination of government services with tribes.

TRIBAL EXCLUSION FROM REGIONAL POLICYMAKING

The causes of regional conflicts between tribes and states and local governments date back to treaty days and to federal policies that sought to permanently alter the nature of many Indian reservations. The General Allotment Act of 1887 in particular allowed for the division and sale of Indian lands and made possible the ownership and occupancy of reservation lands by non-Indians and the imposition of state and local government authority over those lands.[4] Many Indian reservations contain a complex land tenure that includes federal trust lands and fee-simple title. In some regions, Indian reservations contain a disproportionate number of non-Indian residents,[5] challenging a tribe's political authority when state and local governments apply their jurisdiction to reservation fee properties. The management of reservation lands and natural resources is often subject to multiple jurisdictions, which creates an impossible scenario that prevents the attainment of consistent policies unless some mechanism for coordination is available.[6] Past Indian litigation often included civil disputes regarding jurisdiction over non-Indians, the application of tax laws, the creation of public-services districts under state laws, and the imposition of state and local government land-use regulations within reservations. These contentious issues affect the interests of tribes as well as of those of state and local governments and non-Indian reservation residents and property owners.

FIRST STEPS IN BUILDING INTERGOVERNMENTAL RELATIONS

The resolution to the historic conflicts in the relationship between tribes and local governments requires new ways of forming meaningful relationships that begin with intergovernmental dialogue in order to understand different policy positions. Many states have embraced negotiation as an alternative to litigation.[7] Although the new state–tribal relationship model was motivated by the need to address tribal interests in the management of natural resources, the process has evolved further to resolve policy inconsistencies in natural resources policies, public service delivery, and the reconciliation of on-reservation land-use conflicts. The trend toward negotiation has evolved further as some states have adopted policies recognizing the legitimacy of tribal sovereignty.[8] This negotiation approach to intergovernmental relations with tribes has led to many successes in resolving historic conflicts. The goals in forming IGAs among tribes and local governments are to mediate disputes, and to achieve a unified regional vision where tribal interests are more fully represented in policymaking. The tribal benefits to successful IGAs is twofold: to deliver governmental services more efficiently in cooperation rather than in competition with other governments and to achieve reservation-wide and region-wide policy consistency that equitably reflects tribal interests.

ISSUES FOR RECONCILIATION IN RELATIONS BETWEEN TRIBES AND STATE AND LOCAL GOVERNMENTS

Tribes interact with states, local municipalities, and counties in myriad ways. These interactions come about as tribes need to have their concerns acknowledged and expressed. The articulation of tribal interests falls into two categories: those actions that affect tribal interests on Indian reservations and those actions that occur off-reservation where Indian treaty rights exist. Several areas of mutual policy interests that affect both tribes and local governments are summarized below.

Land and Reservation Boundary Claims. Land and reservation boundary claim cases filed by tribes have involved claims of ownership to aboriginal land title, adjacent tidelands, and federal actions that altered reservation boundaries. By upholding such claims, courts affirm the tribal status of land areas previously presumed to be free of Indian title. This can raise concerns regarding federal or state liability in transferring original title to those lands.

Water Resources. Treaties implied that sufficient water would be reserved to satisfy the purposes of the reservations. The priority date of this federally reserved water right is the date when the reservation was established. The quantity of the reserved water right, however, has not been determined for most reservations.

Environmental Management. A state's authority over the application of environmental laws on reservations was clarified in *State of Washington v. Environmental Protection Agency* in 1985, holding that states lack jurisdiction over Indians on Indian lands.[9] The U.S. Environmental Protection Agency's (EPA) 1984 Indian policy supports tribal reservation environmental programs, and many tribes have been granted "treatment as a state" status under federal rules. Although many tribal environmental programs operate independently of state program authority, others work cooperatively under mutual agreements with state programs.

Fish, Shellfish, and Environmental Rights. Washington State's fishing dispute involves the three-decade interpretation and implementation of the fishing-rights clause in the Stevens Treaties of 1854–55. In 1974, the U.S. District Court for the Western District of Washington construed the fishing clause to require an allocation between treaty Indians and other citizens on a "50 percent plus" basis and agreed to retain continuing jurisdiction of the case to assure compliance.[10] In *United States v. Washington*, the tribes contended that in addition to their fishing right they also have a right to have the fishery protected from environmental degradation.[11] Since 1984, the environmental-right question has continued to be of serious concern,[12] and its threat has prompted greater cooperation to achieve a solution with tribes through collaborative habitat-protection efforts. Further, in 1994, the U.S. District Court for the Western District of Washington ruled that treaty tribes have a right to harvest 50 percent of the natural production of shellfish in Washington State.[13] A controversial part of the decision concerned the tribal right to cross private property to exercise harvest rights. In this case, the court ordered the state and the tribes to negotiate a joint implementation plan.

Tribal Regulation of Non-Indians. The application of tribal regulatory authority over non-Indians and fee lands within a reservation has presented ongoing conflicts. Tribes maintain that their jurisdiction over non-Indians preempts state and local jurisdiction. The U.S. Supreme Court has analyzed jurisdictional disputes by applying infringement and preemption tests,[14] and has liberally construed the preemption tests in favor of tribal jurisdiction in a number of opinions, but has also affirmed concurrent state jurisdiction over certain reservation activities unless that jurisdiction is expressly preempted by federal law.

Taxation. State taxation over property owned by Indians has historically been the subject of conflict. The states' early position was that a state's taxing authority was valid unless expressly preempted by federal law or treaty. Although the U.S. Supreme Court affirmed the exclusion of state taxation of Indian personal property within a reservation, it raised questions regarding the state's authority to impose a tax on non-Indians within reservations where a tribal tax on the same transaction already exists.[15]

Gaming. Indian tribes have expanded their reservation economies through gaming activities, resulting in a series of litigations. In 1988, Congress intervened in tribal gaming activities to require tribes and states to negotiate compact agreements regarding certain types of gaming and to foster state and tribal regulatory cooperation.

MEDIATING THE IGA

Mediation organizations play an important role in facilitating the resolution of intergovernmental disputes. Washington State and the tribes supported such mediating efforts by forming the Northwest Renewable Resources Center (NRRC) in the 1980s to resolve conflicts regarding natural resources. The NRRC served as a catalyst for devising solutions to a treaty-rights fisheries decision based on the view that conflicts over policy can be addressed through direct communication between adversaries in their search for common ground. The process served to facilitate the formulation of policy involving tribes, the state, and local and regional governments in a broad range of complex issues, ranging from land use and environmental regulation to taxation and service delivery. Table 1 identifies several agreements negotiated among tribes and state and local governments, illustrating a growing trend that emphasizes cooperative approaches in intergovernmental dispute resolution.

HOW TRIBES AND LOCAL GOVERNMENTS VIEW INTERGOVERNMENTAL PARTNERSHIPS

A national survey of tribal and county planning departments identified several solutions for improving intergovernmental coordination.[16] Tribal respondents almost uniformly supported regional cooperation between tribal and county governments. They agreed that greater understanding about tribal sovereignty and treaty rights was needed. Counties generally acknowledged that their obligations to multiple stakeholders often conflicted with tribal interests, and that issues associated with reservation non-Indian land and residency continue to be problematic. Tribes emphasized the importance of the relationship based on a government-to-government basis before intergovernmental coordination

Table 1. Examples of Intergovernmental Negotiated Solutions in Washington State

TRIBAL PARTICIPANTS	NON-TRIBAL PARTICIPANTS	AGREEMENT TOPIC
Suquamish Tribe; Muckleshoot Indian Tribe	City of Seattle	Mitigation of impacts to marine habitat
Confederated Tribes and Bands of the Yakima Nation; Nez Perce Tribe; Confederated Tribes of Warm Springs	U.S. Department of Agriculture, U.S. Forest Service, Washington and Oregon Counties	Protection of cultural resources and treaty rights
Puyallup Tribe of Indians	Port of Tacoma; Pierce County; Cities of Tacoma, Fife, and Puyallup	Resolution of tribal land claims
Tulalip Tribes	Snohomish County	Aquatic resource protection plan
Muckleshoot Indian Tribe	City of Seattle	Fisheries-habitat-restoration plan
The Confederated Tribes of the Colville Reservation; Spokane Tribe of Indians	Spokane County; Washington State; federal agencies	Cooperation in regional planning
Skokomish Indian Tribe	Mason County	Reduction of on-reservation jurisdictional conflict
Upper Skagit Tribe; Sauk-Suiattle Indian Tribe; Swinomish Indian Tribal Community	Seattle City Light	Mitigation of cultural resources
Swinomish Indian Tribal Community	Skagit County	Cooperation in land-use planning; law enforcement cross-deputization agreement
Swinomish Indian Tribal Community; Quinault Indian Nation	Skagit and Clallam Counties	Cooperation in land-use planning and timber management
Port Gamble S'Klallam and Skokomish Indian Tribes	Kitsap, Mason, and Jefferson Counties	Restoration plan for Hood Canal waterways

can proceed. The survey identified several measures to overcome the barriers in tribal–county relationships:

- *Regular Meetings.* Both governments identified the importance of regular meetings to identify and stay informed about current issues and to build trust.
- *Continuing Education.* Both governments recognized the need to gain knowledge about their respective governing systems, Indian policy history, and community priorities.
- *Formal Agreements.* IGAs were identified as critical first steps for institutionalizing a working relationship.
- *Topics of Interest for Future Collaboration.* Survey respondents indicated a strong interest in pursuing collaboration in the following areas: land use, environmental protection, natural resources, public safety, transportation planning, public services, and utilities.

PRINCIPLES AND PROCEDURAL CONSIDERATIONS IN IGAS

The emerging precedent favoring negotiated solutions offers an important pathway for reconciling the historic exclusion of tribes in regional governance and building more culturally tolerant and diverse regional communities. Intergovernmental cooperation depends on the acceptance of a paradigm shift toward inclusionary tribal participation in regional affairs and an institutional structure based on a government-to-government approach. The following points, adapted from the principles and structure of "cooperative federalism" and state–tribal accords,[7] can serve as a guide in the formulation of IGAs to support on-reservation collaboration and to expand tribal participation in off-reservation policymaking.

- *Definitions.* The IGA should describe the geographical boundaries subject to the agreement as well as the participating government parties.
- *Purposes and Intent.* The parties' intent should emphasize consultation and cooperation with the aim of developing coordinated plans, programs, and policies to improve the health, safety, and welfare of all citizens; to provide for efficiencies in services; and to protect cultural and natural resources.
- *Tribal Participation in Regional Governance.* Indian tribes that elect to become parties to the agreement voluntarily join in the regional governance process, and the parties recognize their respective sovereign status and commit to cooperate on a government-to-government basis.
- *Lands Not within Reservations.* The parties recognize that tribes have interests and rights regarding treaty-protected cultural and natural resources that may occur off reservations and therefore agree to formulate policies that are respective of such treaty rights.
- *Lands within Reservations.* The parties may desire to enter into a collaborative planning process with tribes to address policy inconsistencies affecting Indian reservation lands and resources. The parties may engage in a coordinated planning process to develop consistent policies and service programs that will not limit any degree

of jurisdiction held by either party or be misconstrued as a recognition of jurisdiction by one party over another.

- *Regional Policy Collaboration Structure.* A Regional Policies Committee (RPC) should be formed among the parties to develop policies pertaining to topics identified in the IGA. The committee should be composed of the parties' elected and appointed representatives to the RPC. The RPC should appoint two co-chairpersons representing local government(s) and tribe(s). A technical advisory committee may be established at the direction of the RPC. Decisions should be made by consensus or by a supermajority vote of members present when consensus cannot be reached.

- *Public Education, Participation, and Ratification.* As part of the collaborative process, the education of the parties and citizens of the region should emphasize understanding about tribal history, culture, treaty rights, and institutions. Meetings of the RPC should be public and provide opportunities for public comment. After the RPC has referred the draft recommendations, each party should provide the opportunity for public review and ratification by its constituency.

- *Withdrawal, Amendment, and Termination.* Any party may withdraw from the IGA by providing written notice to the other parties. The parties may terminate the agreement by unanimous vote. Changes to the agreement may be made by a majority vote of RPC members.

- *Term.* The IGA should commence on the date that is approved by all of the parties and remain in effect for a period described in the IGA. The agreement may automatically renew for a prescribed period unless terminated.

- *Jurisdiction.* Nothing in the agreement should limit or waive the regulatory authority or jurisdiction of any of the parties to this agreement.

- *Good-Faith Efforts.* The parties should seek in good faith to resolve any dispute arising out of or relating to the agreement. In the event a dispute arises, the parties agree to make a good-faith effort to work toward the successful completion of the activities envisioned by this agreement.

- *Dispute Resolution.* If in disagreement with any RPC recommendation, the disputing party may provide the RPC co-chairs with a written notice of such disagreement, identifying the nature of and the circumstances that caused the disagreement. If the disagreement is not resolved, the IGA should provide procedures to invoke nonbinding alternative dispute-resolution (ADR) procedures. The IGA should identify the method, rules, and cost-sharing obligations of the parties for the ADR procedure.

IGAs as Strategic Planning

The approach used by the Swinomish Indian Tribal Community in Washington State to achieve intergovernmental coordination through agreements with regional governments has proved strategic in advancing tribal goals, eliminating conflict, enhancing service-delivery efficiencies, and strengthening tribal sovereignty. As a first step in taking this approach, the tribe acknowledged that effective reservation planning could not occur in isolation from its surrounding political region. Tribal initiatives fostering intergovernmental cooperation resulted in effective outcomes to reconcile a history of regional conflict. The tribe's experiences demonstrate that through the incorporation of multiple interests in public-policy development, efficient and cost-effective utilitarian relationships can result.

The Treaty of Point Elliott of 1855 set aside the Swinomish Indian Reservation as a permanent tribal homeland. Like many reservations, the Swinomish Indian reservation was severely affected by the General Allotment Act, which allowed allotted tribal members' land parcels to be sold to non-Indians, and other federal actions that declared certain reservation lands as surplus, thereby diminishing the size of the original reservation. The process of reservation-land division and removal of land from federal trust occurred over several decades and produced a checkerboard pattern of fee simple and federal trust reservation land tenure.

Maintaining governance within the reservation became a primary objective of the Swinomish Tribe when reservation land tenure emerged as a central cause of jurisdictional conflict as state and local governments imposed regulatory policies that impeded the ability of the tribe to manage its reservation.[18] Non-tribal government authority operating on the reservation concerned civil and criminal jurisdiction, roads and utilities, taxation, and the zoning of fee-simple reservation lands. The tribe's inherent jurisdictional authority over its reservation had been preempted through a series of intrusions by the state and local governments. The tribe recognized that in order to control its reservation development, it needed to affirm its powers of self-government and to engage with regional governments.

IGAs Advancing Swinomish Self-Determination

Regaining control of the reservation was the first step toward strengthening the tribe's self-determination. Beginning in the early 1980s, when I was employed as the tribe's planning director, a two-phase strategy was adopted by the tribal council: first, enacting sufficient self-governing powers to preempt state- and county-asserted jurisdiction, and second, negotiating IGAs. The tribe was aware that jurisdictional tensions would continue unless a dramatic shift occurred in the way regional governance was conducted. A change was needed to ensure that tribal interests were fully considered both on the reservation and throughout the region. By enacting policies that asserted its own authority in matters concerning reservation development, the tribe sought to disrupt the political status quo and the application of non-tribal government rules on the reservation. By pursuing a strategy of cooperation, the tribe sought to reverse conflicting reservation policies as well as to increase its influence in off-reservation policymaking in support of its treaty-based interests.

Since 1984, the Swinomish Tribe has negotiated a wide range of IGAs with county, municipal, and regional governments as well as with state and federal agencies to foster intergovernmental cooperation. These agreements have effectively bolstered the tribe's interests both on the reservation and throughout the region. This approach to regional cooperation replaced the previous system of unilateral non-tribal authority with a bilateral system of cooperative management. The cooperative approach began by addressing on-reservation land-use planning and regulation and later expanded to many other areas of public service delivery.

Reservation Land Use. The checkerboard land-tenure conditions on the reservation created two separate regulatory schemes, resulting in development on reservation fee lands that conflicted with tribal policies. Rather than litigate the validity of the county's jurisdiction over reservation fee lands, the tribe and county agreed to resolve policy conflicts by embarking on a collaborative planning program. An IGA was approved in 1987 to begin joint land-use planning based on a view that if the tribe and county could agree on a consistent land-use policy, matters regarding jurisdiction would become a secondary concern. The governments sought to develop identical but jurisdictionally separate plans and regulations as well as a system for joint administration. Tribal- and county-elected officials recognized that historical events had created a situation whereby Indian and non-Indian interests were intertwined on the reservation, and that neither government could act unilaterally without incurring objections from the other party and the threat of litigation. An advisory planning board was established with equal representation, and a neutral facilitator guided the effort. The board's members attended work sessions on federal Indian policy and law, the functions of tribal and county governments, and consensus-based problem-solving techniques to broaden understanding about the cultural and political differences between the two communities. The board developed a draft comprehensive land-use plan for review and approval by each government. The plan articulated goals and policies to guide the stewardship of the reservation and outlined a process for joint implementation. Although the tribe continues to assert its jurisdiction on all reservation lands, the approach provides for county participation in reservation decision-making on certain matters.

Tribal Water Authority. In 1984, the tribe, county, state, and regional water purveyors participated in the state's first water-supply coordinated planning program that included an Indian tribe under the state's laws.[19] In carrying out its authority as the reservation's utility provider, the tribe constructed a public water-supply system that serves the majority of the reservation's Indian and non-Indian population under common regional utility standards. To overcome the inefficiencies associated with operating small state-established private water associations within the reservation, the tribe also agreed to incorporate these water associations under tribal utility laws, thus removing the presumption of a valid state authority that had originally created the reservation water associations.

Wastewater Treatment. A regional wastewater-treatment facility, managed under agreement with the tribe and a local municipality, serves to meet the reservation's growth demands. Reservation utility services required compliance with tribal policies, furthering the tribe's control over reservation development. In addition, a reservation residential community petitioned the tribe in 1993 to reconstitute its private wastewater utility, established under state laws, as a tribal sewer utility district, which eliminated the state's jurisdiction on the reservation and ensured compliance with tribal policies.

Public Safety. To overcome the complexity of law enforcement jurisdiction and to reduce duplicative public-safety programs, the tribe, county, and area municipalities established cross-deputizing commissions that authorize tribal and non-tribal police officers to act under dual local and tribal authority with consistent law enforcement procedures and standards. Tribal law enforcement provides first response for calls on the reservation, reducing the response time from forty-five minutes to less than five minutes.

Transportation Planning. A state highway intersection on the reservation experienced a high occurrence of traffic accidents and fatalities and was recognized as a public-safety issue. In the 1990s, the tribe conducted a study to identify cost-effective solutions and assumed the lead-agency role for coordinating project planning. The state, the county, and the regional transportation authority supported the tribe's highway-improvement project, and federal funds were matched with state and regional funds to complete the improvements in 2003.

Water Rights. In 1996, the tribe joined two other tribes, regional water purveyors, the county, and the state to establish a process for securing water rights from the Skagit River in order to meet future water-supply demands and conservation needs. The resulting agreement established in-stream flow rates necessary to protect treaty fisheries. The agreement represented the first program in the state for resolving in-stream flows to protect threatened and endangered salmon resources.

Environmental Protection. Several agreements were entered into with the U.S. Environmental Protection Agency (USEPA) to develop the tribe's capacity to protect the reservation environment. In 1996, a Tribal Environmental Agreement was signed to assist the tribe in assessing environmental threats and to provide funding and technical assistance for environmental programs to address water- and air-quality protection, invasive-species management, and the remediation of toxic dumpsites on the Swinomish Reservation. In 1996, the tribe, the state, and the USEPA agreed to the joint administration of a federal water-quality permit where the tribe contracts with the state to perform technical analysis for

National Pollution Discharge Elimination Systems permit applications on the reservation. The agreement redefines the state's role from a permitting agency to a consultative agency under tribal and federal authority, further removing the state's jurisdictional presence from the reservation.

Public Parks. A joint-ownership agreement was signed in 2010 by the tribe and the state for the purchase of Kiket Island, the first jointly owned and managed Tribal State Park in Washington State. The Kukutali Preserve and adjoining tidelands are home to endangered and threatened species and important shellfish resources.

While the benefits of negotiation often outweigh the costs of litigation, other circumstances may preclude the parties from accepting compromises, such as in cases where neither the state nor a tribe may concede its sovereign rights to control land. Despite the long-term success in the Swinomish Tribe–Skagit County relationship, conflicts between the governments still persist. The agreements have survived administrative appeals, filed in the 1990s, by both the county and the tribe. The tribe appealed the county's Critical Areas Ordinance for failing to adequately protect fisheries resources in the region. The county appealed the federal government's decision to accept a reservation fee parcel into tribal trust ownership for a tribal economic development project.[20] Even though the governments have worked tirelessly to maintain consistency in their mutual land use policy, these separate appeal actions illustrate that consistency is not always attainable. Both legal actions followed failed attempts to negotiate a compromise solution, yet illustrate how the institutionalized cooperative relationship can endure even when other conflicts cannot be settled amicably through negotiation. As the 1987 Tribal-County IGA had anticipated and provided for, and as these legal appeal proceedings demonstrate, deference to a third-party mediator is sometimes necessary.

PRACTITIONER PERSPECTIVE

In my role as the Swinomish Tribe's general manager and planning director between 1980 and 2000, I helped advise the tribe's governing body in devising strategic actions that included entering into over a dozen intergovernmental agreements. As a result, the tribe's interests in its on-reservation affairs have evolved from a state of political dormancy and control by county and regional governments to becoming the primary governing authority on the reservation. Its participation in regional policymaking had reversed its isolation from this policymaking with outcomes that have been beneficial not only for the tribe but also for the entire region. As the Swinomish case and other examples from Washington State illustrate, the cooperative approach to intergovernmental relations can represent a constructive approach to reversing a history of jurisdictional and policy conflict by simultaneously promoting the interests of both tribal and non-tribal communities. From a regional perspective, IGAs represent a pathway to promote equitable regional diversity that is inclusive and respectful of the interests of tribal nations. The process of intergovernmental cooperation serves to broaden a tribe's political influence both on and off the reservation, thereby greatly enhancing its interests.

NOTES

1. The term intergovernmental agreement (IGA) is used throughout this chapter as an umbrella term to include memorandum of agreement (MOA), memorandum of understanding (MOU), compacts, contracts, accords, or other forms of written agreement made between tribes and state and local governments to address problems of mutual concern, including the management of natural resources, coordinated law enforcement, delivery of human services, tax revenue sharing, and the regulation of gaming activities.
2. 384 F. Supp. 312 (W.D. Wash., 1974), aff'd, 520 F. 2d. 676 (9th Cir. 1976), cert. denied, 423 U.S. 1086 (1976).
3. Wisconsin's intergovernmental cooperation law requires local governments within metropolitan areas to sign compact agreements with neighboring governments for the provision of joint public services (Wisconsin Statutes, chap. 66, subchap. III). Washington State mandated local government cooperation when it enacted the Growth Management Act in 1990, requiring land-use plans to be consistent with adjoining local jurisdictions.
4. 25 U.S.C. sec. 331–34, 339, 341, 348, 349, 354, 381.
5. The Puget Sound region of Washington State contains sixteen federally recognized Indian reservations, with a combined reservation population of about seventy thousand. These reservations have about 85 percent non-Indians.
6. In 2002, the U.S. Court of Appeals for the Ninth Circuit upheld a tribe's land-use jurisdiction over reservation fee-simple lands held by an individual Indian person (*Gobin & Madison v. Snohomish County v. The Tulalip Tribes of Washington*, 2002 [No. 00-36031, D.C. No. CV-99-01432-RSL]). The court affirmed that by making this person's fee lands

freely alienable, Congress did not expressly authorize county jurisdiction over those lands, nor did circumstances warrant county jurisdiction to apply.

7. Although the benefits of negotiation often outweigh the costs of litigation, other circumstances may preclude the parties from accepting compromises, such as in cases where neither the state nor a tribe would have to concede its sovereign rights to control land or resources.

8. Such as in the Centennial Accord of 1989 and the Millennium Agreement of 1999 between Washington State and twenty-nine recognized tribal governments, which acknowledged tribal sovereignty and committed to a working relationship based on the federal government-to-government relationship model.

9. 752 F.2d 1465 (9th Cir. 1985).

10. *United States v. Washington*, 384 F. Supp. 312 (W.D. Wash. 1974).

11. *United States v. Washington*, 506 F. Supp. 187 (W.D. Wash. 1980), en banc appeal dismissed (9th Cir. No. 91-3111, Dec. 17, 1984).

12. The U.S. Supreme Court left standing a lower court ruling that the State of Washington must redesign and rebuild road culverts to uphold Native American treaty rights to fish. See Docket no. 17-269; 584 U.S. _; 138 S. Ct. 1832; 201 L. Ed. 2d 200.

13. In *United States v. Washington*, sub proceeding no. 89-3.

14. *McClanahan v. Arizona State Tax Comm'n*, 411 U.S. 164 (1973). Preemption analysis is based on the principle of balancing competing state, federal, and tribal interests.

15. *United States v. Anderson*, 425 U.S. 463 (1976); *Washington v. Confederated Tribes of the Colville Indian Reservation*, 447 U.S. 134 (1980).

16. The survey was conducted between 2018 and 2019 by Western Washington University. Survey respondents included seventy-three tribes and sixty-seven counties in twenty-two states.

17. The term "cooperative federalism" refers to the federal–state partnership established by the EPA for the delegation and coordination of federal environmental programs. The policy was later extended to authorize tribes with the delegated authority over environmental programs affecting Indian reservations. The Centennial Accord of 1989 and the Millennium Agreement of 1999 by Washington State and twenty-nine tribes proclaim a government-to-government relationship between the governments. Both agreements have improved the way federal and state agencies work with tribes to resolve conflict issues.

18. Nicholas C. Zaferatos, "Planning the Native American Tribal Community: Understanding the Basis of Power Controlling the Reservation Territory," *Journal of the American Planning Association* 64 (4): 395–410.

19. Tribes are considered public agencies, so state and local agencies are permitted to enter into agreements with tribes for cooperative efforts to promote "mutual advantage" (State of Washington, RCW 39.34.010).

20. In 1998, the tribe filed an appeal before the Washington State Growth Management Hearings Board (*Skagit Audubon Society et al. v. Skagit County and Agriculture for Skagit County et al.*, No. 00-2-0018c) claiming that the county inadequately protected critical resource areas for fisheries resources. The board affirmed the tribe's claim and remanded back to the county. In 1999, the county sought to reverse a Bureau of Indian Affairs decision (United States Department of the Interior, Office of Hearings and Appeals, Interior Board of Indian Appeals, Docket No. IBIA 02-1002-A) to accept 350 acres of fee land owned by the tribe into trust ownership for tribal economic development. The major issues that were raised concerned the conversion of farmland to urban uses.

GLOSSARY

Cooperative federalism. The term cooperative federalism refers to the federal–state partnership established by the EPA for the delegation and coordination of federal environmental programs. The policy was later extended to authorize tribes with the delegated authority over environmental programs affecting Indian reservations.

General Allotment Act of 1887. A congressional act that allowed allotted tribal members' land parcels to be sold to non-Indians, and declared certain reservation lands as surplus, thereby diminishing the size of the original reservation. The process of reservation-land division and removal of land from federal trust occurred over several decades and produced a checkerboard pattern of fee-simple and federal-trust reservation land tenure.

Gobin & Madison v. Snohomish County v. The Tulalip Tribes of Washington, **2002.** In 2002, the U.S. Court of Appeals for the Ninth Circuit upheld a tribe's land-use jurisdiction over reservation fee-simple lands held by an individual Indian person.

Intergovernmental agreements (IGAs). The term intergovernmental agreement (IGA) is an umbrella term to include memorandum of agreement (MOA), memorandum of understanding (MOU), compacts, contracts, accords, or other forms of written agreement made between tribes and state and local governments to address problems of mutual concern.

Northwest Renewable Resources Center (NRRC). Washington State and the tribes supported mediating efforts by forming the Northwest Renewable Resources Center (NRRC) in the 1980s to resolve conflicts regarding natural resources. The NRRC served as a catalyst for devising solutions to a treaty-rights fisheries decision based on the view that conflicts over policy can be addressed through direct communication between adversaries in their search for common ground.

Skagit Audubon Society et al. v. Skagit County and Agriculture for Skagit County et al. In 1998, Swinomish Tribe filed an appeal before the Washington State Growth Management Hearings Board claiming that the county inadequately protected critical resources areas for fisheries resources. The board affirmed the tribe's claim and remanded back to the county.

Washington Centennial Accord of 1989. The Washington State Centennial Accord of 1989 between Washington State and twenty-nine recognized tribal governments acknowledged tribal sovereignty and committed to a working relationship based on the federal government-to-government relationship model.

Washington Millennium Agreement of 1999. The Millennium Agreement of 1999 between Washington State and twenty-nine recognized tribal governments provided the mechanism to implement the Centennial Accord of 1989.

Tribal Influence in Federal and State Politics

Michael D. O. Rusco, Kirsten Matoy Carlson, and Patrice Kunesh

THIS CHAPTER WILL LAY OUT OPTIONS ON HOW TRIBES CAN PARTICIPATE POLITically in federal and state governments. Tribes should determine what options are best for their own situation. The chapter includes a discussion of the benefits of lobbying, the costs of lobbying, basic advice, things to avoid, a list of online resources, and perspectives from an experienced practitioner.

BEST PRACTICES SUMMARY

- Identify the problem and how you want it resolved. Make your request to policymakers concise and easy to understand.
- Know who you need to approach and how to approach them.
- Build relationships with policymakers before asking them for help.
- Build coalitions with other Indian nations, national and regional Indian organizations, local and state governments, and other interested parties.
- Always act with honesty and integrity when engaging with federal or state policymakers, coalition partners, and other stakeholders.

INTRODUCTION: BENEFITS AND COSTS

There are lots of advantages to lobbying at both the state and federal levels. Lobbying is a form of political participation.[1] Tribes can create beneficial partnerships, influence federal and state legislation and policy, and head off adverse actions through lobbying.

Tribes are in a unique position. They are part of and subject to the federal government, but many tribes have more complicated relationships with state governments.

Tribes have interacted with the federal government in various ways over the past five centuries.[2] Until 1871, Indian nations used the treaty-making process to retain their existing governmental and property rights. They also petitioned and sent delegates to Washington, DC, to meet with members of the executive branch and Congress.[3] Since 1871 and increasingly over the past fifty years, Indian nations have used litigation, diplomacy, the occupation of federal lands, and lobbying to assert sovereignty and treaty rights.[4]

Two scholars—Prof. Robert Odawi Porter and Prof. John LaVelle—represent the breadth of tribal attitudes toward broad-based participation (voting, legislative representation, and lobbying) in non-tribal politics. Prof. Porter sees tribal participation in state or federal government as a categorical negative that will ultimately destroy tribal identity and sovereignty.

> Maintaining dual political allegiance has a negative effect on the loyalty that one has to a political community. Failure to hold absolute political allegiance toward one nation can compromise one's political loyalty to either or both of the nations of which the individual is a citizen. This can be a threat to both of the nations extending citizenship status. . . . This effect can be even more destructive if one of the two nations is small and weak in relation to the other.
>
> Because forcing American citizenship upon Indigenous peoples undermines the loyalty that one has to one's Indigenous nation, as the commitment of Indigenous citizens to their Indigenous nation diminishes, dual citizenship will have the effect of destroying the Indigenous nation from within. . . .
>
> Participating in the American political system wholly abandons the notion of Indigenous sovereignty and the nation-to-nation relationship established by the treaties with the United States. Voting in American elections, running for political office and lobbying American officials totally concedes to the United States the

controlling authority that it has long sought. . . . Foreign nations do not direct their citizens to vote in American elections, nor do they fund American political candidates to effectuate their agendas with the American government; they send ambassadors and engage in diplomatic relations.[5]

Prof. LaVelle disagrees and urges increased broad-based participation at both the state and federal level. In a response to Prof. Porter, Prof. LaVelle wrote:

Indian activists within the American political system work constantly to secure *respect* for that nation-to-nation relationship, by educating non-Indian political operatives with whom they interact about the crucial need for recognizing and affirming the sovereignty of tribal nations. . . . [W]hen Indian people engage [voting, running for office, and lobbying American officials], they typically do so precisely for the purpose of leveraging the institutions of American government to *support* the political self-determination and autonomy of Indian nations, or at least to induce the United States to stop undermining tribal sovereignty through the application of coercive instruments of "federal Indian control law." It is simply untrue that by participating in American politics, Indian people "undervalue the fact that Indians also have their own Indigenous governments and political processes." In reality, Indian political activists *highly* value the unique and enduring nation status of Indian tribes; indeed, they *actively manifest* this supreme value by working energetically to remind federal policymakers of the importance of this status—and within precisely those spheres of political influence and power where that reminder is desperately and constantly needed.[6]

One of the authors here sees a middle path between Prof. Porter's and Prof. LaVelle's positions. "No one can deny that tribes and their citizens have had greater success in non-tribal politics in recent years, becoming better able to influence legislation and policy targeting tribes."[7] This success has created considerable opportunities and benefits for tribes, and helped defeat adverse laws and policies. That said, tribal citizen participation in non-tribal politics by voting and legislative representation in non-tribal elections has a downside that lobbying does not.

In essence, because democracies are based on consent and voting forms a type of consent, voting by reservation residents in non-tribal elections invites states to apply their laws on reservation lands. This is contrary to tribes' long-standing efforts to exclude state jurisdiction from tribal territories.

Thus, whether to participate in non-tribal politics becomes a strategic choice each tribe must make after fully assessing the long-term potential costs and benefits. It boils down to whether a particular tribe will get more out of participating than it might lose by participating in the long run. Fortunately, lobbying by tribes is a modern version of the diplomatic relations tribes have always maintained with the federal government. Therefore, lobbying does not imply consent to non-tribal authority.[8]

Basic Advice: What You Need to Know Before Lobbying

Tribes need to know several things before trying to influence federal, state, or local officials. Here are the top five most important ones:

Know Your Audience, the Process, and the Players

Familiarize yourself with the process and the players. If the tribe needs legislation from Congress to settle a water-rights claim or an increase in federal appropriations to improve social services to the community, learn about the federal legislative process and the two committees with primary jurisdiction over Indian affairs: the Senate Committee on Indian Affairs and the House Subcommittee for Indigenous Peoples in the United States.[9] If you need to approach a state or federal regulatory agency, such as the Bureau of Indian Affairs, educate yourself about that agency, including what it does and how it does it.[10] As you learn about the process, also learn as much as possible about the people involved in it. For example, find out about your local member of Congress, including what committees she serves on, what issues she cares about, and how she has handled similar issues in the past.[11] This knowledge will help you determine how to engage both the people and processes that can help you resolve your issue.

Know Your Ask

Identify why you are lobbying and what it is that you want done. Consider what you expect to get out of lobbying. Do you have a specific goal in mind, like particular legislative or administrative action, or are you interested in engaging more broadly? Having a clear sense of what you want to get out of your engagement will help you devise a clear message to share with policymakers and determine the effectiveness of your efforts. Be realistic in framing your goals. Messaging is extremely important. Policymakers and their staff are short on time, so your message should be clear, short, and simple. Develop a way to explain it concisely to another person in a one-page briefing paper because many public officials will only have time to read one page.

Build Relationships

Successful advocacy often develops out of solid relationships built with public officials. Relationship building may take time, but it is worth the effort. Relationships are important because in an effective advocacy effort, information flows two ways: from the advocate to the policymaker and the policymaker to the advocate. The two collaborate to resolve problems effectively.

Start building relationships before you need policymakers to do something for you, and continue the relationship after you engage policymakers on a specific issue. In other words, do not just show up in policymakers' offices when you need something. Try to get to know them and their staff. Invite them to visit your community and to attend important community events (e.g., pow wows or groundbreaking ceremonies). Be patient, calm, and positive. Expect to have to educate and reeducate policymakers and their staffs as they change over time. Do not accept "no" as a final answer. If a policymaker cannot attend an event, invite her to another one. If a policymaker rejects your first proposal for solving an issue, rethink your approach and try again. If a policymaker needs more information on an issue, offer to provide information, especially if it is about your community.

Always Act with Integrity

Integrity is essential to effective advocacy. An effective advocate is someone whom public officials and their staff trust. Public officials and their staff expect advocates to be honest and trustworthy. Tribal governments should be too. Never deliberately mislead staffers or falsify information (or hire anyone who does). You do not have to emphasize all the substantive or political pitfalls in your argument, but you have to be honest about what you are asking for and how it will impact others. You and anyone else advocating on behalf of the tribe should know the substantive and political arguments that are against your proposal and represent the opposition's arguments fairly. Even if you cannot persuade a policymaker and their staff on a specific issue, your integrity will help you build a relationship with them. Public officials and staffers who trust that you provide honest and sound advice will ask you for information in the future.

Build Coalitions

In all advocacy efforts, there is power in numbers. Strong national and regional tribal advocacy organizations exist in Indian Country. Join the advocacy opportunities organized by the National Congress of American Indians,[12] and regional organizations, like the Midwest Alliance of Sovereign Tribes,[13] United South and Eastern Tribes,[14] or The Affiliated Tribes of Northwest Indians.[15] Action or impact days sponsored by these organizations may provide opportunities to contact policymakers that are otherwise unavailable. These organizations have staffs that may have advice on how to approach policymakers. Do not limit your outreach to tribal organizations. Local governments, businesses, and other organizations may have similar concerns or support your position.

DEVELOPING AN ADVOCACY PLAN

Indian nations lobby for a variety of reasons and have several choices to make in deciding to lobby at the state or federal level.

Establish Your Goals

Think about what it is that the tribe wants to get out of engaging in lobbying. Tribes typically participate in political processes for one or more of the following reasons:

- A tribe has a particular problem that it has to take to Congress or an administrative agency to have fixed. For example, if a tribe buys a parcel of land and wants it taken into trust, the tribe has to request that the BIA take the land into trust for them.
- A tribe may be interested in monitoring legislative and/or administrative actions because Congress or an agency is considering an issue important to them. For example, some tribes have monitored the federal legislative process because Congress has considered various bills that could affect gaming enterprises. The Native American Rights Fund has a Legislation Bulletin that it regularly updates to help tribal governments monitor the federal legislative process.[16]
- A tribe may want to join a wider coalition on an issue that affects Indian Country as a whole. For example, many tribes participate in efforts to reauthorize the Violence Against Women Act because it includes provisions that protect Indians.
- A tribe may want to educate policymakers about an issue or problem.
- A tribe may want to develop relationships with policymakers to increase their influence in the political process more generally.

Carefully consider which of these reasons (and it may be more than one) are motivating your tribe's involvement in the political process. It is easier to devise strategies and evaluate effectiveness if you know why you are engaging in the political process. For example, if you have a specific problem that the tribe needs resolved, that will inform the policymakers you target and the strategies you use.

Devise a Strategy

Once you have determined why you want to engage in the political process, think about how you can best achieve your goals. Tailor your engagement in the political process to the goals you hope to achieve for your community. You will want to think about three aspects of your strategy: who can help you meet your goals; the best way to approach them; and who else should engage in the advocacy effort.

Consider what public officials are in the best position to address your issue. Many issues faced by tribes have to be addressed at the federal level through either Congress or an administrative agency. Others are local and would be better handled by the state, county, or municipal government. You may want to engage local, state, and federal public officials, especially if you have an issue, like land into trust or environmental issues, that affects the local community but has to be resolved through a federal process. You may also want to target your efforts at various institutions. For example, if you are having a problem with an administrative agency, you may want to enlist the help of your member of Congress.

Develop a basic understanding of the processes that you plan to engage in—e.g., legislative process. Decide on the best way to influence decision-makers. There are several options or tactics for influencing the political process, including donating to electoral campaigns; joining or establishing a political action committee (PAC), an organization formed specifically to collect money and make contributions to candidates for public office; lobbying; and/or launching efforts to increase voter registration and voting during local, state, and federal elections.

Strategies may vary within each of these tactics. For example, lobbying efforts may occur at local, state, and federal levels and across legislative and administrative branches. Lobbying may involve multiple activities, including personal contact with policymakers and their staffs; mobilizing tribal members to write letters or emails to policymakers; testifying before congressional committees or administrative bodies; writing letters to policymakers; drafting legislative or regulatory language; commenting on legislative or regulatory language; drafting and disseminating policy papers to policymakers and the public; and/or holding press conferences to educate policymakers and the public. You may combine different lobbying tactics depending on your goals.

Also think about who will do the advocacy or lead the advocacy effort. Most elected officials prefer to hear from elected tribal leaders, so you may be more successful if you get your tribal council involved. If you are knowledgeable about intergovernmental relations or have in-house personnel who are, you may want to represent yourself. Alternatively, you may want to hire a lawyer, lawyer-lobbyist, or a lobbyist to assist you.

If you want to hire someone to help you in your advocacy, consider different advocates' qualifications and approaches. Not all advocates are the same. Each client-advocate relationship is unique and these relationships often differ. Some tribes want to hire an expert who will develop a strategy for the tribe to establish its goal. These advocates devise a plan, implement the plan, and report the results to the tribe, sometimes with little tribal input or oversight. Other tribes prefer an advocate who lets tribal leadership lead the advocacy effort. These advocates build close relationships with their tribal clients, often visiting the tribe's territory and meeting with tribal leadership. The advocate and the tribe work together to establish goals, devise a plan, and implement the plan. The advocate often monitors the political situation but expects tribal leadership to represent themselves at meetings with policymakers.

Take your time in choosing an advocate. In the past, tribes have lost millions of dollars to unscrupulous lobbyists who were interested in making money rather than representing tribes. Interview advocates thoroughly to avoid hiring one that does not suit your needs, share your values, or intend to advocate effectively on your behalf. Some qualities to look for in an advocate include:

- A leadership style and advocacy philosophy similar to your own.
- Qualifications, including how long they have been an advocate and whether they have worked for a legislator or served in an agency.
- Thought-out reasons for advocating for tribes.
- Possible conflicts of interest, including whether they represent another tribe or industry that competes with the tribe for federal dollars or market share.
- The advocate's reputation for acting with integrity.

You also have choices in how you hire an advocate to represent the tribe. Advocates may be hired in-house, on limited contracts (sometimes called contract lobbyists), or on long-term contracts.

PRACTITIONER PERSPECTIVE

Attorney Patrice Kunesh (Standing Rock Lakota descent) directs Peȟíŋ Haha Consulting, a social enterprise committed to building more engaged and powerful Native communities.[17] She has also held appointments as the deputy under secretary for Rural Development at the U.S. Department of Agriculture and as the deputy solicitor for Indian Affairs at the U.S. Department of the Interior. In addition, she has served as in-house counsel to the Mashantucket Pequot Tribe and on the faculty at the University of South Dakota School of Law.

Lobbying is really about the ability to persuade. My elevator speech to a tribal leader is sharing a story that best describes what is the need, what is the community or cultural context of that need, and why it is important for this particular legislator to care about that need. Often tribes have to tell policymakers why something matters and how Indian Country is different from state and local governments—there's something special and unique about Indian Country. And sometimes that brings up issues of hardship and vulnerability and disparities. But, I often like to talk about the strengths and the assets of the tribal community and how that community is going to be able to succeed and prevail notwithstanding these challenges. And that's why the appropriation for a particular project, or to address a particular grievance or legal wrong can be really impactful.

Oftentimes tribal leaders lead with the litany of "here's this problem and that problem." Historically tribes have been left out of funding considerations, or not included in them, so those conversations start with more of a negative perspective. I find that the person on the receiving end (and I've been one of those on the receiving end) really wants to know: what is the issue, what is the solution that you're proposing (and it needs to be a mutual solution), and why is it important? Their statements need to be short, crisp, and precise. And I think they should have a "can-do" perspective.

So, it obviously matters what kind of appropriation is involved and what is being asked for. If there's a settlement of a legal claim, there will be lots of issues involved in addressing that legal wrong. If it's appropriation for an essential central governmental service, like Indian Health Service or Bureau of Indian Education or Violence Against Native Women, it also is very helpful to have some data around that particular issue. If it's an appropriation that's more nonspecific, I think the strength of the elevator speech is really in its description of the utility of how the funds are going to be used and how the use of those funds will enhance, maybe even exponentially, the benefits to that Native community or Indian Country.

To get something into a bill requires a lot of groundwork, a lot of preparation, and just knowing that it will require an enormous amount of persistence. It also requires having or making contacts with people who matter.

One example is the CARES Act appropriations request. I was part of the broader effort to get relief to Indian Country for economic impacts caused by COVID-19. That work required contacting all of my elected representatives, both U.S. senators as well as congressional representatives from my state. And not only did I contact those people specifically, I also contacted their staff. I laid out the issue, as I said earlier: the case for the need and why it's important to Minnesota for them to support this request in both the Senate and in the House of Representatives. Then I had personal conversations, one-on-one, with their staff to discuss details specific to Minnesota and the importance of supporting the larger effort that often accompanies these bills.

This means joining forces with national Native-serving organizations, such as the National Congress of American Indians (NCAI), the Native American Financial Officers Association (NAFOA), and other subgroups that are pursuing their unique issues, be it education or health care or gaming—these all raise economic issues. It's a lot of coordination, networking, and follow-up. But I do believe the personal connections are incredibly important as well. Your senator and congressional representative must really know why it matters.

Most importantly, don't do it alone. This is a heavy lift. It is a heavy lift for anyone—Indian Country at large or a single tribe. You need advocates, influencers, and people to share your vision, mission, and your pain, so to speak. You need partners, and those partners could be other tribes or national organizations like NCAI. You have to understand the broader impact and find the right team members who can help carry the message and gather support. I just wouldn't do it alone because it takes so much work and requires a lot of persistence. And you're in it for the long haul, meaning it may not work this budget year, it may not work the next budget year.

It also is important to look at the executive branch and various government agencies as other opportunities for funding. For example, the U.S. Department of Agriculture, Rural Development agency has hundreds of millions of dollars available for housing infrastructure, community facilities, and broadband. The

Departments of Commerce and Housing and Urban Development (HUD), the Environmental Protection Agency, and the Administration for Native Americans all have dedicated programs and funds for Native community projects. With this diversity of funding options, you need to get your administrative team ready to apply for the grants and loans, to administer and report on that funding, and then obviously to distribute those funds and make sure they are being used. It's a multipurpose, multiplatform kind of work.

CONCLUSION

Tribal governments may want to engage federal, state, and local governments for various reasons, including to educate policymakers about a particular problem, to monitor issues important to them, to prevent the enactment of policies harmful to their people or lands, or to develop relationships and influence policy more generally. Each tribe has to determine what works best for it. This chapter has provided some guidance for how tribes can effectively engage in political participation at the federal and state levels.

NOTES

1. Political participation can be broadly divided into categories: direct participation, lobbying, and diplomacy. Direct participation means voting, running for office, and service in office. Lobbying is where citizens or subjects of a particular government advocate to their government in an effort to influence decisions and actions of that government. Diplomacy is similar to lobbying, except the people advocating are not advocating on behalf of the citizens of the government to which they are advocating. The individuals and entities doing the advocacy are instead advocating on behalf of outside governments, entities, and individuals seeking to influence decisions and actions of a government they are not a part of. Tribes have historically engaged in diplomatic relationships with the U.S. government. Some continue to characterize their relationship with the United States government as diplomatic.
2. David Wilkins and Heidi Stark, American Indian Politics and the American Political System, 165–70, 189–209 (2011).
3. Frederick Hoxie, This Indian Country: American Indian Activists and the Place They Made (2012); Dale Mason, Indian Gaming: Tribal Sovereignty and American Politics (2000).

4. Kirsten Matoy Carlson, *Lobbying against the Odds*, 56 Harv. J. Legis. 23 (2019).

5. *The Demise of the Ongwehoweh and the Rise of the Native Americans: Redressing the Genocidal Act of Forcing American Citizenship upon Indigenous Peoples*, 15 Harv. Blackltr. L.J. 107, 169–71 (1999).

6. *Strengthening Tribal Sovereignty through Indian Participation in American Politics: A Reply to Professor Porter*, 10 Kan. J.L. & Pub. Policy 533, 550 (Spring 2001).

7. Michael D. Oeser, *Tribal Citizen Participation in State and National Politics: Welcome Wagon or Trojan Horse?*, 36 Wm. Mitchell L. Rev. 793, 800 (2010).

8. *Ibid.*

9. https://www.indian.senate.gov; https://naturalresources.house.gov/subcommittees/subcommittee-for-indigenous-peoples-of-the-united-states.

10. https://www.bia.gov.

11. See https://www.congress.gov/members/find-your-member.

12. http://www.ncai.org/.

13. http://m-a-s-t.org.

14. https://www.usetinc.org.

15. https://atnitribes.org.

16. See https://narf.org/nill/bulletins/legislation/116_uslegislation.html.

17. Patrice Kunesh, attorney, director of Peȟíŋ Haha Consulting, and major gifts officer, Native American Rights Fund.

GLOSSARY

Diplomacy. Efforts on behalf of a government to influence the decisions and actions of a foreign government.

Direct participation. Participation in the political process of a government through voting, running for office, or service in office.

Lobbying. Efforts by the citizens or subjects of a government to influence decisions and actions of that government.

Political action committee (PAC). In the United States, an organization that pools money from private donors and spends it to influence elections or legislation. Typically, PACs are nonprofits.

Political participation. Participation in the political process of a government through voting, running for office, service in office, lobbying, and diplomacy. Political participation can be broken down into three categories: direct participation, lobbying, and diplomacy.

About the Contributors

Laural Ballew, ses yehomia/tsi kuts bat soot, is a member of the Swinomish Tribe located on Fidalgo Island near La Conner, Washington. She earned an associate's degree from Northwest Indian College, a bachelor's degree from Western Washington University, and a master's in public administration–tribal governance from The Evergreen State College. She is currently working toward a doctorate of Indigenous development and advancement with Te Whare Wananga O Awanuiarangi. Her thesis is titled "Pathway for Tribal Governance: A Model for Preparing Indigenous Leaders" as a combination of research for tribal governance curriculum and her personal academic journey. She is currently at Western Washington University as the first executive director of American Indian/Alaska Native and First Nation Relations and tribal liaison to the president. Her position represents the president and Board of Trustees as liaison and envoy to American Indian/Alaska Native and First Nations governments. She continues her work to advocate for the support and success of Native students at Western, and she serves as liaison to the twenty-nine federally recognized tribes of Washington. She serves as consultant for the recruitment and retention of American Indian/Alaska Native, First Nation students and expanding the university's ability to provide resources for their academic success.

Joseph Bauerkemper serves on the faculty in the Department of American Indian Studies at the University of Minnesota Duluth and as affiliate faculty for the University of Minnesota Twin Cities Humphrey School of Public Affairs. His scholarship, outreach, and teaching emphasize Indigenous governance, federal and state policy regarding American Indian nations, and Native literatures. Joseph teaches undergraduate courses in UMD's BA programs in American Indian Studies and Tribal Administration & Governance, and graduate courses in UMD's Master of Tribal Administration & Governance and Master of Tribal Natural Resource & Environmental Stewardship programs. He also serves as lead facilitator for an intergovernmental collaboration providing training on tribal-state relations for State of Minnesota departments and agencies, and provides governance programming for tribal staffers and administrators.

Kirsten Matoy Carlson is associate professor of law and adjunct associate professor of political science at Wayne State University. She is a leading authority on federal Indian law and legislation. Her interdisciplinary, empirical research focuses on legal advocacy and law reform, with particular attention on the various strategies used by Indian nations to reform federal Indian law and policy effectively. It has been funded by the National Science Foundation (NSF) and the Levin Center at Wayne Law. Her articles have appeared in the *Michigan Law Review, Minnesota Law Review, Indiana Law Review, Harvard Journal on Legislation, Law and Society Review,* and *American Indian Law Review.* Carlson serves on the State Bar of Michigan Standing Committee on American Indian Law and is a fellow of the American Bar Foundation. Prior to joining Wayne Law, she advocated nationally and internationally to protect the rights of Indian nations as a staff attorney at the Indian Law Resource Center and clerked for the Hon. Diana E. Murphy of the U.S. Court of Appeals for the Eighth Circuit. Carlson earned a PhD in political science and a JD from the University of Michigan and was a Fulbright Scholar in New Zealand.

Julie Clark is a citizen of the Oneida Nation in Wisconsin. She received her master's degree in organizational development from Silver Lake College. She has worked for her nation's casino, Oneida Casino, for thirty-three years. Her experience ranges from a frontline cashier in the late 1980s to her most recent role as organizational development specialist. She has worked with the Oneida Nation and the Oneida Casino's strategic planning and execution. Julie was also certified as a ToP's, FranklinCovey, and AchieveGlobal facilitator. Her experiences range from training, employee orientation, strategic planning, team building, to building balanced scorecards. Julie resides in Green Bay, Wisconsin, within the boundaries of the Oneida reservation. She has recently begun basket making as a new hobby to help preserve a traditional craft of her nation.

Wayne Ducheneaux (Cheyenne River Sioux) is the executive director of the Native Governance Center, which he joined in 2016. Prior to that Wayne was a District Four Tribal Council representative from 2012 to 2016 for his nation and served two years as vice-chairman from 2012 to 2014. He has also served his nation as administrative officer (2010–12) and general manager of the Cheyenne River Motel, a Cheyenne River tribal enterprise. Wayne has served on numerous local, regional, and national boards for multiple organizations. He is married to Megan Swan and is father to Veda, Aiden, and Alexander Ducheneaux; they currently reside on the Cheyenne River Reservation.

Donald Eubanks is an associate professor and field director for the social work program at Metropolitan State University in St. Paul, Minnesota. Don has broad experience in tribal and state government, which includes commissioner of Health and Human Services for the Mille Lacs Band of Ojibwe Indians, director of multicultural affairs for the Chemical and Mental Health Services Administration, and director of the Chemical Health Division, both for the Minnesota Department of Human Services. Don has consulted for the Substance Abuse and Mental Health Services Administration and served as treasurer for the National Association of State Alcohol and Drug Abuse Directors. He has served on multiple state and federal task forces and boards, including the Tribal Self-Governance Advisory Committee, the Midwest Alliance of Sovereign Tribes, St. Paul Indians in Action, and the American Indian Family Center. Don has a master's in social work from the University of Minnesota, a bachelor's in social work from Metropolitan State University, and a liberal arts degree from Minneapolis Community College. He is a member of the Mille Lacs Band of Ojibwe Indians and resides in Roseville, Minnesota, with his family.

Linda Bane Frizzell has extensive experience and practice as a provider and administrator with Indian Health Systems. She holds a doctorate degree in physiology, education administration, and gerontology, and a post-doctorate in epidemiology. Her endeavors have included a broad range of professional preparations both in medicine and education, dedicated to improvement of quality of life across the lifespan. She has provided numerous testimonies in regard to health care policy, health issues, public health, cultural attunement, and tribal consultation. Her specialties include health services administration; clinic management; rural and Indian health policy and legislation; public health and wellness; cultural humility; health and education research and assessment; behavioral health; community assessment and survey development; evaluation; gerontology services, assessment, and avocation; exercise physiology; health education; physical rehabilitative therapy; service learning administration; Senior Corps administration; and therapeutic recreation. She currently serves on the governing board of the Minneapolis Indian Health Board. She is a Global Health Faculty associate and an associate professor at the University of Minnesota, where she developed an American Indian studies graduate minor and a Regents certificate for American Indian public health and wellness. She also teaches and provides presentations on tribal public health and wellness.

Amy Gould previously worked as a public servant in transportation, is a non-Native ally, and is currently in her sixteenth year as a full-time faculty member at Evergreen State College in Washington State. Amy teaches in the Master of Public Administration program and the tribal governance concentration. She is passionate about the intersections of identity and conformity, cultural norms, positionality, and postcolonial feminism. She earned a PhD in political science from Northern Arizona University.

Wendy Helgemo, a member of the Ho-Chunk Nation, has dedicated her career to serving American Indians, Alaska Natives, and Native Hawaiians and protecting tribal sovereignty. She is especially devoted to increasing Native representation in the halls of the United States Capitol. She is senior legislative attorney at Big Fire Law & Policy, based in Washington, DC. Prior to that, she was senior advisor on Indian Affairs to United States Senator Harry Reid (D-NV) and helped to secure passage of critical tribal provisions in the Violence Against Women Act of 2013 and legislation conveying more than 71,000 acres of much-needed land to six Indian tribes in Nevada. As inaugural director of the AT&T Center for Indigenous Politics and Policy at George Washington University, Wendy continued to develop her relationships across Washington,

DC, placing Native students into internships in the United States Congress, national tribal organizations, and federal agencies. She hopes these training grounds inspire Native students to make their careers and lives in Washington, DC. Wendy received a BA in English from St. Olaf College and a JD from the University of Colorado.

Annamarie Hill is Ojibwe and a member of the Red Lake Nation. She is also of fourth-generation Finnish descent. Annamarie's undergraduate degree is in music performance and business administration. In 2017, she fulfilled a dream and obtained a master's in tribal administration and governance (MTAG) from the University of Minnesota-Duluth. Annamarie works in community engagement at the University of Minnesota Medical School-Duluth Memory Keepers Medical Discovery Team (MK-MDT), and is responsible for assisting MK-MDT in developing and maintaining respectful research relationship partnerships with tribal authorities, tribal members, communities, and agencies. Annamarie has enjoyed a long career in public service devoted to the American Indian/Indigenous tribal nations, holding the position of executive director for the Minnesota Indian Affairs Council (2006–15) as well as providing lengthy service in the state legislature and as a lobbyist for the Red Lake Nation. In 2015, she was appointed to serve on the Minnesota Humanities Center board by Governor Mark Dayton in 2015 and was reappointed by Governor Tim Walz in 2018. Whether at remote work or leisure, Annamarie most enjoys spending her days with her children and grandchildren close by. She also loves visiting with her amazing eighty-nine-year-old mother and many family and friends. Annamarie makes her home in beautiful White Bear Lake, Minnesota.

Jason Hollinday, Duluth, Minnesota, is a member of the Fond du Lac Band of Lake Superior Chippewa and had worked for the Band the last twenty-five years in the Planning Division. In those years he spent eleven as the economic development planner and the last fourteen years as the planning director. Working in the Planning Division, Jason has written a large number of grants, and administered projects and project development. Among the projects are the Fond du Lac Fiber to the Home, Land Use Plan, Strategic Plan, Assisted Living, WGZS Radio, among others. Currently, he serves on the Northland Foundation Board of Trustees, ARDC Board of Directors, MNDOT-Area Transportation Partnership, and the MNDOT-Advocacy Council on Tribal Transportation. Jason completed the certificate program in tribal administration from the University of Minnesota, Duluth (2018); in 2012 he completed a yearlong training course sponsored by the Bush Foundation called Native Nation Rebuilders. Jason graduated from the University of Minnesota, Duluth in 1992 with a degree in geography and urban & regional studies, with a minor in history.

Jo Anne House is a member of the Oneida Nation. She is currently the Nation's chief counsel, which includes parliamentarian duties at General Tribal Council meetings. She has a doctorate degree focusing on deliberative democracy. Her time spent with the Oneida Nation has shifted from legislative drafting and analysis to providing policy and leadership for the Oneida Nation through the nation's law offices. Her focus is on providing legal opinions and research papers on subjects of interest to the membership at General Tribal Council meetings, to the operations, and to the Oneida Business Committee in terms understood by a broad variety of individuals in order to foster informed discussion.

Toni M. House from the Oneida Nation resides on the Oneida Reservation in Wisconsin. Her grassroots education began in midwifery, where she was licensed in the states of New Mexico and Texas, followed by a practice in Wisconsin. She and her husband homeschooled their three children in order to prioritize the Oneida language and culture. She is also a certified yoga instructor. Her undergraduate studies were in human development with a special emphasis in lay-midwifery and a minor in Spanish from the University of Wisconsin Green Bay. Her master's was in community counseling from the University of Wisconsin Oshkosh. Finally, her PhD was in human services, with a nonprofit management certificate from Capella University. Her sixteen years of employment history with the Oneida Nation include nurse's aide; fitness instructor; children and women's advocacy; domestic violence education and prevention; psychotherapy, where she acquired an Independent Clinical Social Worker license; and a continuous improvement specialist (CIMS). As CIMS she was trained and trained others in the following areas: team building, meeting facilitation, consensus building, conflict resolution, leadership training, system redesign, and program planning. She is currently an associate professor for the Department of Human Services Leadership at the University of Wisconsin Oshkosh.

Krystal L. John grew up in Milwaukee, Wisconsin, making frequent trips to the Oneida Reservation to visit family. She completed her bachelor's and juris doctorate in Milwaukee at Marquette University and Law School. After a brief stint working in-house for Oneida Total Integrated Enterprises, she found "home" working and living on the Oneida Reservation. She works in-house for the Oneida Law Office and has represented areas such as gaming, housing (residential leasing, foreclosures and evictions, and legislative representation), retail (commercial real estate acquisitions), land (commercial and agricultural leasing, easements, and land acquisitions), zoning (intergovernmental relations and enforcement), engineering, and public works, focusing counsel on business law, residential and commercial real estate, and legislative review and analysis. She takes pride in being able to do a job she loves right in her Oneida community. More than anything, she loves her boys, Landry and Nicolas, and her dog Mabel—they keep her hands and her heart full.

Tadd M. Johnson is the University of Minnesota's first senior director of American Indian Tribal Nations Relations. In this role, he serves as the liaison between the entire University of Minnesota system and the regional tribal nations. An enrolled member of the Bois Forte Band of Chippewa, Johnson served as a tribal attorney for more than thirty years, but has also served as a tribal court judge and a tribal administrator. He is a frequent lecturer on American Indian history and federal Indian law. He spent five years with the U.S. House of Representatives, ultimately becoming staff director and counsel to the Subcommittee on Native American Affairs. In 1997, President Clinton appointed Johnson to chair the National Indian Gaming Commission. Johnson earned his BA from the University of St. Thomas and his law degree from the University of Minnesota. He has served as a faculty member of the National Judicial College and has served on the board of the Minnesota Chamber of Commerce. He is currently on the board of the Native Governance Center, serves as director of the Tribal Sovereignty Institute, and is on the board of trustees of the Udall Foundation.

Katie Johnston-Goodstar is associate professor and the director of undergraduate studies in the School of Social Work at the University of Minnesota. Drawing on Indigenous, decolonial, and social justice frameworks, she collaborates with youth and communities in participatory action research (PAR) to study the social, political, and historical contexts of Indigenous youth and to build community wellness. She is particularly interested in how Indigenous and minoritized young people experience institutions like youth organizations, schools, and universities as unsafe spaces, engaging them in a process of collective transformation and in revitalizing Indigenous knowledge and practices with youth.

Patrice Kunesh, of Standing Rock Lakota descent, is the founder and director of Pehíŋ Haha Consulting, a social enterprise committed to building more engaged and powerful Native communities, and the major gifts officer at the Native American Rights Fund (NARF). Prior to starting Pehíŋ Haha Consulting, she established and led the Center for Indian Country Development at the Federal Reserve Bank of Minneapolis, an economic policy research center, where she developed national initiatives and advanced publications on housing, education, and financial institutions. Patrice also held appointments as the deputy under secretary for Rural Development at the U.S. Department of Agriculture and as the deputy solicitor for Indian Affairs at the U.S. Department of the Interior. In addition, she served as in-house counsel to the Mashantucket Pequot Tribe and on the faculty at the University of South Dakota School of Law.

Lorna LaGue is an enrolled member of the Minnesota Chippewa Tribe (MCT)–White Earth Reservation where she was born and raised. She received a business management degree from the University of Minnesota Crookston and an MPA from Capella University. Lorna has spent most of her career working in various capacities for White Earth, including the tribal government, IHS, and gaming. She is currently the president of the White Earth Tribal and Community College, a two-year higher education institution rooted in the Anishinaabe values, language, and culture. Lorna has worked on various projects with reservations throughout the state of Minnesota. She is a Native Nation Rebuilder and cofounder of Zaagibagaang, a grassroots group to provide educational materials on the MCT Constitution. She is passionate about tribal government reform for the betterment of reservations and future generations. Lorna lives with her husband, Bill, and has two grown children. In her free time, she enjoys spending time with her grandchildren, reading, and beading.

Paul Ninham's Haudenosaunee name is Watho ha hunko (He Has Come across a Path); he is wolf clan from the Oneida Reservation in Wisconsin. Paul earned a BS degree in physical education from Arizona State University and a master of tribal administration and governance from the University of Minnesota Duluth. In August 2014, Paul completed his duties and responsibilities as an elected tribal councilman for the Oneida Nation, proudly serving his community and nation for twelve years. As one of five legislators serving on the nine-member Business Committee, the nation's governing body, Paul's primary duties were to draft and present for approval the nation's laws, codes, and ordinances. Paul also served six years on the board of directors for the Native American Rights Fund, including three years as its vice-chairman. Moreover, he has served on the board of regents for Haskell Indian Nations University, as vice-chairman for the Wisconsin Tribal Conservation Advisory Council, as Midwest Region representative for the Tribal Leader/Department of Interior Trust Reform Task Force, and currently serves as a board member for the Oneida Youth Leadership Institute. Paul's passions include hunting, fishing, teaching Native American traditional games, and nurturing emerging tribal leaders.

Jon Panamaroff is the chief executive officer of Command Holdings, a sustainable, self-sufficient economic development arm of the Mashantucket Pequot Tribal Nation. Before joining Command Holdings, Jon had spent his professional career in finance and Native American economic development working with/for Native-owned corporations, Community Development Financial Institutions, the federal government, and banks. He has held such positions as the former chief compliance and business integration officer of Koniag Government Services, president and CEO of the Kodiak Brown Bear Center, Colville Tribal Solutions Corporation, Willapa Bay Enterprises Corporation and First Nations Oweesta Corporation, Northwest Zone credit manager for the Office of Indian Energy and Economic Development–Division of Capital Investments at the Department of the Interior, and vice-president at Native American Bank. Jon holds a bachelor of arts in business administration and a bachelor of arts in psychology with departmental honors in both disciplines from Eastern Washington University (EWU). Jon also graduated with a master of public administration from EWU. He has completed industry-focused programs at the University of Washington, the Graduate School of Banking at Colorado, and Harvard Business

School. He is currently completing his PhD at the Daniels College of Business at the University of Denver.

Laura Paynter has a master of public policy degree from the University of Minnesota and a master of arts in history from the University of California, Riverside. She has worked in environmental policy, historic preservation, and regional planning policy. At the Greater Wellington Regional Council in New Zealand, she had the privilege of convening a group of Indigenous Māori *kaitiaki* (guardians) to advise the council on the significance of Māori values and the recognition and protection of them in the regional natural-resources management plan. Laura identifies as a settler, and believes it's important for everyone to honor and respect Indigenous people and values. She contributed to this handbook as part of a graduate internship under Tadd Johnson in the Tribal Sovereignty Institute at the University of Minnesota.

Kris Peters is the chairman of the Squaxin Island Tribe in Washington State. Before his appointment as the tribal chair, Kris worked for three years as the tribal administrator at Squaxin, and has nearly twenty years of experience working in public safety and social work in Indian Country. He has also worked as an adjunct faculty member at Evergreen State College in Indigenous studies. Kris holds a bachelor of arts degree with an emphasis on federal Indian law and tribal governance, and a master of public administration, tribal governance degree from Evergreen State College.

Michael J. Poitra is an enrolled member of the Turtle Mountain Band of Chippewa located in Belcourt, North Dakota. Growing up on the reservation, he was taught to value the importance of education. Following high school, he pursued education in the area of business, attending Minot State University. Relying upon cultural and family values helped him learn to adapt and explore further educational opportunities, leading to a bachelor of science degree in business administration at the University of Mary. With an interest in human resources, Poitra decided to return to school and earned a master of science degree in this area of study. His commitment and passion to return to his reservation soon followed, where he joined colleagues in the development of the Ogimaawiwin Leadership and Business Management of Arts Program at the Turtle Mountain Community College. He could not have pursued these endeavors without the support of his fiancé, who also returned home to serve our community as a clinical psychologist. Together, they have a four-year old son, who is their greatest accomplishment. They enjoy the outdoors, spending time fishing, camping, and making s'mores under the clear, bright stars of the North Dakota skies.

Lawrence S. Roberts is a professor of practice and executive director of the Indian Gaming and Tribal Self-Governance Programs at Arizona State University's Sandra Day O'Connor College of Law. Roberts is a citizen of the Oneida Nation (Wisconsin). Roberts has spent much of his career in federal service. He was appointed by President Obama in 2012 to leadership positions in the Assistant Secretary for Indian Affairs' Office, including as the deputy assistant secretary for policy and economic development and the principal deputy assistant secretary. In these positions he managed all programs and offices that report to the assistant secretary, including the Bureau of Indian Affairs and the Bureau of Indian Education. Roberts ultimately served as the acting assistant secretary for Indian Affairs and led Indian Affairs for the final year of the Obama administration. During his tenure, Roberts advised the secretary of the Interior on a broad spectrum of Indian Affairs matters—from tribal self-governance to education, and Native youth to tribal reserved treaty rights. During the Obama administration, Indian Affairs restored over 500,000 acres of homelands to tribal nations, including homelands in Alaska, and revised regulations to advance tribal self-governance and self-determination in the areas of the Indian Child Welfare Act and tribal homelands. Prior to leading Indian Affairs, Roberts served as general counsel of the National Indian Gaming Commission. Roberts advised NIGC on all matters concerning Indian gaming, including ensuring that tribes maintain the sole proprietary interest in their gaming. Roberts began his legal career as a trial attorney with the United States Department of Justice. His work included litigation protecting tribal rights.

Michael D. O. Rusco, Cooweejamįnąk (Ho-Chunk for "Sits in Front"). Enrolled in Cherokee Nation. Associate professor, Southern University Law Center. Senior fellow, SULC Native American Law & Policy Institute. Rusco has spoken, published, taught, and practiced tribal law and federal Indian law extensively. He has published articles on political participation by tribes and on tribal citizenship. He has advised tribal businesses and governments on a variety of high-stakes matters, including commercial contracts, business structures, construction law, constitutional law, employment law, gaming, taxation, natural resource defense, code drafting, U.S. Supreme Court appeals, and collection of tribal court judgments. Prior to joining SULC, Rusco served as senior tribal counsel to the Ho-Chunk Nation, a tribe with more than 7,700 citizens and 3,300 employees. Rusco's primary area of responsibility was advising the nation's Department of Business, the Ho-Chunk office that oversees the nation's lucrative gaming, retail, and smoke shop enterprises. In that capacity, he provided advice on contract review and enforcement, construction law, employment law, RFPs/RFIs, and taxation. Rusco also teaches civil procedure, conflict of laws, legal writing, legal research, oral advocacy, contract law, contract drafting, business structures, and constitutional law.

Candice Skenandore is an enrolled member of the Oneida Nation and has worked for the nation since 2011. Candice currently serves as the nation's Office of Self-Governance coordinator and previously worked as a legislative analyst. Candice holds a master's degree in public administration, a bachelor's degree in political science, and a post-baccalaureate certificate and associate's degree in paralegal studies.

Kekek Jason Stark is an assistant professor with the Alexander Blewitt III School of Law at the University of Montana. He is a Turtle Mountain Ojibwe and member of the Bizhiw (Lynx) Clan. Kekek is a former president of the Minnesota American Indian Bar Association, a former Bush Foundation Leadership Fellow and alumnus of Hamline University School of Law. Kekek worked as an assistant professor with the American Indian Studies Department at the University of Minnesota–Duluth as well as an adjunct faculty member at several institutions. In addition to his teaching experience, Kekek served as the attorney general for the Lac Courte Oreilles Band of Lake Superior Chippewa Indians, as a policy analyst in the Division of Intergovernmental Affairs for the Great Lakes Indian Fish and Wildlife Commission, and as a policy analyst for the Bad River Band of Lake Superior Tribe of Chippewa Indians. As a practitioner of Indigenous law, Kekek has firsthand experience in training students how to work productively with Indigenous principles and procedures. Along the way, he has helped build institutions grounded in Anishinaabe law and has helped students and communities forge better relations between Indigenous and non-Indigenous institutions and peoples, strengthening tribal sovereignty.

Lois Stevens is a mother, teacher, researcher, geographer, and an enrolled member of the Oneida Nation in Wisconsin. She is an assistant professor of First Nations studies and the First Nations Education Doctoral Program at the University of Wisconsin–Green Bay. Growing up on the Oneida Reservation, she is a product of the community that raised her and helped her develop a deep appreciation for ancestral knowledge and understanding of her impact on Mother Earth. As a mother, she works on transferring this knowledge to her three daughters. As a researcher and geographer, her research interests involve the effects of environmental and climatic change on Indigenous food systems and place-based adaptation within Indigenous communities. She is also invested in empowering Indigenous voices in academia by fostering a love for collaborative research and writing.

Joan Timeche is the executive director of the Native Nations Institute for Leadership, Management, and Policy (NNI) at the University of Arizona (UAz), where she works with Native peoples in strengthening their governance. Her focus at NNI is leadership development, economic development, and youth, and she is a skilled facilitator. A citizen of the Hopi Tribe from the village of Old Oraibi, she received a BS in social work and an MBA from Northern Arizona University (NAU). Prior to joining NNI in 2001, she served as program director of NAU's Center for American Indian Economic Development (CAIED) and concurrently, in 1992–95, as co-executive director of the National Executive Education Program for Native American Leadership, a joint project of CAIED and the Harvard Project on American Indian Economic Development. Timeche also worked eight years as director of the Hopi Tribe's Department of Education. She is actively involved in the community, has extensive experience developing organizations and serving on boards, has received a number of awards recognizing her work, and currently serves on the boards for the National Center for American Indian Enterprise Development, the Economic Development Authority of the Tohono O'odham Nation, and Native Women Lead.

Eric S. Trevan is an assistant professor at California State University San Marcos and just ended his position of Visiting Scholar of Innovation, Business and

Economic Policy for Tribal Nations for the California Indian Culture and Sovereignty Center, California State University San Marcos. Previously, he served as a member of the faculty (tenure-track) for the master's of public administration program at The Evergreen State College. In 2020, he was awarded the prestigious Executive Leadership Fellowship for two years to provide research funding and guidance to the Community Development Society. Currently, Trevan serves as president of aLocal Solutions, a new AI market-research software platform; on the board of directors of Northern Initiatives, a Community Development Financial Institution (CDFI); a Tribal Economic Development Board for Noo-Kayet Development Corporation (Port Gamble S'Klallam Tribe) and Cheyenne and Arapaho Business Development Corporation (Cheyenne and Arapaho Tribes); as well as a policy advisor to the Treasury Tribal Advisory Committee (TTAC) with the U.S. Department of Treasury. He earned his PhD at Arizona State University, Watts College of Public Solutions and Community Solutions, Community Resources and Development (local and tribal economies); master's degree in administration (public administration) from Central Michigan University; and a bachelor's degree in public administration/economics from Western Michigan University. He is a tribal citizen of the Match-E-Be-Nash-She-Wish Band of Pottawatomi Indians, Gun Lake Tribe.

Cary B. Waubanascum is a member of the Oneida Nation of Wisconsin, Wakeny^ta (Turtle Clan), with ancestral roots in the Menominee, Forest County Potawatomi, and Stockbridge-Munsee Band of Mohican Nations of Wisconsin. She is a wife to Lance and Aknulha to a son, daughter, and many nephews. Before entering the PhD program at the University of Minnesota-Twin Cities, she worked ten years as a social worker with Indigenous families and communities in Northeast Wisconsin. Her dissertation, "Indigenous Kinship Stories as Epistemic De-Linking: Implications for Decolonizing Social Work," critically examines the influence of colonialism on Indigenous kinship and seeks to illuminate stories of Indigenous caregivers to recover kinship knowledge and practices.

Rebecca M. Webster is an enrolled citizen of the Oneida Nation in Wisconsin. She is an assistant professor at the University of Minnesota Duluth in their American Indian Studies Department. She teaches undergraduate and graduate courses in their Tribal Administration and Governance programs.

Prior to joining the American Indian studies team at Duluth, she served the Oneida Nation as an attorney for thirteen years, where she provided legal advice for the nation's administration on government relations, jurisdiction concerns, and a wide variety of tribal land issues. Her research interests focus on tribal and local intergovernmental relationships, best practices in tribal administration, and Indigenous food sovereignty. She currently serves on the Oneida Land Commission, an elected tribal body responsible for setting land use and acquisition priorities for the Oneida Nation. In addition to her academic interests, she grows heirloom traditional foods with her family on their ten-acre farmstead Ukwakhwa: Tsinu Niyukwayayʌthoslu (Our food: Where we plant things) and with Ohe·láku (among the cornstalks), a co-op of Oneida families that grow Iroquois white corn together. She received her BA, MPA, and JD from the University of Wisconsin-Madison and her PhD in public policy and administration from Walden University.

Brandon Yellowbird-Stevens is the vice-chairman for the Oneida Nation of Wisconsin. Elected in 2008, he served as a councilman on the Oneida Business Committee for three consecutive terms while continuing with his second term as the vice-chairman. Yellowbird-Stevens serves as the president of the National Haskell Board of Regents for Haskell Indian Nations University, the Midwest delegate for the National Indian Gaming Association Executive Board, and appointee for President Obama's Nation Convening Council and Advisory Council of the My Brother's Keeper Alliance. He earned his associate's degree from the United Tribes Technical College in Bismarck, North Dakota; bachelor of science in business administration from Haskell Indian Nations University, and master of business administration in finance at Lakeland University.

Nicholas C. Zaferatos, PhD, AICP, is a professor of urban planning at Huxley College of the Environment, Western Washington University. His teaching emphasis on urban planning, sustainable development, Native American planning and governance, and environmental policy complements his regional and international applied teaching and research interests. Zaferatos serves as the director of the Urban Planning Program at Huxley College, a program accredited by the Planning Accreditation Board. Over the past two decades, Zaferatos has directed several service learning programs in planning and sustainable development both regionally and internationally. His professional practice in planning spans over forty-five years and includes positions as planning director, executive managerial positions, and civic appointments on boards and commissions with local, regional, and Native American governments and international organizations. He served as planning director and general manager for the Swinomish Indian Tribal Community for a period of two decades. His recent publications concerning Native American planning include *Planning the Native American Reservation: From Theory to Empowerment* (2017) and *Washington Indian Tribes and the Growth Management Act: Toward Inclusionary Regional Planning* (2020). He has a BA in geography from the State University of New York, Buffalo; an MS in regional and environmental planning from Western Washington University; and a PhD in urban design and planning from the University of Washington.

Index

11, 22, 195, 248, 255, 260 (n. 5), 262

General Tribal Council (GTC): citizen engagement in, 12–13; decision-making in, 24–25; members, 23; negativity at, 26; as Oneida governing body, 12, 32; operation of meetings, 23–24; reacquisition of land on Oneida Reservation, 12; restructuring of, 26–27; social media, 26; stipend, 23, 25, 26

Gila River Arena (Gila River Indian Community), 140

Gila River Indian Community, Gila River Arena, 140

Gobin & Madison v. Snohomish County v. The Tulalip Tribes of Washington (2002), 262

governance: best practices using Great Law of Peace, 3–4, 19–20; and clan systems, 10; colonization as perpetuated in, 152; and determination of budget priorities, 232; expansion of, approaches to include intergovernmental agreements, 247; Haudenosaunee Confederacy, 7, 8–9, 10; and inherent sovereignty of Native nations, 53, 204; and IRA, 11–12; of Mille Lacs Band of Ojibwe Indians, 155–56; models, 40–42; Oneida, 12, 20, 22–23; within operating and authorizing environments, 40; over non-Natives, 248, 250, 260 (n. 5), 261 (n. 14); regional, 253; teaching, 13, 15; traditional knowledge as means to promote, 51–54;

traditional principles of, 11–12, 156; and tribal constitutions, 204; and tribal politics, 88; of United States and Haudenosaunee, 19. *See also* General Tribal Council (GTC)

Great Law of Peace (Kayanlásla?kowa): adoption process, 10; basic facts about, 64; best governance practices, 3–4, 19–20; and corn, 13; decision-making process, 7, 14; and ethical spaces, 27–29; Five Nations acceptance of, 4; and membership in and unity of Haudenosaunee, 10; principles of, 3, 21, 22, 29, 30, 32; and sustenance, 13, 14; variations of, 4–5, 10, 20

Great White Pine, 7

gross domestic product (GDP), 129

gross profit margin (%), 116

Growth Management Act (Washington State, 1990), 260 (n. 3)

Gun Lake Investments (Match-E-Be-Nash-She-Wish Band of Pottawatomi Indians), 141

Gun Lake Trust Reaffirmation Act, 217–18

Gwayakwaadiziwin (Honesty), 156

Hard Rock (Seminole Tribe of Florida), 140–41

Haudenosaunee (They Make a House) Confederacy: and General Allotment (Dawes) Act, 11, 22; governance, 7, 8–9, 10; and Peacemaker story, 20; relocation of, 11, 22; Revolutionary War,